ABRAHAM AND HAWTREY'S

PARLIAMENTARY DICTIONARY

ABRAHAM AND HAWTREY'S

PARLIAMENTARY DICTIONARY

THIRD EDITION

BY

S. C. HAWTREY, C.B., M.A.

CLERK OF THE JOURNALS

HOUSE OF COMMONS

AND

H. M. BARCLAY, M.A.

A DEPUTY PRINCIPAL CLERK

COMMITTEE OFFICE

HOUSE OF COMMONS

LONDON

BUTTERWORTHS

1970

ENGLAND: BUTTERWORTH & CO. (PUBLISHERS) LTD.
LONDON: 88 KINGSWAY, WC2B 6AB

AUSTRALIA: BUTTERWORTH & CO. (AUSTRALIA) LTD.
SYDNEY: 20 LOFTUS STREET
MELBOURNE: 343 LITTLE COLLINS STREET
BRISBANE: 240 QUEEN STREET

CANADA: BUTTERWORTH & CO. (CANADA) LTD.
TORONTO: 14 CURITY AVENUE, 374

NEW ZEALAND: BUTTERWORTH & CO. (NEW ZEALAND) LTD.
WELLINGTON: 49/51 BALLANCE STREET
AUCKLAND: 35 HIGH STREET

SOUTH AFRICA: BUTTERWORTH & CO. (SOUTH AFRICA) (PTY.) LTD.
DURBAN: 33/35 BEACH GROVE

ISBN 0 406 10101 9

PRINTED IN GREAT BRITAIN
SPOTTISWOODE, BALLANTYNE AND CO. LTD.
LONDON AND COLCHESTER

PREFACE TO THE THIRD EDITION

THE years which have passed since the second edition of this work was published have seen an unusually large and varied amount of change in parliamentary procedure. The House has shown a constant readiness to experiment with new forms of procedure, mostly with the object of facilitating the despatch of business. Some of these new forms (such, for example, as the opening of the sitting at 10 a.m.) have been abandoned after trial, but most of them appear likely to be permanent. Among them two, at least, may be mentioned; first, the transfer of certain proceedings on some public bills—second reading debates and the consideration of bills on report—from the floor of the House to standing committees, and secondly, the abandonment of the rule requiring financial business to originate in a committee of the whole House, which has resulted in the abolition of the Committees of Supply and Ways and Means and of all " money committees ".

As the second edition was the last which our former colleague, Mr. L. A. Abraham, C.B., C.B.E., M.A., helped to prepare, we wish to take this opportunity to record our gratitude for the unique contribution which his scholarship and industry have made to this work.

We also wish to express our thanks for valuable help and advice which we have received from Mr. J. C. Sainty, Clerk of the Journals, and Mr. M. F. Bond, O.B.E., Clerk of the Records, House of Lords.

S. C. H.
June, 1970. H. M. B.

PREFACE TO THE FIRST EDITION

THE addition of another work on parliamentary procedure to the number of those already in existence needs a few words of explanation, if not of apology. The justification of the present work is, we believe, that it attempts to provide the general reader with most of the information which he is likely to want, for every-day use, about our parliamentary machinery, in the form most convenient for easy reference. To this end we have collected all the subjects discussed under headings alphabetically arranged; we have tried to define and explain all the commoner parliamentary expressions, ranging from the colloquial to the technical, and we have included articles dealing at greater length with the main branches of our subject. We have not tried to avoid a certain amount of repetition, believing that, in a subject of such complexity, where the different topics treated constantly overlap one another, repetition is less harassing to the reader than a too elaborate system of cross-references. We have not attempted to supply references or examples for all our statements, considering that they are not called for in a work of this scope; for such the reader is referred to Erskine May's "Parliamentary Practice", which is the standard treatise on this subject, and to the General Indexes to the Journals of both Houses.

We are conscious that in such a work as this many errors may be discovered, in spite of the care with which we have checked every statement that we have made. For these we beg our readers' indulgence, and ask that our mistakes may be pointed out to us.

Except in those passages which deal specifically with the House of Lords, the book must be understood, unless the context obviously requires otherwise, to refer to the House of Commons.

We wish to express our gratitude for the help which we have received from a number of our colleagues and others, to whom we are indebted for much valuable information and many useful suggestions: in particular, to Sir Edward Fellowes, K.C.B., C.M.G., M.C., Clerk of the House of Commons, who, in addition to contributing a foreword, has read through the whole work in typescript and pointed out a number of errors, and has, moreover, given us much useful information that only an incumbent of his office can supply; to Mr. K. R. Mackenzie, Principal Clerk of Standing Committees; to Mr. T. G. Odling and Dr. E. S. Taylor, Senior Clerks, House of Commons; to Major-General I. T. P.

Hughes, C.B., C.B.E., D.S.O., M.C., Deputy Serjeant at Arms, and Lieutenant-Colonel P. F. Thorne, Assistant Serjeant at Arms, House of Commons; to Air Vice-Marshal Sir Paul Maltby, K.B.E., C.B., D.S.O., A.F.C., Serjeant at Arms, House of Lords; to Mr. A. H. Jeffreys, Reading Clerk and Chief Clerk, Committee and Private Bill Office, and Mr. C. F. L. St. George, C.B.E., Clerk of the Journals, House of Lords; and to Mr. T. G. Seager Berry, President, Society of Parliamentary Agents.

L. A. A.

May, 1956. S. C. H.

A PARLIAMENTARY DICTIONARY

ABSENCE, LEAVE OF

Members of both Houses of Parliament who were unable to attend or desired to absent themselves from the House to which they belonged formerly applied to the House* for leave of absence, which, if granted, suspended their obligations to attend the House and to discharge any duties imposed upon them by it. Such applications continued to be made long after the attendance of members (except at election committees and committees on opposed private bills where it was obligatory) had ceased to be enforced. The trial of controverted elections was transferred to the courts in 1868, and though members of committees on opposed private bills were (and are) still obliged to attend†, the gradual decline in the number of private bills reduced the likelihood of a reluctant member being compelled to serve on one of these committees and as time went on applications for leave of absence became less and less frequent and none has been made since 1901, when a fortnight's leave of absence was given to Mr. Bignold on account of domestic affliction.

Since 1948 members who are to present maces, Speakers' chairs, and other gifts from the House to Commonwealth legislatures have been given leave of absence without their asking for it. This expedient has been resorted to because the House, having no funds at its disposal for the purpose, has to present an address praying the Sovereign to make the gift to the legislature in question on its behalf, and the gift thus being the Sovereign's, the House cannot *impose* the duty of making the presentation on the members who have been chosen to make it.

The obligation of members of the House of Lords to attend their House, or, if they cannot do so, to obtain leave of absence, and the right of the House of Lords to grant or refuse such leave as it thinks fit, were re-affirmed by that House in 1958. The relevant

* Attendance in Parliament being in origin a duty owed to the Crown, leave of absence had at first to be obtained from the King. In 1515, however, power to license members to depart or absent themselves from Parliament before the end of the session was conferred by statute upon "the Speaker and the Commons". The power of excusing the attendance of peers in Parliament was assumed by the House of Lords during the seventeenth century with the tacit consent, or at least the acquiescence, of the Crown.

† So recently as 1931 a member who had absented himself from a committee on opposed private bills was ordered to attend the committee at its next sitting.

ABSENCE, LEAVE OF—*continued*

standing order as then amended states, however, that a member who is unable to attend regularly is not required to apply for leave of absence if he proposes to attend as often as he reasonably can. A member may apply for leave of absence at any time during a Parliament; he may apply for leave of absence for a session or for the remainder of the current session, or for the remainder of the Parliament.

Before the beginning of each session letters are sent by the Lord Chancellor to all members whose leave of absence expired with the preceding session or who, though not granted leave of absence, did not attend the House during the preceding session (except in order to take the oath of allegiance), asking them whether or not they wish to apply for leave of absence. Members who fail to reply within twenty-eight days are deemed to have applied for leave of absence for the remainder of the Parliament, and the necessary orders are made.

Members who have been granted leave of absence are expected not to attend the House (except in order to take the oath of allegiance) until their leave has either expired or been terminated by the House. A member who wishes to attend before his leave of absence has expired is expected to give at least one month's notice to the Clerk of the Parliaments of his desire to do so, in which case his leave ends one month from the date of his notice or sooner if the House so directs.

ABUSE OF THE RULES OF THE HOUSE

A term used in several standing orders of the House of Commons. It may be defined as the use by a member for an improper purpose (*e.g.* to impede the transaction of business or to prevent the minority from giving utterance to sentiments unpalatable to the majority or which they do not wish to be voiced) of his right to move motions. For a member who has been speaking on a question to conclude his speech by moving the closure would probably be considered to be an abuse of the rules of the House.

ACT OF PARLIAMENT

A bill passed by one House of Parliament, agreed to by the other either without amendment or with amendments to which the first House has agreed, and assented to by the Queen. Under the provisions of the Parliament Acts 1911 and 1949 a bill passed by the House of Commons may receive the royal assent and become an act without the agreement of the Lords (*see* BILL, PUBLIC). Acts of Parliament are divided into public general acts, local and personal acts and private acts. In the legal vocabulary Acts of Parliament are referred to as statutes.

ADDRESS

When either House wishes to make known its desires or opinions to the Sovereign, it does so by means of an address. A motion is made, beginning with the words " That an humble address be presented to Her Majesty ", and setting forth the request or sentiments to be communicated. This is treated like any other motion ; it may be amended, debated, and divided upon. If an address is agreed to by the Commons, an order is thereupon made " that the said address be presented to Her Majesty by such Members of this House as are of Her Majesty's Most Honourable Privy Council or of Her Majesty's Household " ; in practice it is conveyed by one of the Government Whips holding a Court appointment, who may have to travel to Balmoral to wait upon the Queen.

In the Lords an address is usually ordered to be presented by " the Lords with white staves ", that is, the Lord Steward and the Lord Chamberlain, who are members of the royal household.

An address which has been ordered to be presented by members of either House is answered by message from the Queen. This message is usually brought to the Lords by the Lord Chamberlain, who wears levee dress and carries a white staff, and in the Commons by a Government Whip holding an appointment in the Royal Household. In either case the proceedings are interrupted while the messenger reads Her Majesty's answer.

Occasionally in either House members may be specified by name to present an address ; but this is rarely done nowadays.

Either House may resolve that an address shall be presented by the whole House. This is a ceremonial reserved for special occasions, such as the victorious end of a war. The members go to Buckingham Palace (or such other place as may be appointed) to attend the Queen ; the Lord Chancellor or the Speaker, as the case may be, is at their head and reads the address, afterwards handing it to Her Majesty, kneeling upon one knee. The Queen delivers her answer to the address, after which the peers or members depart.

It was formerly not uncommon for a single address to be jointly agreed to by both Houses on important occasions. In such cases one House first agrees to a resolution for an address, which is then communicated to the other House by message (a blank being left in the address for the name of that House) and its concurrence desired thereto. The other House then agrees to the address, filling up the blank, and sends a message to the first House, acquainting it that it has agreed to the address and has filled up the blank by inserting its own name. The Lords order one of their own members, holding an office in the Royal Household, to " wait upon Her Majesty humbly to know where and at

ADDRESS—*continued*

what time Her Majesty will please to appoint to be attended with the address ". When the place and time have been announced to the Lords, they send a message to inform the Commons.

The presentation of a joint address may be by both Houses in a body, or by members appointed by each House to undertake the duty, or by the Lord Chancellor and the Speaker. When members are named for the purpose, the Lords, in announcing by message to the Commons the place and time for the address to be presented, state at the same time whom they have appointed to attend the Queen with the address ; and they ask the Commons to appoint " a proportionate number " of their members for the same purpose. The House then appoints four of its own members to accompany the two peers appointed by the Lords, and sends a message to that effect (showing their names) to the House of Lords.

The ceremony of joint presentation is like that of presentation by the whole House, except that the Lord Chancellor and the Speaker walk side by side, each followed by the members of his own House, the Speaker being on the Lord Chancellor's left. The address is read by the Lord Chancellor.

The last occasion when a joint address was presented by the two Houses together was in 1842 ; and no joint address has been agreed to since 1880. In recent years the custom has been, on occasions of national rejoicing such as the victorious conclusion of war in 1918 and 1945, for separate addresses to be presented in the same place one after the other (the Sovereign having appointed the same time and place for both Houses). The Commons arrive first. When the Queen has arrived, the Lord Chancellor reads the Lords' address, and after the Speaker has read that of the Commons the Queen delivers her reply to both addresses. In recent years these ceremonies have taken place in Westminster Hall; the last one, on June 22, 1965, celebrated the seven hundredth anniversary of Parliament.

So far as subject matter is concerned, addresses may be divided into two classes : (*a*) those of the more formal sort, expressing the joy or sorrow of the House at an event of public importance (such as the victorious end of a war) or on some matter of more personal significance to the Sovereign (such as the birth, marriage or death of a member of the royal family, including her relations in the royal families of foreign countries) ; and (*b*) those which either express the opinions of the House or request the statutory exercise of the royal power with regard to some matter of public policy.

The legislative powers of the Queen are exercised by means of Orders in Council ; Orders, that is, which are made by the Queen at meetings of the Privy Council, by whose advice she acts. Many of these are now made under the authority of various statutes, which provide that orders may first be made in draft by a minister and presented to both Houses (or the House of Commons only, if they concern finance); if both Houses (or the House of Commons only, in the case of a financial Order) agree to an address praying that an Order be made in the form of the draft laid before Parliament, the Queen then makes an Order in Council which has legislative effect. Statutes may also provide for the annulment of orders, statutory instruments, etc., on the presentation to the Queen of an address praying for such action. Motions for addresses for the annulment of statutory instruments are often called "prayers" by members because they "pray" for action by Her Majesty.

The great majority of addresses in both Houses nowadays are in the last category; that is, they are moved under the provisions of a statute. But one other address, which is regularly voted every session, may be noted; the address of thanks which is moved in answer to the speech with which the Queen opens Parliament at the beginning of each session. This provides the occasion for a general debate—commonly known as the "debate on the Address"—on the policy of the Government as announced in the Queen's speech, and amendments are regularly moved by the Opposition, expressing regret at the absence from the speech of the mention of policies favoured by them. Although these amendments are keenly debated and voted upon, it is contrary to parliamentary etiquette to vote against the address itself.

ADJOURNMENT OF THE DEBATE, MOTION FOR

A motion for the adjournment of the debate may be moved at any time during a debate (except, of course, while another member is speaking). It may be moved by any member who has not exhausted his right to speak to the question under debate and succeeds in catching the Speaker's eye. Thus the adjournment of the debate on a substantive motion could be moved by the member who had moved the motion provided that he had done so without making a speech—by raising his hat or in some other formal manner. A motion for the adjournment of the debate on any question cannot be moved before that question has been proposed from the chair, but it may be moved immediately after the question has been so proposed.

The motion must be simply "that the debate be now adjourned", and not that it be adjourned till any particular time. If the Speaker considers that such a motion is an "abuse of the rules of the House", he may either refuse to accept it, or accept the motion and put the question on it at once without allowing it to be debated. Members speaking on the motion must confine themselves to giving reasons why the debate should or should not be adjourned. They cannot continue to discuss the motion, debate on which is proposed to be adjourned.

ADJOURNMENT OF THE DEBATE, MOTION FOR—*continued*

A motion for the adjournment of the *debate* cannot be moved while a motion for the adjournment of the *House* is under discussion.

If a motion for the adjournment of the debate is defeated, a second motion to the same effect cannot be moved unless some other motion or an amendment has in the meantime been moved.

The mover of a motion for the adjournment of the debate has no right of reply and if the motion is *defeated* he loses his right to speak to the original motion. If, however, the motion is *carried*, the mover does not forfeit his right to speak when the debate is resumed provided that, in moving the adjournment of the debate, he confines himself to giving reasons why the debate should be adjourned ; and if he rises directly the question is again proposed, the Speaker will call upon him in preference to other members. If the motion is carried, the mover of the original motion must name a day for resuming the debate, otherwise it will lapse.

If the discussion on a motion for the adjournment of the debate continues until the Speaker interrupts the business in pursuance of the standing order, the motion lapses, but the mover does not lose his right to speak on the original motion when the debate is resumed.

In theory a motion for the adjournment of the debate, if carried, merely defers the decision of the question. In the case of a private member's motion or bill the carrying of such a motion is likely to be fatal as only a limited amount of time is available for business initiated by private members and any that remains will usually have already been bespoken.

A motion for the adjournment of the debate can only be made in the House ; in a committee of the whole House the corresponding motion is " That the Chairman do report progress and ask leave to sit again " (*see* PROGRESS, MOTION TO REPORT).

ADJOURNMENT OF THE HOUSE

The adjournment whether of the House of Lords or of the House of Commons means the termination of the sitting of that House with a view to holding the next sitting of that House the following or some later day. In the House of Lords this can be effected only by the carrying of a motion " That this House do now adjourn ". The adjournment of the House of Commons usually takes place as a result of a motion " That this House do now adjourn " being carried or, in the following circumstances, of its merely being moved. If such a motion is moved at or after 10 p.m. on a Monday, Tuesday, Wednesday or Thursday, or on a Friday at or after 4 p.m., after the orders of the day have been disposed of, or immediately after an order has been disposed of and before the next one is read, and the motion is not agreed to within half an hour, the Speaker adjourns the House. Similarly when a motion to suspend a sitting until the following morning has been agreed to (*see* SUSPENSION OF SITTING), a motion for the adjournment of the House follows immediately upon the proceedings on the motion to suspend the sitting; in this case the Speaker leaves the Chair without putting any question on the adjournment motion at the time that it is debated (i.e., before the sitting is suspended), and adjourns the House without putting any question at the conclusion of the resumed proceedings on the following day. The adjournment of the House may also take place as the result of the number of members present falling below forty (*see* QUORUM), or of grave disorder arising (*see* ORDER IN THE HOUSE).

The House cannot be adjourned on Mondays, Tuesdays, Wednesdays or Thursdays until questions are finished.

When a motion " That this House do now adjourn " is carried, or the House is adjourned by the Speaker, it stands adjourned till the following day (or the same day if the House is adjourned between midnight and the normal time for opening the next sitting but if the following day is a Saturday or Sunday, the House stands adjourned till the following Monday) unless it has previously passed a resolution that it will at its rising adjourn till some other day. Such a resolution may be passed earlier in the sitting or at a previous one.

Either House may be summoned by its presiding officer to meet before the day to which it stands adjourned if he is satisfied that an earlier meeting is required by the public interest. In the case of the House of Lords the initiative rests formally with the Lord Chancellor, who is, however, required, before summoning the House to meet, to consult the Government. The Speaker of the House of Commons acts only on representations being made by the Government. The Lord Chancellor is given the power by a sessional order, the Speaker by standing order. Should either the Lord Chancellor or the Speaker be unable to act owing to sickness or any other cause, the power may be exercised as regards the House of Lords by the Chairman of Committees and as regards the House of Commons by the Chairman of Ways and Means or the Deputy Chairman. The standing order provides that the business on the day on which the House of Commons meets in these circumstances shall be such as the Government appoints subject to the publication of notice in the order paper circulated that day; any Government orders of the day and notices of motions that stand in the order book are automatically appointed for the day of the resumption.

When both Houses stand adjourned for more than six days they may be summoned by royal proclamation to meet on any earlier day not less than six days from the day of the date of the proclamation. Under the Emergency Powers Act 1920 if a proclamation is made of a state of emergency and Parliament is

ADJOURNMENT OF THE HOUSE—*continued*

separated by an adjournment or prorogation which will not expire within five days, a further proclamation must be made for the meeting of Parliament within five days. The Act makes no explicit provision for the arrangement of business on the day on which the House meets; but in such circumstances proceedings would normally begin with the communication of a message from the Queen announcing the issue of the original proclamation and a debate on the message would follow.

On the death of a Sovereign neither House transacts anything but formal business (notably the taking of the oath of allegiance to the new Sovereign by members) for several days. Either House sometimes adjourns as a mark of respect on the occasion of the death of other members of the royal family, or of a distinguished member or ex-member or of the death of a member within the precincts during a sitting. Formerly the House of Commons adjourned on the death of a former prime minister only if he was not a peer at the time of his death, but since 1928 the House has adjourned as a mark of respect to the memory of former prime ministers who have been raised to the peerage. The period for which the House adjourned on the death of Sir Winston Churchill was from January 26th to February 1st, 1965. The House adjourned for the remainder of the sitting on the deaths of the Earl of Oxford and Asquith (1928), Earl Lloyd George (1945) Earl Baldwin (1947) and Earl Attlee (1968). It also adjourned for the remainder of the sitting on January 22 1963, as a mark of respect to the memory of Mr. Gaitskell, who at the time of his death was leader of the opposition. On April 12, 1945, the House of Commons adjourned as a mark of respect to the memory of President Roosevelt; on November 25, 1963, the House adjourned after voting an address to the Queen expressing its sorrow at the assassination of President Kennedy; these are the only occasions on which the House has adjourned on the death of the head of a foreign state. In such cases the adjournment is normally moved at the commencement of public business and the House adjourns for the rest of the day as soon as formal speeches have been made.

ADJOURNMENT OF THE HOUSE, MOTION FOR

May not be made on Mondays, Tuesdays, Wednesdays or Thursdays until questions are finished. It may be moved before the orders of the day or notices of motion are entered on, or between two orders of the day, *i.e.* after one order of the day has been disposed of and before the next one is read, only by a member of the Government. It can be moved during the debate on any question, except while the House is in committee, by either a private member or a member of the Government, but when it is moved in these circumstances the Speaker may put the question on it forthwith or may decline to propose the question on it. It can also be moved by a private member for the purpose of discussing a specific and important matter that should have urgent consideration provided he has previously obtained the leave of the House to do so. The debate on a motion for the adjournment of the House cannot be adjourned, nor can such a motion be made while a motion for the adjournment of a debate is under discussion; but a motion for the adjournment of the House can be interrupted by, or anticipated by another motion for the adjournment if the latter motion is moved with the leave of the House for the purpose of discussing a specific and important matter that should have urgent consideration. If the debate on a motion for the adjournment of the House continues until 10 p.m. or, on Fridays, until 4 p.m., the motion lapses. If a motion for the adjournment of the House is made at or after 10 p.m. (4 p.m. on a Friday) between two orders of the day, or after the orders of the day have been disposed of, it cannot be debated for longer than half an hour. The Speaker must then adjourn the House, or, in the case where a motion to suspend the proceedings of the day's sitting has already been agreed to, suspend the sitting till the following morning.

Motions for the adjournment of the House may be classified as (1) *substantive, i.e.* motions for the adjournment of the House moved when no motion or order of the day is under consideration, including motions moved with the leave of the House for the purpose of discussing a specific and important matter that should have urgent consideration; and (2) *dilatory, i.e.* motions for the adjournment of the House moved during a debate on a motion or an amendment or during proceedings on an order of the day.

A substantive motion for the adjournment of the House normally takes the form " that this House do now adjourn ". It cannot be amended except by adding the words " until such and such a day " or " until such and such a day at such and such an hour ". The mover has the right of reply.

Any subject for which the Government is immediately responsible may be discussed on such a motion provided that it does not entail legislation. It is, however, out of order on a motion for the adjournment of the House to discuss the subject matter of any bill which has been introduced or notice of the intended introduction of which has been given, or the subject matter of a motion or an amendment of which notice has been given. (*See* ANTICIPATION, RULE AGAINST.) The Speaker has, however, discretion to allow *incidental* reference to be made to matters involving legislation, provided that they are relevant to the subject under discussion. It is out of order to discuss the conduct of the Sovereign, governors-general of Commonwealth countries, members of either House of Parliament, judges and certain other

ADJOURNMENT OF THE HOUSE, MOTION FOR—*continued*

persons on a motion for the adjournment of the House. Motions for the adjournment of the House are occasionally moved by the Government in order to afford a minister an opportunity of making a statement of policy or some other announcement, and are commonly moved to provide an opportunity for debating a matter without committing the House in any way.

In theory a member who wishes to raise a matter on the motion for the adjournment of the House which is made at each sitting after the interruption of business, or at the conclusion of exempted business, or before the proceedings are suspended till the following morning, has only to catch the Speaker's eye. In practice the subjects to be discussed on this motion on Mondays, Tuesdays, Wednesdays and Fridays are selected by ballot, while those to be discussed on Thursdays are selected by the Speaker. When the selection rests with the Speaker he endeavours to give priority to (*a*) individual or constituency grievances and (*b*) matters of immediate topical interest.

Ballots are held on Thursdays during the session; a member who wishes to raise a matter on the adjournment on some day in the period from the next Tuesday to the following Monday must write to the Speaker before 10 p.m. on the preceding Wednesday stating the subject he proposes to raise and the minister concerned. On Thursdays the Speaker considers the letters he has received on this matter since the previous ballot, and allocates the subject to be raised on the motion for the adjournment on the following Thursday. The names of the members who have not been selected by the Speaker are, if eligible, put into the ballot for the privilege of raising a matter on the adjournment on the Tuesday, Wednesday, Friday and Monday. A member whose name is drawn in the ballot is not eligible to ballot for the following week, but he is not precluded from submitting his name and subject for the Speaker's selection. A member may not have more than one application current at the same time, and if a further application is received from a member the original application is treated as withdrawn. An oral notice of a member's intention to raise a matter on the adjournment will not be considered by the Speaker unless it is confirmed in writing. A member is not allowed to change a subject selected by the Speaker for an adjournment debate except with the Speaker's consent; for changes in other (balloted) subjects forty-eight hours' notice is required. The list of subjects proposed to be raised is published with the notice paper on the day after the ballot is held and again in the order book published on Saturday mornings, and any alteration is notified from time to time.

A motion for the adjournment of the House for the purpose of discussing a specific and important matter that

should have urgent consideration can be made only with the leave of the House. Only one such motion can be made at a sitting. If a member wishes to move the adjournment of the House for this purpose, he must give notice to the Speaker by noon if the urgency of the matter is then known; if the urgency is not then known he must give the Speaker notice as soon as practicable. He must then rise after questions and before the Speaker calls on the first member who has given notice of his intention to present a bill or move a motion " at the commencement of public business ", or, if no such notice has been given, before the Speaker directs the Clerk to read the orders of the day. He must then " ask leave to move the adjournment of the House for the purpose of discussing a specific and important matter that should have urgent consideration ", stating what it is. Lastly he must hand to the Speaker a statement in writing of the matter he wishes to discuss. The Speaker states whether or not he is satisfied that the matter is proper to be discussed or, if he so wishes, defers giving his decision till a named hour. If he is satisfied that the matter is one proper to be discussed, the Speaker asks whether the member has the leave of the House to move the adjournment for the purpose of discussing the matter. If no member objects, the leave of the House is taken to be given for the member to move the motion. If any member objects, the Speaker asks the members who support the motion to rise, and if not less than forty members rise, again the motion can proceed; but if less than forty but not less than ten members rise a division may be held to determine whether the motion shall proceed.

If it is decided in any of these three ways that the motion shall proceed, it normally stands over until the commencement of public business on the following day (or on the following Monday if leave to move the motion is obtained on a Thursday); but it may stand over until 7 p.m. of the day on which leave was obtained if the Speaker directs that the urgency of the matter so requires.

Debate on the motion must be confined to such topics as would be in order if the motion were a motion to take note of the subject under discussion. The mover of the motion has no right of reply.

A dilatory motion for the adjournment of the House must be simply " that this House do now adjourn ", and cannot be amended. It may be moved at any time during a debate (except, of course, while another member is speaking). It may be moved by any member who has not exhausted his right to speak to the question and succeeds in catching the Speaker's eye (*see* DEBATE). Debate on the motion must be confined to giving reasons why the House should or should not adjourn. If the Speaker considers that the motion is an " abuse of the rules of the House " (*q.v.*), he may either refuse to accept it, or accept it and put the question

ADJOURNMENT OF THE HOUSE, MOTION FOR— *continued*

on it at once without allowing the motion to be debated. If a motion for the adjournment of the House is made during a debate but is defeated, (1) the mover cannot speak when the debate on the original motion is resumed, and (2) a motion for the adjournment of the House cannot be moved again during the debate unless the question on some other motion has in the meantime been proposed from the chair.

If a motion for the adjournment of the House is carried during the debate on a substantive motion or an amendment to such a motion, the substantive motion drops and, if it is desired to resume the discussion, notice of the motion must be given afresh. Similarly, if a motion for the adjournment of the House is carried during the proceedings on an order of the day, the consideration of the bill or other matter which was the subject of the order cannot be resumed unless it is made an order for a future day (*see* DROPPED ORDER).

ADMONITION

A mild form of reprimand (*q.v.*). The last instance of the Speaker's being directed to admonish an offender occurred in 1930 when Mr. Sandham, a member, was directed to be admonished for making a speech at a public meeting reflecting on the character of the House of Commons.

AFFIRMATION

A solemn declaration which a person, who objects to taking an oath either because he has no religious belief or because the taking of an oath is contrary to his religious belief, is allowed by Act of Parliament to make instead of taking an oath. A member may make an affirmation that he will be faithful and bear true allegiance to the Queen, her heirs and successors according to law instead of taking the oath of allegiance, and when evidence before a committee of either House of Parliament is given on oath, *e.g.* in a committee on an opposed private bill, a person called as a witness, instead of taking an oath, may make an affirmation that he will speak the truth.

ALLOTTED DAY

Twenty-nine days are allotted by standing order to the business of Supply during the session. These "allotted days", as they are called, must all occur before August 5. They are in the nature of a minimum provision of time for this business, since there is nothing to prevent Supply being considered on other days, as in fact happens from time to time. The status of an allotted day is governed by certain conditions, failure to observe which means that the day will not count as such, with the result that another day has to be set aside for the purpose. Some of these conditions may, however, be waived for a particular occasion, as will be explained below.

Supply must be the first order of the day on an allotted day, and, with three exceptions, no other business may be taken before 10 p.m., nor may Supply be taken after that hour (save that on three days, as explained below, the proceedings are subject to interruption by the fall of a guillotine at 10 p.m. and must be brought to an end even if the process of completing them extends beyond that hour. The three exceptions are (1) motions for the adjournment of the House on a specific and important matter that should have urgent consideration; (2) opposed private business set down by direction of the Chairman of Ways and Means (either of these may interrupt any business at 7 p.m. and the first may also precede the business of Supply and continue until that hour); and (3) matters of privilege suddenly arising and requiring immediate action by the House.

The business of Supply, as defined for the purpose of an allotted day, includes not only proceedings on all estimates of any sort (except votes of credit or votes for supplementary or additional estimates for war expenditure) but also proceedings on substantive motions and motions for the adjournment of the House and the consideration of reports from the Committee of Public Accounts and the Estimates Committee. The modern tendency is for the allotted days, or Supply days as they are also called, to be used progressively less for debates on the estimates and more for debates on general matters of current interest which take place either on substantive motions or on motions for the adjournment. The latter motions are sometimes preferred for general debates since a decision of the question does not commit the House to the formal expression of an opinion. It is usual, however, for the three service votes "A", authorising the numbers to be employed in the Navy (including Royal Marines), Army and Air Force respectively, to be debated each on an allotted day and for another such day to be devoted to all three services together. On three of the allotted days, moreover, the House must consider (even if it does not debate) various parts of the estimates and on these days a guillotine is provided to ensure that the business shall not fail to be concluded for lack of time (see FINANCE; SUPPLY). On these three days no motion for the adjournment of the House may be made before the consideration of Supply, nor may the business be interrupted by a dilatory motion, that is, a motion for the adjournment of the House or of the debate.

An allotted day may be taken in the form of two half-days; in this case Supply must be the first order and occupy the first half of the day and no business of Supply may be taken after 7 p.m.; not more than one half-day may be taken in two consecutive months and if an odd half-day remains to be taken, when the last allotted day is reached, it is ignored and the previous half-day

ALLOTTED DAY—*continued*

counts as a whole day. Two Fridays count as one day for the purpose of reckoning allotted days; but Fridays are now rarely used as Supply days. The rule requiring that nothing but Supply shall be considered before 10 p.m. on an allotted day is sometimes suspended by order of the House, either to enable other business to be taken if the business of Supply should be disposed of early or to make time for business not included within the definition of Supply. On such an occasion the leader of the House (or some other minister) moves "That this day business other than the business of Supply may be taken before ten o'clock"—a motion of which notice must appear on the paper on the day on which it is to be moved.

By custom, the Opposition have the right to choose the subject to be discussed on an allotted day and, although Supply is Government business, an allotted day is really "Opposition time". The Opposition may sometimes be called upon, in effect, to give up an allotted day, being part of the time at their disposal, as their contribution to an arrangement made to suit the general convenience.

The expression "allotted day" is also applied to a day allotted by order of the House to the consideration of a specified part of a bill or other business under a guillotine or allocation of time order.

AMENDMENT

An alteration proposed or made in a motion or bill. It must take the form of a proposal either to insert certain words in the motion or bill, or to leave out certain words or to leave out certain words and to substitute others. It is permissible by way of amendment to move to leave out all the words of a motion except the initial word "That" and substitute other words to give the motion a completely different sense.

Notice of an amendment is required only in the case of amendments proposing the substitution of an alternative name for one of those on the list of proposed members of a select committee, of amendments to instructions to committees on bills (*q.v.*) which would widen the scope of the instruction and of amendments to the question for the third reading of a public bill. In the latter case, notice is not effective unless signed by not less than six members. Nevertheless notice of amendments is normally given wherever practicable.

When giving notice of an amendment it is important to remember than an amendment to leave out from (a certain word) to (a certain word) will be construed as a proposal to omit the intervening words only.

An amendment may be moved to a motion at any time after the question has been *proposed* from the chair and before it is *put*. Subject to the power of the Speaker to select which amendments, if any, shall be proposed to the motion, any member who catches the Speaker's eye may move an amendment.

A member who wishes to move an amendment must catch the Speaker's eye. Even though he may have given notice of an amendment the Speaker will not call upon him to speak unless he rises. Nor will the Speaker necessarily call on him in preference to any other member who rises to speak at the same time.

When an amendment proposes to leave out some only of the words of a motion and insert other words instead of them, only the words proposed to be omitted (as well, of course, as those proposed to be substituted) may be discussed, not the whole of the original motion. If, however, the amendment is, in effect, a counter-motion, *e.g.* where it takes the form of a proposal to leave out all the words of the original motion except the initial word " That " and substitute words of a different tenor, the original motion, as well as the alternative proposition, may be discussed. Debate on an amendment to leave words out of, or insert words in, a motion must be confined to the words which it is proposed to omit or insert.

No amendment may be moved after the previous question (*q.v.*) has been moved. After an amendment has been moved, the Speaker, after stating what the original question was and how it is proposed to amend it, proposes the question in the form " That the amendment be made ". (But in the particular case where an amendment is proposed to leave out the word " now " in the question that a bill be now read a second or third time, the question for the amendment is put in the form " That the word ' now ' stand part of the question ".) In the House of Lords the question put on an amendment of whatever type is " That this amendment be agreed to ".

When the House has resolved that an amendment shall or shall not be made, no amendment may be moved to any preceding part of the motion. No amendment may be moved to an amendment once the House has decided that it shall be made.

An amendment may be withdrawn by the mover with the leave of the House or committee. An amendment cannot be withdrawn in the absence of the mover, except that one member of the Government may act for another; and when an amendment has been moved to a motion, the motion cannot be withdrawn until the proposed amendment has been withdrawn.

An amendment must be relevant to the motion to which it is moved.

The following amendments are out of order: an amendment which refers to the conduct of a person whose conduct cannot be discussed except on a substantive motion; an amendment which is

AMENDMENT—*continued*
substantially the same as a proposition upon which the House has already expressed its opinion during the session, or which deals with the subject matter of a bill or other matter appointed for consideration or with the subject matter of a motion of which notice has been given; an amendment which is at variance with or inconsistent with words which precede the point at which the House has already taken a decision on an amendment, or with an amendment which has already been made; an amendment which is so worded that, if carried, it would make the motion to which it is moved unintelligible or ungrammatical; an amendment which is merely an expanded negative.

No amendment may be moved to a motion " That this House at its rising this day do adjourn till . . . " except an amendment proposing that the House should adjourn till a different day or that the House should adjourn to an hour other than the usual hour of meeting on the day on which its sitting is to be resumed.

The only amendments which may be moved to a motion for the second or third reading of a bill are (i) an amendment to leave out the word " now " and add the words " upon this day three months (or six months) " at the end of the question, or (ii) an amendment to leave out from the word " that " to the end of the question and add words placing on record reasons for not giving a second or third reading to the bill. An amendment of the latter type is known as a " reasoned amendment ".

The Speaker has power to select what amendments, if any, shall be proposed to any motion. If he thinks fit he may call upon any member who has given notice of an amendment to explain its object so as to enable him to decide whether to select it or not.

The Chairman of Ways and Means when acting as Deputy Speaker has no power to select amendments unless the Clerk has previously informed the House of the unavoidable absence of the Speaker; accordingly if the Speaker has made no selection, the Deputy Speaker is obliged to call any amendment which is offered, so long as it is in order. Similarly the Deputy Chairman of Ways and Means when acting as Deputy Speaker cannot exercise the power of selecting amendments unless the Clerk has previously informed the House of the unavoidable absence of the Chairman of Ways and Means as well as of the Speaker. When the House is in committee, however, both the Chairman and Deputy Chairman can exercise the power.

The procedure for amendments to bills, whether in committee or in the House, is similar to that for amendments to motions; and questions are put on them in the same way. But unlike a member who wishes to move an amendment to a motion, a member who wishes to move an amendment to a bill has not to catch the chairman's (or the Speaker's) eye. He must, however, give notice of the amendment, or at any rate apprise the chairman (or the Speaker) of his wish, and hand him the terms of the amendment. If the chairman (or the Speaker) selects the amendment for consideration, he calls upon the member by name when the appropriate point is reached in the consideration of the bill.

A member who has given notice of an amendment is not obliged to move it, but if he does not do so, any other member may. The amendments which are selected for consideration are considered in priority of place in the bill. (Amendments of which notice has been given are printed on the notice paper in this order). An amendment which proposes to leave out certain words and to insert others is given priority over an amendment which proposes merely to leave out the same words.

Amendments proposed to bills in committee must be relevant to the clause or schedule to which they are moved, and must not be inconsistent with a previous decision of the committee whether come to on the clause (or schedule) under consideration or on an earlier clause (or schedule). In committee it is not in order to move to leave out a clause or schedule, because the same object can be achieved by voting against the question " that the clause stand part of the bill " (or " that this be the (*n*th) schedule to the bill "). The rules as to what amendments are in order and what are not on the report stage of a bill are much the same as those with regard to amendments in committee. An amendment to leave out a clause or schedule is, however, in order at the report stage.

The former practice of the House of Commons was for different forms of question to be proposed depending on the form of the amendment. If the amendment sought only to insert words, the question was proposed " that those words be there inserted "; if the amendment sought to leave out words, the question was proposed " that the words proposed to be left out stand part of the question (or clause, etc.); if the amendment sought to leave out words and insert other words in their place, the question was first put " that the words proposed to be left out stand part of the question (or clause, etc.), and if that question was negatived, a further question was put " that the proposed words be there inserted ".

When questions were proposed in this form, the rule was that, once words had been ordered to stand part, neither the words preceding them nor the words themselves could be further amended. In cases where amendments sought to alter some words which were proposed to be omitted altogether by other amendments, it was the practice to call first the amendment which proposed to leave out all the words but to " save " the amendment which sought to alter only some of the words concerned by proposing the question " that the words proposed to be left out to the word so and so (the first word proposed to be altered by the latter

AMENDMENT—*continued*

amendment) stand part of the Clause ". If that question was agreed to, the second amendment could still be moved, as all that had been decided was that the words specified in the question should stand part of the clause. If, however, the question was negatived, it was held to have been decided that not only the words specified in the question, but all the words to which the amendment related, should be struck out, and the second amendment dropped.

The present practice of the House of Commons of proposing the question on amendments in the form " That the amendment be made " was adopted in 1967. The Lords' practice of proposing the question " That this amendment be agreed to " is of much longer standing; it was adopted by that House because the chair has no casting vote and it was desirable to achieve consistency within the rule that when the votes are equal the question is decided in the negative.

AMENDMENT, CONSEQUENTIAL

An amendment which requires to be made to a bill (or motion) as a consequence of the making of an amendment in an earlier part of the bill (or motion).

AMENDMENT, REASONED

A reasoned amendment may be moved on second or third reading of a bill and on certain other occasions, as stated below. This form of amendment seeks, by substituting other words for those of the question " That the bill be now read a second (third) time ", either to give reasons why the House declines to give a second or third reading to the bill, or to express an opinion with regard to its subject matter or to the policy which the bill is intended to fulfil. Like an amendment which seeks to put off the second reading of a bill for six months, a reasoned amendment is actually moved in the form of an ordinary motion. The question is put in the normal form for amendments, *i.e.* in the form " That the amendment be made "; but if the question for the amendment is not carried in the House of Commons the Speaker is required to put the main question, *i.e.* " That the Bill be now read a second (third) time ", forthwith.

AMENDMENT TO A PROPOSED AMENDMENT

A proposed amendment to insert words in or add words to a motion, bill, clause or schedule may be amended in the same way as a motion, etc., *i.e.* some of the words proposed to be inserted (or added) may be struck out, or words may be inserted among the proposed words, or some of the words which it is proposed to insert (or add) may be struck out and others substituted. But where it is proposed to leave out words, the proposed amendment can be amended only by leaving out some of the words which it is proposed to omit from the motion, etc., thereby restoring them to the original text.

An amendment can be moved to the proposed amendment directly the Speaker or the chairman has proposed the question on the original amendment. The procedure is similar to that on an amendment to a motion. When the amendment to the proposed amendment has been moved, the Speaker (or the chairman) proposes the question " That the amendment (*i.e.* to the proposed amendment) be made ", and when this question has been decided, puts the question on the original amendment or on the original amendment as amended, as the case may be.

Subject to the same rules and limitations as apply in the case of amendments to motions, several amendments may be moved in succession to a proposed amendment. An amendment to leave out all the words proposed to be inserted would be out of order.

ANTICIPATION, RULE AGAINST

When the House has ordered a bill or any other matter (*e.g.* an adjourned debate on a motion) to be considered upon a certain day, it is out of order for a member on an earlier day to move a motion or an amendment dealing with that matter. He may not even discuss it on a motion for the adjournment of the House (whether moved under Standing Order No. 9 or not) or on any other question on which a corresponding latitude of discussion is permitted, *e.g.* on the second reading of a Consolidated Fund Bill or the Appropriation Bill.

It is also out of order for a member, when notice has been given of a motion for a future day, to raise the subject of that motion in the form of an amendment to another motion (*e.g.* to the address in reply to the Queen's speech) on an earlier day, or to discuss the subject to which the motion relates on a motion for the adjournment of the House or on any other question on which debate is not required to be relevant to the question which has been proposed from the chair. This rule formerly applied even though notice of the motion anticipated had been given for a day on which notices of motions did not have precedence or simply for " an early day ".

This rule made it possible for a member to prevent a motion, for which precedence had been obtained in the ballot, from being discussed by introducing a bill dealing with the same subject, or to prevent a matter from being discussed on a motion for the adjournment of the House by giving notice of a motion on the matter for an early day or for a day on which there was no likelihood of the motion being reached. This abuse has been partially remedied by a standing order (No. 11) which directs the Speaker, in deciding whether a matter sought to be discussed is out of

ANTICIPATION, RULE AGAINST—*continued*

order on the ground of anticipation, to have regard to the probability of the business which is alleged to be anticipated being brought before the House within a reasonable time.

APPEAL COMMITTEE

Two Appeal Committees are appointed by the House of Lords at the beginning of every session. Their function is to consider and report on petitions for leave to appeal from the Court of Appeal, petitions for leave to sue *in forma pauperis* and opposed petitions on any matter connected with an appeal. They consist of all the lords who have been or shall be present during the session. As a rule only the Lords of Appeal in Ordinary attend. The quorum is three. Petitions for leave to appeal are heard in public unless the committee decides otherwise.

APPELLATE COMMITTEE

Two Appellate Committees are appointed by the House of Lords at the beginning of each session. They consist of all the lords qualified under section 5 of the Appellate Jurisdiction Act 1876, as amended by later Acts of Parliament, *i.e.* the Lords of Appeal (*q.v.*). The majority of appeals to the House of Lords are referred to these committees which hear argument on behalf of the parties. When the hearing is over the Committee makes a formal report to the House of Lords, which is ordered to be considered on a specified day. On the order of the day for considering the report being read, the presiding lord formally moves, " That the report of the Appellate Committee be now considered ". When this motion has been agreed to, each of the law lords who have heard the appeal in turn, instead of reading his speech, merely states that for the reasons given by him in a speech which is now available in print* he is of opinion that the appeal should be allowed (or dismissed),† after which the presiding lord moves " that the report be agreed to ". When this motion has been agreed to, the presiding lord puts the question " that the order appealed from be reversed (or affirmed) " and any further questions necessary to dispose of the appeal. The committee was originally appointed because the noise caused by building work made it difficult to hear cases in the House of Lords itself, but the practice has continued because the House of Lords frequently meets for legislative business at 2.30 p.m. instead of at 4 or 4.15 p.m. as it did before the late war. The delegation to a committee of the hearing of argument enables legislative and judicial business to be transacted simultaneously.

* Copies of the speeches are made available to counsel who are appearing in the appeal, at least an hour beforehand.

† This practice was introduced at the beginning of session 1963–64. Previously the law lords had given their reasons for allowing or dismissing the appeal orally. Adoption of the procedure is not obligatory ; any law lord who wishes to deliver his opinion orally to the House may do so.

APPROPRIATION

It is one of the cardinal rules of the system of public finance that no money may be spent for any other purpose than that for which it was authorised by Parliament. The allocation of a sum of money for expenditure on any object is called " appropriation ", and money is said to be " appropriated " by Parliament for a particular purpose. It follows that any surplus on a vote remaining in the hands of a department must be surrendered to the Exchequer at the end of the financial year even though there may be a deficit on some other vote.

APPROPRIATION ACCOUNTS

The accounts of the spending of the money (sometimes called " supplies ") voted by Parliament in the estimates; the issuing of this money from the Consolidated Fund (*q.v.*) for the purpose for which it was voted and for no other purpose is annually sanctioned by the Appropriation Act, and accordingly the Appropriation Accounts for each financial year precisely reflect the estimates for the year concerned.

APPROPRIATION IN AID

When a department receives moneys from sources other than the Exchequer, it may be allowed to retain them, instead of surrendering them to the Exchequer, and set them off against its expenses. This transaction is known as an " appropriation in aid " and the amount must be duly shown in the estimates, and authorised like any other expenditure ; and any surplus above the amount authorised must be surrendered in the ordinary way. Fees received from the public are often allowed to be retained by departments as appropriations in aid.

BACK BENCHER

A member who, neither holding office in the Government nor belonging to the inner councils of the party in opposition, occupies a seat in the Chamber on any but the two front benches above the gangway. Although a supporter of the party to which he belongs, he is generally regarded as being freer to differ from its policy than his colleagues on the front benches. The term therefore conveys a suggestion of what Mr. Gladstone called " the greater freedom and less responsibility " belonging to the rank and file of the parliamentary armies.

BALLOT

The ballot, that is, the drawing of lots, is used in the House of Commons to determine precedence among private members desiring a share of the limited amount of parliamentary time available to them (known as " private members' time "). Since government business has precedence at most sittings, there are

BALLOT—*continued*
always more members wishing to introduce bills and move motions than can possibly be accommodated in the limited time available; ballots are therefore held at intervals to allot the opportunities afforded on those days. Ballots are also held unofficially for opportunities of raising matters on the adjournment and on the second reading of Consolidated Fund Bills (*q.v.*).

The number of days on which private members' bills and motions have precedence is laid down by standing order, ten Fridays being allotted to bills and ten to motions, with an additional four days other than Fridays on which precedence is given to private members' motions until 7 p.m.; but the proportion of the Friday sittings to be devoted to bills and motions respectively has frequently been varied by orders of the House passed early in recent sessions. Bills may be considered after motions on the Fridays allotted to motions, and if unopposed have a chance of making progress on those days. Of the days allotted to bills under the standing order, the first six are reserved for second readings, and on the last four the bills must be so arranged on the order paper that those at the most advanced stage come first, and so on according to the progress they have made, second readings being taken last; but when the proportion of Fridays allotted to bills has been varied, the proportion of the days when second readings and later stages respectively have precedence has also been varied. The standing order provides for the ballot for private members' bills to be held on the second Thursday on which the House sits during the session and for ballots for motions to be held on days to be appointed by order of the House. A sessional order is required soon after the beginning of each session to fix the days allotted to each kind of business during that session, and this order also names the days on which the ballots for motions are to be held, and provides that no motions shall be handed in for any of these days allotted to motions in anticipation of the ballots. A standing order provides that no bills may be presented by private members and no motions may be moved by them for leave to introduce bills until after the day (*see below*) on which the members who have been successful in the ballot have the opportunity to present their bills and name a day for the second reading.

The ballot for private members' bills is held by the Chairman of Ways and Means, usually in a committee room. A member wishing to take part signs his name at some time during the two preceding sittings on a numbered list kept in one of the lobbies by a clerk. A member may sign on behalf of another, but in so doing he loses the right to take part on his own account. Numbers corresponding to those opposite members' names on the numbered list are drawn from a box by the Chairman. Successful members must afterwards give notice of the titles of their bills, and must either appear to present the bills on the fifth Wednesday on which the House sits during the session or alternatively nominate other members in writing to present the bills on their behalf.

When the ballot for bills is held enough numbers are drawn to provide three or more members with possible opportunities to move the second readings of their bills on each of the days on which second readings have precedence. Those members whose numbers are drawn first have the opportunity to get their bills placed first on the order paper on these days, but other bills have the chance of being debated on second reading through the ones in front of them being dropped before their day comes or securing a second reading without a full day's debate.

The ballots for private members' motions are held after question time in the chamber. In these cases the list is available from 2.15 p.m. for signing in one of the division lobbies. After questions a box with numbers corresponding with the names of members who have signed is taken to the Table, where the Clerk Assistant draws three numbers, which he calls out, and the Speaker reads the corresponding names. The successful members may announce the subjects which they wish to raise immediately but are not obliged to do so. The terms of the notices of motions must be given to the Clerks at the Table or Table Office not less than nine days before the day of the debate.

In addition to the above ballots, weekly ballots are held unofficially in the Speaker's office for the privilege of raising matters during the half-hour's debate on the motion for the adjournment which concludes the day's proceedings in the House on the following Tuesday, Wednesday, Friday and Monday (*see* ADJOURNMENT OF THE HOUSE, MOTION FOR).

Select committees were formerly sometimes chosen by ballot, *i.e.* by secret voting, not by drawing lots. The last instance of this was in 1819. The use of the ballot in the modern sense, that is, of drawing lots, first occurred on December 6, 1774.

BAR OF THE HOUSE

In the House of Commons chamber the bar of the House, that is, the line which persons who are not members may not cross during the sittings of the House, and beyond which members may not speak, is marked by a broad strip of leather laid across the carpet on the floor of the chamber between the benches. Brass rails may also be drawn across the same spot. The bar is the place to which persons are brought, in order that the Speaker may address them on behalf of the House.

The Duke of Wellington, desiring in 1814 to express his thanks in person for the resolution of the House thanking him for his services " to his Majesty and to the Public ", came to the House, and was attended to the bar by the Serjeant at Arms, bearing the mace, and given a seat just within the bar.

BAR OF THE HOUSE—*continued*

Persons summoned to attend in order to answer charges are brought to the bar by the Serjeant in the same way, and stand there while they answer the Speaker's questions. When the House orders a person to be reprimanded or admonished, he is brought to the bar by the Serjeant, who stands beside him with the mace on his shoulder while the Speaker delivers the reprimand or admonition. A famous case of the latter occurred in 1892, when the directors of the Cambrian Railway Company (including a member of the House) were admonished for the offence of censuring one of their employees who had given evidence before a select committee of the House. The most recent case was on July 24, 1968, when a member was reprimanded for the premature disclosure to the press of evidence taken before a select committee.

Persons who were not members of the House also sometimes attended at the bar in former times, either to be examined as witnesses or to bring papers or returns which were afterwards laid upon the Table for the information of members.

In the House of Lords the bar is a wooden barrier, which, as in the Commons, excludes persons who are not peers. It is also the place at which members stand when the House of Commons is summoned to the House of Lords to hear a speech from the Throne or the royal assent to bills.

BILL

A draft Act of Parliament presented to one or other House of Parliament. It consists of (1) the title, (2) the enacting words and (3) the body of the bill, divided into clauses. After the clauses schedules are sometimes inserted. A preamble is sometimes interpolated between the title and the enacting words. Bills are of two kinds, public and private. Both kinds formerly required to be agreed to by the Queen, the Lords and the Commons, but since the passing of the Parliament Act in 1911 the agreement of the Lords may in certain circumstances be dispensed with in the case of public bills. A public bill which affects the private interests of a particular person or corporate body, or a number of persons or corporate bodies, as distinct from the private interests of all persons or bodies of the same category or class is called a hybrid bill. Bills for confirming provisional orders, though dealing with matters of a nature akin to those dealt with by private bills, are technically public bills.

BILL, HYBRID

A public bill (whether introduced by a member of the Government or by a private member) which affects the private interests of particular persons or corporate bodies as distinct from the private interests of all persons or bodies in the particular category to which those individuals or bodies belong. The standing orders which require that, before a private bill is introduced, certain preliminary steps shall be taken, including the giving of notices and deposit of documents, apply to hybrid bills. If a public bill which has been introduced into the House of Commons appears to affect particular private interests in the manner already described, the Examiners of Petitions for Private Bills are ordered to examine the bill "with respect to the applicability thereto of the standing orders relative to private business". Whether the Examiners shall be ordered to examine a public bill is, in practice, decided by the Public Bill Office.

The order for second reading of the bill continues to appear among the orders of the day, but the second reading is not taken until the Examiners have made their report. If the Examiners report that standing orders relative to private bills are applicable and have been complied with, the bill is proceeded with as a "hybrid" bill. If the Examiners report that standing orders relative to private bills are applicable but have not been complied with, their report is referred to the Standing Orders Committee. If this Committee reports that the standing orders ought to be dispensed with, the bill is proceeded with as a "hybrid" bill. If, however, the Standing Orders Committee reports that the standing orders ought not to be dispensed with, the order for reading the bill a second time is automatically discharged. If the Examiners report that none of the standing orders relative to private bills is applicable, the bill is proceeded with in the ordinary manner as a public bill.

A hybrid bill is usually committed to a select committee, some of the members of which are appointed by the House and the remainder by the Committee of Selection. An order is made that all petitions presented against the bill within a certain time shall be referred to the committee, that the petitioners praying to be heard by themselves, their counsel or agents shall be heard and that counsel shall be heard in favour of the bill against such petitions. The order further provides that if no petition is deposited within the time specified, the order for the committal of the bill to a select committee shall be automatically discharged, and the bill shall be committed to a committee of the whole House or to a standing committee.

In a select committee on a hybrid bill the petitioner makes his case first. The promoters are then heard. If they call evidence the petitioner has a right of reply. A petitioner is not allowed to argue on matters which cannot give him a *locus standi*. Subject to this, he may traverse the principle of the bill. This procedure may, however, be modified, at the discretion of the committee, to meet the requirements of the particular case.

A hybrid bill when reported from a select committee is recommitted to a committee of the whole House unless the House

BILL, HYBRID—*continued*

orders otherwise, and thenceforward pursues its course as a public bill.

In the House of Lords petitions against a hybrid bill can be presented within ten days of its first reading. Unless it has been decided to refer the bill to a joint committee, it is referred after second reading, if unopposed, to the Lord Chairman. If opposed, the bill is referred either to a select committee or a joint committee and the procedure in committee is similar to the procedure on a private bill. When reported, the bill is recommitted to a committee of the whole House and proceeds as a public bill.

Proceedings on a hybrid bill have been suspended and resumed in the next session.

BILL, PRIVATE

Must not be confused with a private member's bill (*q.v.*). A private bill is a bill for the particular interest or benefit of some person or body of persons, *e.g.* the shareholders of a company or the inhabitants of a borough, city or county, as distinguished from a measure intended for the general benefit. Certain public corporations such as the British Railways Board and the Electricity Authority, however, are authorised by Act of Parliament to promote private bills though the interests which it is the object of such bills to promote can scarcely be said to be the interests of individuals rather than those of the community.

Private bills are not introduced by members. The parties who desire the enactment of a private bill (called " the promoters ") present a petition, to which a copy of the proposed bill is attached, praying that leave may be given to bring it in. Petitions for private bills are presented to the House of Commons except in the case of personal bills (*q.v.*) petitions for which are always presented to the House of Lords. Private bills are not presented to the House by members as public bills are, but are deposited in the Private Bill Office (*q.v.*) by the promoters' agents (*see* PARLIAMENTARY AGENT). No petition for a private bill will be received after November 27 without the sanction of the Chairman of Ways and Means.

A private bill usually, though not invariably, affects the private rights or interests of particular persons or corporate bodies. In order to prevent such persons or bodies from being taken by surprise and to give them an opportunity, if they wish, of defending their rights or interests, the standing orders of both Houses of Parliament require notice of the proposed measure to be published in local newspapers and the "London Gazette" and, in some cases, to be served upon persons whose rights and interests are affected by it. The promoters of a private bill are also required by these standing orders to take other preliminary steps, varying according to the nature of the proposed measure.

These notices have to be published and served and the other preliminary steps have to be taken within certain fixed periods in the autumn and the petitions for the bill must be presented by November 27. The introduction of private bills is consequently restricted to one period of the year except in proved cases of urgency when these requirements are relaxed on the recommendation of the Standing Orders Committees (*q.v.*) of the two Houses.

Petitions for private bills are referred to the Examiners of Petitions for Private Bills (*q.v.*) for inquiry and report whether the standing orders referred to above have or have not been complied with. Before pronouncing his decision the Examiner who deals with the particular petition hears any parties who have deposited memorials in the Private Bill Office alleging that the promoters have failed to comply with standing orders. The Examiners' findings are communicated to both Houses. If the Examiner by whom a particular petition is dealt with reports that the standing orders have not been complied with, his report is referred by each House to its Standing Orders Committee which decides whether compliance with the standing orders shall be dispensed with and the parties permitted to proceed with their bill.

Although the petitions for the bills are addressed to the House of Commons, about half the bills are introduced in the House of Lords. The object of this is to secure a proper distribution of the business of private legislation between the two Houses. The Lord Chairman and the Chairman of Ways and Means decide in which House each bill shall begin.

If the bill has not been allocated to the House of Lords, it is laid on the table of the House of Commons on January 21 or the first day on which the House sits thereafter unless the Examiner has reported that the standing orders have not been complied with, in which event the bill is not laid on the table unless and until the Standing Orders Committee reports that the standing orders ought to be dispensed with. When laid on the table the bill is deemed to have received its first reading.

A private bill passes through the same stages as a public bill, but is considered at a special period of the sitting called "the time of private business". An interval of a certain number of days is required to elapse between the various stages. Thus there must be at least four clear days between the first and second reading; and at least three clear days between the reporting of a bill from committee and its consideration by the House. (However, where time is of importance towards the close of the session or owing to the near approach of the summer recess, standing orders are frequently suspended and particular bills are permitted to pass through the consideration and third reading stages on the same day or the interval between the reporting of a bill and the

BILL, PRIVATE—*continued*
report stage is curtailed, or the required period of notice for third reading or consideration of Lords amendments is dispensed with.) Subject to these rules the date on which a private bill is set down for second or third reading or, where a bill is reported with amendments, for consideration as amended, is fixed, in the first instance, by the agent for the bill, not by the House.

Motions for proceeding with a private bill at each of its several stages are usually moved by the Chairman or the Deputy Chairman of Ways and Means. The second and third readings as well as the report stage of a private bill usually pass without debate. Occasionally, however, bills are discussed and even rejected. If the bill is promoted by, or confers certain powers on, a company, it is referred, after second reading, to the Examiners for proof that the bill has been consented to by resolutions of meetings of the shareholders. Amendments proposed by the promoters on the consideration or the third reading of a bill are usually agreed to *en bloc*.

The constitution, functions and procedure of committees on private bills depend on whether the bills are opposed or unopposed. By an opposed bill is meant, not a bill which has been opposed in the House, but a bill against which a petition praying to be heard has been deposited in the Private Bill Office within the time allowed by Standing Order and has not subsequently been withdrawn, or a bill which the Chairman of Ways and Means has reported should be treated as an opposed bill although no petition has been presented against it. Except in specified cases petitions against bills originating in the House of Commons must be presented on or before January 30.

The committee on an opposed bill consists of four members who must have no personal or local interest in the bill. They are appointed by the Committee of Selection, which at the same time appoints one of the members as chairman and fixes the date and time of the first meeting and, if several bills are referred to the same committee, decides which bills shall be considered at that meeting. Members appointed to serve on a committee on an opposed bill are required to sign a declaration that they have no personal or local interest in the bill and that they will not vote on any matter without having duly heard and attended to the evidence thereon. The chairman votes like any other member and, if the votes are equal, gives a second or casting vote. The attendance of members is compulsory, and members who are not present within an hour of the time of meeting or absent themselves from their duties are reported to the House. A committee can, however, proceed with business so long as three members are present. If no quorum is present within one hour of the time of meeting, or the number of members present falls below three and a quorum is not again formed within an hour, the committee must adjourn till the next day on which the House sits. If a committee adjourns over a day on which the House is sitting, it must report to the House why it is has done so. The public are admitted except while the committee is deliberating.

Although any person or body may petition against a bill, only those persons or bodies whose property or interests are directly and specially affected by the bill are entitled to be heard. If the promoters object to a petitioner's being heard on the ground that he has no *locus standi* (*q.v.*), the matter is determined by the Court of Referees (*see* REFEREES, COURT OF). The Court has additionally a discretion to admit petitions from societies representing amenity and other interests who have no absolute right to be heard.

The parties respectively promoting and opposing the bill are usually represented by counsel. Counsel for the promoters states the case for the bill and calls witnesses to prove it. Evidence is given on oath. Each witness may be cross-examined by counsel who appear for petitioners who have prayed to be heard against the preamble of the bill, but not as a general rule by counsel who appear for parties who have prayed to be heard against particular clauses only or for the insertion of protective clauses. After being cross-examined witnesses may be re-examined by counsel for the promoters. When the case for the bill is closed, the case against it is stated by the petitioners or their counsel, who may also call evidence. Witnesses called by petitioners or their counsel may be cross-examined by counsel for the promoters, and re-examined by or on behalf of the party who called them. Members of the committee may also put questions to witnesses called by either side. If any of the opposing parties have called witnesses or put in documentary evidence, counsel for the promoters has a right to reply, but only to those parties who have called witnesses or put in documents.

When the case for and against the bill is closed, the committee room is cleared and the committee decides whether the preamble of the bill has been proved, *i.e.* whether a case has been made out for the bill. The parties are then called in and informed of the committee's decision by the chairman.

Where particular parts of a bill dealing with a number of different subjects are opposed, but not the bill as a whole, it is the practice to consider each part which is objected to separately, and to decide whether "so much of the preamble as relates" thereto has been proved, proof of the remainder of the preamble being postponed until after the clauses of the bill have been considered. The reason for this is that the preamble may require to be amended in order to make it consistent with the bill as passed by the committee.

If the committee decides that the preamble of the bill has not been proved, it so reports to the House and the bill is not further

BILL, PRIVATE—*continued*

proceeded with. If, however, the committee decides that the preamble has been proved, it turns to the clauses. Clauses which are opposed by petitioners or which they seek to amend are first considered, the petitioners being heard in support of their objections or amendments.

Officers of government departments which have made reports on the bill may be heard, if the committee thinks fit, in explanation of any recommendation made in the report, but may not cross-examine the witnesses called by the parties or be themselves cross-examined by the parties or their advocates. The promoters of a private bill cannot be forced to proceed with it against their will. If, therefore, the committee insists on making an amendment or inserting a clause to which the promoters object, the promoters may drop the bill, in which case the committee can take no further action except to report the fact to the House.

Where a committee is unanimously of opinion that a petitioner has been unreasonably or vexatiously subjected to expense in defending his rights, or that the promoters have been vexatiously subjected to expense by opposition thereto, it may order his or their costs or part of them to be paid by the promoters or the opponent, as the case may be. Costs are, however, not often awarded.

A committee on an unopposed bill consists of the Chairman and the Deputy Chairman of Ways and Means and three other members chosen by the Chairman of Ways and Means from a panel appointed by the Committee of Selection at the beginning of each session. The committee does not, as a rule, require the promoters, who are represented by their agent, to satisfy it of the general expediency of the bill, but contents itself with requiring him to make out a case for those provisions in the bill to which the committee's attention is directed either by reports from government departments or by the Speaker's Counsel (who assists the committee), or which seem to members of the committee objectionable in a public point of view.

When the bill reaches the House of Lords it is given a first reading as a matter of course and is referred to the Examiners for inquiry whether any further standing orders applicable to the bill have been complied with. The subsequent proceedings in reference to the bill are similar to the proceedings in the House of Commons. Some differences are mentioned below. Petitions against the bill may be presented within ten days of the first reading. If any amendments are made to the bill during its progress through the House of Lords, the procedure for obtaining agreement between the two houses is the same as in the case of public bills (*see* p. 39). One clear day's notice must be given by the agent for the bill of the day on which the Lords amendments are to be set down for consideration, but this notice must not be given until after the day on which the bill is returned from the House of Lords. Similar notice must be given of any amendments it is intended to propose to Lords amendments. Lords amendments and amendments proposed by the promoters to such amendments are usually agreed to *en bloc*.

The proceedings with reference to a bill introduced in the House of Lords are much the same as the proceedings on a bill originating in the House of Commons. If the standing orders have been complied with, the bill is presented to the House by the Lord Chancellor on the day on which the Examiner's certificate to that effect is laid on the table of the House or on one of the next seven sitting days. If the standing orders have not been complied with, and the Standing Orders Committee reports that they ought to be dispensed with, the bill is presented to the House on the day on which it agrees that the bill shall be allowed to proceed. Petitions against the bill must be deposited in the Committee and Private Bill Office of the House of Lords on or before February 6 (not later than the tenth day after the bill was presented to the House, in cases where the standing orders have not been complied with).

The chief differences between the procedure on private bills in the House of Lords (whether they have come from the House of Commons or began in the House of Lords) and the procedure on such bills in the House of Commons are (1) committees on opposed bills consist of five members and the chairman has no casting vote; (2) unopposed bills are referred to the Lord Chairman; (3) questions of *locus standi* are determined by the committee on the bill; (4) the committee decides whether the bill may proceed, not whether the preamble has been proved; (5) bills do not have to go through a consideration stage; (6) amendments of substance may be made on third reading.

When a private bill which began in the House of Lords reaches the House of Commons it is automatically read a first time and referred to the Examiners for proof that any standing orders which are applicable and have not been previously inquired into have been complied with. Petitions against the bill must be deposited in the Private Bill Office within ten days of the first reading of the bill. In other respects the procedure is the same as on a bill which began in the House of Commons. When the bill has passed through all its stages it is returned to the House of Lords. If amendments have been made to the bill, these are considered by the House of Lords in the same manner as Lords amendments to a bill which originated in the House of Commons are considered in that House.

In both Houses fees are payable by promoters whenever a bill passes through a stage in the House and by both promoters and opponents whenever they appear before any committee or one of the Examiners or the Court of Referees, or deposit any document

BILL, PRIVATE—*continued*

in the Private Bill Office of the House of Commons or the Committee and Private Bill Office of the House of Lords. The amount of the fees payable by the promoters depends upon the amount of money which is to be raised or expended under the authority of the bill. Tables of the fees are to be found at the end of the printed standing orders of each House.

When it is clear that the private business cannot be completed before Parliament is prorogued or dissolved, standing orders are made by both Houses permitting the promoters of private bills to suspend further proceedings on them and providing in effect that in the next session of Parliament proceedings on the bills shall be resumed at the point at which they were suspended.

BILL, PRIVATE MEMBER'S

A public bill introduced by a private member; that is, a member who is not a minister. It must be carefully distinguished from a private bill (*q.v.*). Private members' bills have precedence of government business on certain days during the session only (*see* BALLOT).

BILL, PROVISIONAL ORDER

A bill to confirm, *i.e.* give the force of law to, an order made by a minister of the Crown under powers conferred on him by an Act of Parliament. Such orders are usually made on the application of local authorities or statutory bodies. Procedure by way of provisional order was introduced with the object of reducing the expense incurred by parties in promoting private bills and at the same time lightening the burden thrown on members by delegating the duty of considering the application to a government department and holding the inquiry locally. It has now been largely superseded by procedure by special procedure order (*q.v.*) except in Scotland.

By the Private Legislation Procedure (Scotland) Act 1936 procedure by way of provisional order is substituted, save in certain exceptional cases, for procedure by private bill so far as Scotland is concerned. The procedure under this Act (*see* SCOTTISH PRIVATE LEGISLATION) differs in important respects from the ordinary provisional order system.

A provisional order bill may be introduced into either House of Parliament. One or more orders may be contained in a single bill. A provisional order bill may not be introduced after May 15 if the current session began in a previous year. It is introduced in the same way as a public bill (*see* BILL, PUBLIC) by either the minister who made the order or the parliamentary secretary of the department concerned, but its introduction and all subsequent proceedings on it in the House take place at the time of private business (*q.v.*).

A provisional order bill, after it has been introduced, is referred to the Examiners of Petitions for Private Bills to ascertain whether certain standing orders are applicable to the bill and, if so, whether they have been complied with, and the bill does not come before the House for second reading until the Examiner who dealt with the case has reported either that the standing orders in question have been complied with or that they are not applicable. The subsequent proceedings are generally similar to the proceedings on a private bill, but the standing orders which provide that a certain period must elapse between the several stages of the progress of a private bill through the House and require notice of the days proposed for the second reading, consideration and third reading of such a bill to be given by the agent for the bill in the Private Bill Office do not apply to provisional order bills, and the days for taking each successive stage are fixed by the House at each stage of the bill and not by notice given by agents in the Private Bill Office. If a provisional order is opposed, the conduct of the case therefor before the committee on the bill is usually left in the hands of the parties on whose application the order was made. A committee on a provisional order bill reports, not that the preamble has or has not been proved, but that the order ought or ought not to be confirmed. The procedure on a provisional order bill in the House of Lords is similar to the procedure in the House of Commons except that, after the bill has been reported from the committee, it is recommitted to a committee of the whole House and proceeds as a public bill.

BILL, PUBLIC

In the House of Commons a public bill may be introduced in one of the following ways: (1) by being presented after notice (the most usual method); (2) by order of the House, after the House has come to a resolution or resolutions approving the subject matter of the bill; (3) on a motion "that leave be given to bring in the bill" being carried. In addition, a bill may be brought from the Lords, having been first introduced in, and passed by, that House. The member introducing a bill must obtain beforehand a "dummy bill" from the Public Bill Office. This is a piece of stiff paper bearing the title of the bill and the names of the members presenting and supporting it. These names afterwards appear on the back of the printed copies and may not exceed twelve in number.

(1) Most bills are presented without any other formality than the giving of notice, at the Table or in the Table Office, of the title of the bill, not later than the day before the member intends to present it. On that day he is called by the Speaker at the commencement of public business, on which he comes to the Table from behind the Speaker's chair, and hands the "dummy bill" to the Clerk, who reads out the short title. If the Bill is a Government Bill, the Minister nods when his name is called, the bill

BILL, PUBLIC—*continued*
having already been placed on the Table. The bill is then regarded as having been read the first time and is ordered to be read a second time on a day named by the member. The practice of putting the question for the first reading, thus allowing the bill to be debated and rejected at this stage, has long been abolished.

(2) A bill whose main object was either to authorise the expenditure of money from the Exchequer or to impose a tax was formerly preceded by a resolution of the Committee of Ways and Means, the resolution being reported to, and agreed to by, the House. Since the changes in 1967 and 1968, which saw the abrogation of the rule requiring the initiation of proposals involving expenditure or taxation in a committee of the whole House, and the consequent abolition of the Committees of Supply and Ways and Means, a bill of this nature is preceded by, and founded upon, a resolution of the House itself and is ordered to be brought in upon the resolution. The minister introducing the bill presents it by going to the bar of the House, approaching the Table with the usual three bows and handing the dummy bill to the Clerk, who reads out the short title, and the bill receives its first reading and a day is appointed for the second reading as described above. Other bills, such as those fixing the sovereign's civil list at the beginning of each reign, are occasionally introduced in a similar manner.

(3) The former practice whereby the introduction of a bill was preceded by a motion for leave to bring it in now survives chiefly in the case of bills introduced under the "ten-minute rule", which allows such a motion to be made on certain days of the week at the commencement of public business, and directs the Speaker to put the question thereon after brief statements by the mover and opposer of the motion. This method is used chiefly by the private member who wishes to introduce a bill for which he has not succeeded in drawing a place in the ballot. If the motion is agreed to, the member presents his bill in the manner described in (2) above (*see* TEN-MINUTE RULE).

When a bill has been passed by the Lords, it is sent to the Commons with a message to the effect that the Lords have passed the bill and desire the agreement of the Commons thereto. No further action is taken until a member informs the Clerks at the Table of his intention to take charge of the bill, and names a day for the second reading. The bill is then deemed to have been read the first time, and an entry to that effect duly appears in the Votes and Proceedings for that day. Unless a Lords bill is thus "taken up" by a member it can make no further progress in the Commons.

After the first reading, the bill is ordered by the House to be printed, and it is examined by the clerks in the Public Bill Office, whose duty it is to see that the bill complies with the rules of the

House. In so doing they pay particular attention to the requirement that the contents of the bill shall be covered by the title, and to the rules concerning public money, notably those which require that certain bills must be founded on a Ways and Means resolution and that a clause involving a charge on public funds must be printed in italics. Failure to comply with the rules, whether on the part of a minister of the Crown or of a private member, may result in the withdrawal of the bill, since the Speaker will decline to propose the question for second reading, when his attention is called to the point.

After an interval to give time for the bill to be read and digested by members and other interested persons it is submitted to the House for a second reading. Whereas the first reading is a purely formal stage, it is on the second reading that the House considers the bill's general principle and decides to give or withhold provisional approval. The member in charge of the bill moves " That the bill be now read a second time ". If a member objects to the bill, he may content himself with opposing the question with his voice and vote ; but the usual course is to move an amendment to the question in one of two forms. Either he moves " That the bill be read a second time upon this day six months " (this is a polite way of rejecting the bill, by ensuring that it shall come up again only after the end of the session, " three " being substituted for " six " when the session is sufficiently advanced); or he moves a " reasoned amendment ", giving reasons why the bill should not receive a second reading (*see* AMENDMENT, REASONED).

The procedure differs according to the form of the amendment. If it is in the first of these two forms, the question is first put (in the old manner) " That the word 'now' stand part of the question." If this is agreed to, the bill is declared by the Speaker to be read a second time; if not, the words " upon this day six (three) months " are added at the end of the question and the main question, in its amended form, is put and agreed to without debate. The question on a reasoned amendment is put in the usual way, "That the amendment be made"; if this is negatived, the main question, "That the bill be now read a second time", is put forthwith.

In the case of a bill which applies exclusively to Scotland, the second reading may, in effect, be transferred from the House to the Scottish Grand Committee, if the House thinks fit (*see* SCOTTISH BILLS). Bills of a specialised character are sometimes referred to second reading committees (*q.v.*), with the object of saving the time of the House by transferring the debate from thence to a smaller body. The committee's report consists simply of a recommendation that the bill ought, or ought not, to be read a second time. In the latter case, reasons may be given for the

BILL, PUBLIC—*continued*
decision. When the report has been made, a day is appointed for second reading; and the question for second reading is decided without amendment or debate.

The second reading is followed by the committee stage. This normally takes place in a standing committee, to which the bill stands committed unless (*a*) it is a Consolidated Fund or Appropriation Bill and is therefore, by a practice of long standing, committed as a matter of course to a committee of the whole House, or (*b*) the House, for some reason, decides to commit it to a committee of the whole House or to a joint or a select committee. A motion so to commit a bill (including a motion that it is expedient to commit the bill to a joint committee) must be made immediately after the second reading and may be made without notice; it must be decided without amendment or debate. A motion may similarly be made to commit a bill in part to a standing committee and in part to a committee of the whole House; if this is opposed, the Speaker may allow a brief statement to be made for, and another against, the motion before he puts the question. Bills are rarely committed to joint or select committees. This is done only when it is desired that the committee should hear evidence; for this a joint or select committee, with its small number of members, is a more suitable body than a committee of the whole House or a standing committee. After a bill has been reported from a joint or select committee, it is recommitted to a committee of the whole House.

A committee on a bill may make such amendments thereto as it thinks fit, provided that they are relevant to the subject matter of the bill; but though the House does not interfere with the committee in the exercise of its functions, it may nevertheless dictate to some extent how the committee shall proceed, by means of an "instruction" (for which a motion must be made after second reading). An instruction may be permissive, and allow the committee, if it thinks fit, to do something which it would not otherwise have the power to do, or it may be mandatory, and lay down some action which the committee must take. A mandatory instruction, however, may not be given to a committee of the whole House or to a standing committee (*see* INSTRUCTION).

The procedure of a committee in considering a bill is the same whether it be a committee of the whole House or a standing committee. The bill is gone through clause by clause, from the beginning to the end, each clause being first amended if desired, before the chairman proposes the question "That the clause [as amended] stand part of the bill". Debate may take place on each amendment, and also on the question "That the clause stand part of the bill"; if the chairman thinks that the clause has been adequately discussed on the amendments, he may put the question at once without allowing it to be debated. The schedules, if any, are similarly dealt with. New clauses and schedules may be added to the bill, being first amended if necessary. At the conclusion of the proceedings, which may be protracted over many sittings of the committee, the chairman puts the question " That I do report the bill (as amended), to the House ". This question is usually agreed to without division or debate, and marks the formal end of the committee stage.

If a bill involves the expenditure of public money, the relevant parts must be printed in italics (as stated above) when the bill is introduced and the necessary expenditure must be authorised by a resolution of the House (called a " money resolution ") before the italicised section is considered in committee. This procedure applies not merely when expenditure is incidental to the main purpose of the bill but also to bills having expenditure as their main object; exception is still made, however, in the case of those bills which, as stated above, must be founded on Ways and Means resolutions.

When a bill has been considered by a committee of the whole House, the chairman makes a verbal report to the effect that the committee have gone through the bill and either made amendments thereto or directed him to report the same without amendment, as the case may be. The report from a standing committee to the same effect is laid upon the Table in documentary form by the committee clerk on the chairman's behalf. The subsequent " report stage ", as it is commonly called, or consideration of the bill as reported from the committee, is omitted in the case of bills which have been reported without amendment from a committee of the whole House. Such bills proceed direct to third reading; but all other bills must undergo this further consideration, at which amendments may be moved as in committee. If, on report, the bill is ordered to be considered on a future day, the House enters on such consideration, on the order being read, without any question being put, and proceeds at once to consider any amendments which may be moved to the bill. If, however, the bill is to be considered forthwith, the question " That the bill be now considered " must first be put and agreed to and this question may (except in the case of a Consolidated Fund or Appropriation Bill) be amended and debated. If no amendment is proposed, the third reading is either taken forthwith or appointed for a future day. If amendments are proposed, the House considers them in the same way as in committee; but each clause does not again have to be approved in turn, so that proceedings are usually somewhat shorter than in committee. If new clauses or schedules are proposed, they are considered before the amendments to the bill. Any amendment which imposes a charge upon the revenue or upon local rates may be considered provided that it would have been in order if proposed in committee, *i.e.*, if it is covered by the

BILL, PUBLIC—*continued*
terms of the money resolution authorising the expenditure involved in the bill. Money resolutions are sometimes passed at this stage to allow amendments involving expenditure not originally foreseen.

A bill which has been considered by a second reading committee, or by the Scottish Grand Committee " in relation to its principle ", may, if the House so decides, be referred for consideration on report to a Standing Committee (*see* COMMITTEE TO CONSIDER BILL ON REPORT). The Committee proceeds in the same way as the House itself, making amendments if it thinks fit, and reports that it has considered the Bill and has made amendments or no amendment, as the case may be; on which the bill is ordered to be read the third time on a future day.

The third reading stage is generally similar to the second reading, in that the bill is once more submitted as a whole to the judgement of the House, and a member who objects to the bill may likewise move " That the bill be read the third time upon this day six (three) months " or a reasoned amendment. There is, however, an important difference, in that, unless notice has been given by at least six members either of an amendment to the question for third reading or of a motion that the question be *not* put forthwith, the question must be put immediately and without debate. The question for third reading of a Consolidated Fund or Appropriation Bill must always be put forthwith and decided without amendment or debate. Verbal amendments (*i.e.* amendments which are purely verbal and do not alter the sense of the text) are occasionally made to a bill immediately before the third reading is moved. If the third reading is agreed to the bill is passed, and is sent to the Lords with a message requesting their concurrence.

In the House of Lords a bill may be presented by any peer without notice. After second reading a bill is ordinarily committed to a committee of the whole House, sometimes after previous consideration by a joint or select committee. In certain cases, however, bills may instead be referred to a " public bill committee " in which the procedure is comparable to that observed in a standing committee in the House of Commons. If a bill brought from the Commons remains on the Table for twelve sitting days without any lord giving notice of second reading, it is taken off the paper, and may not be further proceeded with in the same session unless eight days' notice is given of the second reading.

In both Houses it is usual to allow a certain interval to elapse between the more important stages of a bill, in particular between the first and second reading, and between second reading and committee. In the case, however, of those bills, such as Consolidated Fund Bills, to which amendments are never moved, the second reading and committee stages are often taken on successive days. On rare occasions, in case of need, a bill has been passed through all its stages in both Houses in one day. In the House of Commons this only needs the special sanction of the House if the bill involves expenditure, since* it is moreover the practice of the House not to pass a bill† through more than one stage in a day. In the House of Lords, however, a standing order provides that a bill may not pass through more than one stage in a day (except that the report of a bill which has not been amended in committee may be received forthwith); and this standing order must be suspended if it is desired to proceed more quickly. Several bills were thus passed quickly by both Houses in the course of a few hours at the outbreak of war in 1939.

When a Bill is expected to be brought up in the immediate future from the House of Commons, the House of Lords has sometimes agreed to the introduction of a bill in identical terms in anticipation of the arrival of the bill from the Commons. The Lords then by agreement debate the bill as introduced into their own House, and subsequently agree to the Commons bill without Debate; the Lords bill is then not proceeded with.

If the Lords pass a bill brought from the Commons without amending it, they send a message to the Commons stating that they have agreed to it without amendment; if, however, they have amended the bill, they return it with the amendments to the Commons, and ask for their agreement. A further stage, the consideration of the Lords amendments, then ensues in the Commons. The Lords amendments, when they are received by the Commons, are usually ordered to be considered on a future day; in that event the House, on the order for their consideration being read, proceeds with their consideration without any further question being put. The member in charge of the bill may, however, move that they be considered forthwith. It is then open to a member opposing the bill to move as an amendment "That the Lords amendments be considered upon this day six (three) months". When, in either event, the House proceeds to deal with the amendments themselves, the procedure is as follows. The House has twice (once in 1906 and once in 1909) disagreed to the Lords amendments *en bloc;* on each occasion a resolution sanctioning this procedure was previously passed. Ordinarily the question is put on each amendment in turn, or on groups of them if this course is not objected to. Each amendment may be agreed to, amended, or disagreed to, and, if disagreed to, another amendment may be made to the bill in its place. In the latter event it may be necessary to make a consequential amendment to the bill, but, apart from this, only the Lords amendments, and not the rest of the bill, are open to consideration and amendment.

* Proceedings on the bill itself must then be interrupted to allow the passage of a money resolution between second reading and committee.

† Founded on a Ways and Means resolution.

BILL, PUBLIC—*continued*

If all the amendments are agreed to, the bill is sent back to the Lords with a message to that effect, and is then ready to receive the royal assent in its amended form. If they are not all agreed to, the message, in addition to announcing the Commons' decision, gives a reason in every case where they have disagreed to an amendment without making another amendment in lieu thereof.

The Lords then have the choice, in the case of each amendment to which the Commons have disagreed, between (1) insisting on it, (2) not insisting on it (*i.e.* acquiescing in the Commons' decision) and (3) proposing an alternative amendment. In theory the process of trying to reach agreement could continue indefinitely, with each House making amendments to the amendments made by the other. But if the Lords insist on an amendment to which the Commons have disagreed, and the Commons persist in their disagreement, the bill is lost; and this may also happen if the process of reaching agreement is cut short by the prorogation or dissolution of Parliament. Otherwise, when the amendments made by one House are accepted by the other, the bill is presented to the Queen for the royal assent in its amended form.

The procedure in the case of a bill begun in the House of Lords is the same as that described above, but in the reverse order. It should be observed that if one House rejects or does not proceed with a bill passed by the other it does not inform the other House of the fact.

The royal assent, the final stage in the legislative process, follows in due course. Since the passing of the Royal Assent Act 1967 this may be signified in one of two ways, either by a simple notification to each House, by the Lord Chancellor to the House of Lords and by the Speaker to the House of Commons, or, as formerly, by royal commission. Under the first method, which is the one used in most cases since the passing of the Act in April 1967, the notification is usually made at the beginning of the sitting, though it may take place at any time. According to the second method, still used occasionally, a full ceremony takes place in the House of Lords (strictly, the Parliament Chamber) to which the Commons are summoned (see ROYAL ASSENT). A bill becomes law as an Act of Parliament under the first method on the notification being made to the second House and under the second method on the assent being signified to each bill with the words "La Reyne le veult", or in the case of a bill granting aids and supplies "La Reyne remercie ses bons sujets, accepte leur benevolence et ainsi le veult." The royal assent has not been withheld from a bill since 1707, when the Scottish Militia Bill was submitted to Queen Anne; the words used on that occasion were "La Reyne s'avisera"—"The Queen will consider it."

The Commons' privilege in financial matters is recognised in the rule that all bills having expenditure or taxation as their main object must be introduced first in the Commons, and that in the case of bills involving incidental expenditure the relevant sections must be inserted in the lower House. Likewise the House of Lords may not amend a Commons bill in such a way as to place or increase a charge on public funds. The latter rule is sometimes waived by the Commons in minor cases for the sake of convenience, the fact being duly recorded by a "special entry" in the Journal on each occasion.

The Parliament Act 1911 goes further, by giving to the Commons, in effect, the sole right to frame legislation which is wholly concerned with finance. Any bill which the Speaker certifies as being a money bill within the meaning of the Act, *i.e.* as dealing solely with certain subjects (in which are included the imposition or regulation of taxation, the imposition of charges on the Consolidated Fund or the National Loans Fund, or on money provided by Parliament and the appropriation or issue of public money), may, unless it is passed by the Lords within one month of being sent to them by the Commons, receive the royal assent and become law, without the Lords having consented thereto.

The Parliament Act contains a further important provision which deprives the Lords of the power permanently to prevent a bill which the Commons are determined to enact from passing into law. The power of the Lords to reject a bill other than a money bill remains. But if the same bill is passed by the Commons in two successive sessions, it may receive the royal assent and become law, notwithstanding that the Lords have not consented to it, provided that one year has elapsed between the first time that the bill received a second reading in the Commons and the second time that it receives the third reading in that House. The effect of the Parliament Act is therefore to limit the Lords' powers, in opposition to the Commons, to the imposition of one month's delay in the case of a money bill and rather less than one year's delay in the case of other bills. This does not affect the power of the Lords, where the latter class of bill is concerned, of forcing the Commons to compromise in order to secure the immediate passage of a bill.

BLACK ROD, GENTLEMAN USHER OF THE

An officer of the royal household placed by the Sovereign at the service of the House of Lords. He is usually called " Black Rod " simply. He is appointed by the Queen by letters patent. The office of Black Rod apparently dates from St. George's Day, April 23, 1361. By one of Henry VIII's constitutions relating to the Order of the Garter, Black Rod is to have the care and custody of the doors of the " High Court called the Parliament ". He derives the title from his staff of office, a black ebony wand with a golden lion on the top. He is allowed to appoint a deputy

BLACK ROD—*continued*

who is called the Yeoman Usher of the Black Rod. He appoints and controls all the doorkeepers and messengers of the House of Lords. Black Rod or his deputy attends all sittings of the House of Lords. He has a seat below the bar. He issues orders of admission to the Strangers' Gallery. He is responsible for the maintenance of order among strangers who are admitted to the gallery or below the bar. Orders for the arrest of persons charged with breach of privilege or with contempt of the House are carried out by officers acting under his authority. Persons who have been adjudged guilty of such offences are committed to his custody. He assists at the introduction of peers and other ceremonies. He is sent to *desire* or, if the Sovereign is present in person, to *command* the attendance of the House of Commons in the House of Peers at the opening or prorogation of Parliament, and on certain other occasions including any occasion when the royal assent to bills is notified by royal commission in the House of Lords instead of by the Speaker and the Lord Chancellor to each house individually.

When Black Rod approaches the Commons Chamber the attendants shut the door. Black Rod knocks three times on the door with his staff. The Serjeant at Arms opens the grille and asks " Who is there ? " The Gentleman Usher replies : " Black Rod ", and is thereupon admitted. (The practice of shutting the door in Black Rod's face is said to have originated in the attempt of Charles I to arrest the five members in 1642. But this is a myth. In the first place it was not Black Rod but a Serjeant at Arms who was sent to arrest the five members. In the second place, an entry in the Commons Journal of May 10, 1641, records that " exception was taken to Mr. Maxwell, coming to the House with a message, without his black rod, and *coming in before he was called in* ".) When Black Rod is admitted, he advances to the bar and bows to the Speaker ; he then advances up the middle of the House to the Table, bowing a second time when half-way between the bar and the table and a third time on reaching the table. He then delivers his message, bowing to each side of the House when he utters the words " this honourable House ". Having delivered his message, he bows to the Speaker, and walks backwards to the bar, bowing a second time when half-way between the table and the bar, and a third time on reaching the bar.

It may be mentioned that the Gentleman Usher of the Black Rod is one of the officers of the Order of the Garter and is chief of all the Ushers in the Kingdom.

BLOCKING OF BILLS

A bill which has been set down for consideration in the House of Commons for a particular day may in certain circumstances be " blocked ", that is, its consideration at that sitting may be prevented, by a member calling out "object". This applies (1) to private bills, which are normally considered at the beginning of the sitting; if they cannot make any progress in this way, time must ultimately be found for them at the time for opposed private business (*i.e.* 7 p.m.) (*see* PRIVATE BUSINESS); and (2) after the interruption of business (*see* SITTINGS OF THE HOUSE OF COMMONS) to public bills, unless they belong to the class of bills which is exempted by standing order from interruption or are exempted by an *ad hoc* order. Private members' bills, that is, public bills introduced by private members, are especially vulnerable to this form of opposition. If these are not successful in the ballot, their only chance of making progress is in the period after the interruption of business when the orders of the day are gone through and before the adjournment is moved.* When objected to, the bill may be set down for another day if the member in charge so chooses.

A private bill which has thus been deferred, on objection, may be further "blocked" by a member giving notice that on the second reading, consideration, or third reading (as the case may be) of the bill, he will move either that the bill be read a second (or third) time or be considered† "upon this day six (or three) months", or a resolution declining for a stated reason to give a second (or third) reading to, or to consider, the bill, according to the circumstances of the case. Such a notice is effective for a week only and then lapses unless renewed.

BLUE BOOK

A term loosely applied to government publications bound in a blue paper cover. Broadly speaking, the bulkier papers are issued in this form because of their size, so it follows that a blue book, like a white paper, may be any form of government publication. Reports of royal commissions and the more important departmental committees are usually blue books; reports of select committees sometimes take this form.

BREACH OF PRIVILEGE

Strictly speaking, the term breach of privilege means disregard of any of the rights and immunities either of members of Parliament individually or of either House of Parliament in its collective capacity. In practice, however, it is also applied to other contempts, *i.e.* acts or omissions which either directly obstruct either House in the performance of its functions or tend indirectly to

* This opportunity now rarely occurs except on Fridays devoted to private members' bills and motions, since it is usual on other days for the adjournment of the House to be moved as soon as the business which the Government has announced its intention of taking has been concluded, and before the remaining orders of the day are read.

† The consideration or third reading of a bill may also be blocked by giving notice of a motion to re-commit the bill.

BREACH OF PRIVILEGE—*continued*

produce this result by lowering the authority of the House in the eyes of the public. The practice of describing such offences as breaches of privilege gives rise to the misconception that the House of Commons can punish a person only if he has disregarded some specific privilege, and that if it treats misconduct of any other kind as a breach of privilege, it is extending its privileges by its own resolution.

It would take too much space to give a complete list of the acts which have been treated by one or other House as breaches of its privileges, but the following may be regarded as typical:

(*a*) Disorderly conduct on the part of members of the public who have been admitted to the galleries of the House or to sittings of committees.

(*b*) Premature publication of reports of select committees; or publication of evidence given before select committees and not, or not yet, reported to the House.

(*c*) Assaults on, or insulting behaviour to, members on their way to or from the House.

(*d*) Attempts to influence members in their parliamentary conduct by bribes, threats or other improper means.

(*e*) Assaults on, abuse of, or threats against, members on account of their parliamentary conduct.

(*f*) Speeches or writings defamatory of the House or particular members of the House in respect of their conduct as members.

To constitute a breach of privilege a statement reflecting on the conduct of a member in his capacity as a member need not be untrue, but it must tend to lower the House in the eyes of the public.

(*g*) Refusal to attend when summoned as a witness, or to produce documents or answer questions.

(*h*) Tampering with witnesses.

(*i*) Assaults on, abuse of, threats against, or the infliction of pecuniary injury on, witnesses on account of evidence given by them before select committees.

(*j*) Resistance to, or obstruction of, officers of the House in the execution of their duties.

(*k*) Service of process, civil or criminal, within the precincts of the House while it is sitting.

Absence of precedent will not prevent an act from being treated as a breach of privilege.

Some acts which formerly were treated as breaches of privilege are now allowed to pass without notice, *e.g.* the publication of debates or other proceedings of either House or its committees (unless such debates or proceedings have been conducted behind closed doors).

If an alleged breach of privilege is brought to the notice of the House of Commons at the earliest possible opportunity, it will be given precedence over the business of the day, provided that the Speaker is of opinion that the act or conduct complained of *prima facie* constitutes a breach of privilege.* In determining whether this condition is satisfied the Speaker assumes that the facts are as stated by the member who raised the matter. By the earliest possible opportunity is meant at the next sitting of the House at the end of questions and before the public business of the day is entered on. A breach of privilege alleged to have been committed during a sitting of the House may be brought to the notice of the House forthwith if the offence is of such a character as to call for immediate action by the House, as, for instance, an assault upon a member within the precincts of the House. Otherwise it should be raised at the next sitting. A member who intends to bring an alleged breach of privilege to the notice of the House should, if possible, give notice of his intention to do so to the Speaker and, if a member is involved, to that member.

On February 8, 1960, an order was made providing that for the remainder of the session a complaint of breach of privilege might be heard before the commencement of public business on the next sitting day after notice had been given to the Speaker, provided that such notice had been given at the earliest opportunity. This order was interpreted to mean that when a complaint was made the Speaker could defer giving his decision until the next sitting so long as the matter had been raised at the earliest opportunity. Although the order has not been renewed in any subsequent session, the Speaker since then has almost invariably deferred giving his decision until the next sitting day when, if he decides that the complaint satisfies the condition mentioned above, it is given precedence over the business of the day.

If the Speaker decides that the act or conduct complained of *prima facie* constitutes a breach of privilege the member must make some motion in reference to the matter. He† usually moves "that the matter of the complaint be referred to the Committee of Privileges", but he may content himself with moving a resolution to the effect that the act of which he complains constitutes a breach of privilege. This is frequently done in the case of libels on the House or on members. If a member complains of something published in a newspaper, he must produce a copy of

* By refusing to give precedence over the prearranged business to a complaint of breach of privilege on the ground that the act or conduct complained of does not, in his opinion, *prima facie* constitute a breach of privilege, the Speaker does not in any way prejudge the question whether a breach of privilege has been committed. That is a question which only the House can decide. The member who has raised the matter can therefore give notice of a motion regarding the alleged breach of privilege and, if opportunity offers, move it.

† In recent times this motion has regularly been moved by the Leader of the House.

BREACH OF PRIVILEGE—*continued*
the newspaper (a cutting will not do) and the passage complained of must be read out by the Clerk of the House before any motion is made in reference to the matter.

When the matter of a complaint of breach of privilege is referred to the Committee of Privileges it is the function of the Committee to ascertain the facts and to report whether, in its opinion, they constitute a breach of privilege. The Committee usually orders the person alleged to have committed the breach of privilege to appear before it. When he appears he is examined by the Committee. He is not allowed to be defended by a barrister or a solicitor. If he admits his guilt, but makes an adequate apology, the Committee usually recommends the House to accept it. If he denies the charge, the Committee usually allows him to call evidence in his defence. Witnesses are examined on oath or not according to the circumstances of the case. Members of the public are not allowed to be present.

If the Committee reports that no breach of privilege has been committed, the House usually takes no further action. If, however, the Committee reports that a breach of privilege has been committed, and does not recommend the House to accept the apology which the offender has made or to refrain from taking any further action in the matter, the report is usually considered by the House. If the House resolves that it " doth agree with the Committee in their report ", it goes on to determine what punishment shall be inflicted on the offender. He may be committed either to the custody of the Serjeant at Arms or to prison; or the House may content itself with ordering the Speaker to reprimand him. In the latter case, the offender is brought to the bar by the Serjeant at Arms, who stands, with his mace on his shoulder, by the offender whilst the Speaker delivers the reprimand. Offenders are sometimes heard in their defence before the House decides whether to accept the finding of the Committee of Privileges, or, after the finding has been accepted, in extenuation of their offence or in mitigation of punishment.

Persons imprisoned by order of the House of Commons are detained until they petition the House expressing proper contrition for their offences, upon which the House usually orders them to be released, or until the end of the session, when they are automatically released. If, however, the House thinks that an offender who has been automatically released has not been sufficiently punished, it may order him to be re-arrested and imprisoned in the ensuing session. This course was followed in 1880 in the case of Charles Edward Grissell, who, by going abroad, had evaded arrest until two days before the close of the preceding session.

The House of Lords has power to impose a fine instead of, or in addition to, imprisonment, but there is some doubt whether the House of Commons has power to do so. At any rate, it has not exercised the power for nearly three hundred years. The House of Lords, unlike the House of Commons, can inflict a definite term of imprisonment by way of punishment for breach of privilege, in which case the prisoner will not be released if Parliament is prorogued or dissolved before the term has expired.

BUDGET

Soon after the opening of each financial year (April 1), the Chancellor of the Exchequer "opens his budget" with a statement in the House. The word "budget" is derived from a French word meaning a leather bag of the kind used to carry confidential documents; in Parliament it denotes the collection of proposals which the Chancellor puts before the Committee for adjusting the revenue of the State to meet its expenditure, the annual rate of income tax being one of the most important. The speech which he makes on this occasion is known as his "budget statement", and includes a review of the public revenue and expenditure and, sometimes, of the economic state of the nation as well. The budget debate which follows take place on the first of the motions for the budget resolutions, which give effect to the Chancellor's proposals (*see also* FINANCE; WAYS AND MEANS).

BUSINESS, ORDER OF

A list is given below of the different kinds of business which may occur at a sitting, in the order in which they are taken. It will, no doubt, be realised that all the items mentioned are seldom likely to occur at the same sitting; some, indeed, are very rare. It must also be understood that the order is not invariable, occasional departures from it being made for the convenience of the House. Certain items described below, such as questions to ministers for oral answer (except by private notice) and motions for the adjournment of the House under Standing Order No. 9, do not occur on Fridays.

The business of the day is preceded in the House of Commons by prayers, which are read by the Speaker's Chaplain as soon as the Speaker has entered the Chamber. During prayers the Speaker stands at the Table in the Clerk's place and the Chaplain in the Second Clerk Assistant's. Immediately afterwards the Speaker takes the chair and the sitting begins.

Messages from the Queen, usually in answer to addresses, are read to the House by their bearers, usually members who hold office in the royal household, as soon as the Speaker has taken the chair. Communications from other persons or bodies to the House—such as messages of congratulation, condolence, etc.,

BUSINESS, ORDER OF—*continued*

from foreign legislatures—are read by the Speaker and come next in order. The Speaker also normally notifies the Royal Assent to Bills at this time. Then come motions for new writs for the election of members to fill vacant seats. These may be, though rarely are, debated (*see* ELECTIONS); when they are debated, the motion moved at this time is withdrawn, and is moved again after any Government motions relating to the business of the House (*see below*) have been disposed of.

After this comes the time for taking unopposed private business. This is an item of almost daily occurrence during most of the session and includes provisional order bills and amendments to the private bill standing orders in addition to private bills themselves. Since the time is only for *unopposed* business, the single word "object" is enough to cause further proceeding on a bill to be deferred. A bill's progress cannot, however, be blocked indefinitely in this way since the Chairman of Ways and Means may order an opposed bill to be set down for seven o'clock on the same or a future day, when it can be considered at leisure, debated, and, if necessary, divided upon (*see* PRIVATE BUSINESS; BLOCKING OF BILLS).

After private business is over, and before question time begins, two more items may occur. These are, first, the presentation of a public petition by a member who wishes to make a short statement in "explanation" (*see* PETITION) and, secondly, a motion "for an unopposed return", that is, a motion ordering the return to the House of information which a department has signified its willingness to supply. Both these items were formerly much commoner than now.

The next business, the oral answering by Ministers of questions of which notice has been given by members, must begin not later than 2.45 p.m. and end not later than 3.30 p.m. In practice the time available is usually not much less than a full hour. After these have been finished, questions "by private notice" may be asked (*see* QUESTIONS TO MINISTERS).

From this point until the beginning of public business a variety of matters may be dealt with, of which some are omitted from the list since they are too rare to be worth mentioning. The following are the more important.

(1) Statements by ministers about the policy of their departments.

(2) The introduction of new members returned at by-elections (*see* OATH OF ALLEGIANCE).

(3) Requests for leave to move the adjournment of the House, under Standing Order No. 9, on a specific and important matter that should have urgent consideration (*see* ADJOURNMENT OF THE HOUSE, MOTION FOR).

(4) Statements by ministers and other members in commemoration of distinguished persons lately dead.

(5) The holding of ballots for the privilege of moving motions in " private members' time " (*see* BALLOT).

(6) Personal explanations by members, whether ministers or not; that is, explanations of their conduct or actions. The most important of these are the statements made by members who have just resigned government office, explaining their reasons for differing from their colleagues.

(7) Raising matters of privilege. This is the convenient moment for bringing to the notice of the House a matter of privilege which has arisen since the last sitting. A question of privilege requiring immediate action by the House may, however, be raised at any time, and instances have occurred of the business being interrupted at a later stage in the sitting in order that such a matter might be submitted to the House at the earliest possible opportunity.

(8) The presentation of public bills (*see* BILL, PUBLIC).

(9) Government motions relating to the business of the House, other than motions for the suspension of the " ten o'clock rule ". Motions taken at this time include motions for the reference of bills to second reading committees and committees to consider bills on report and of other business to the Scottish and Welsh Grand Committees (*q.v.*).

(10) Motions for introducing bills or nominating select committees under the " ten-minute rule ".

A motion for the adjournment of the House moved by a member of the Government may come next, preceding the " public business ", that is, the orders of the day, and may be, in fact, the real business of the day. Likewise if a member has at a previous sitting obtained the leave of the House to move the adjournment for the purpose of discussing a specific and important matter that should have urgent consideration, that motion will be moved before the orders of the day are entered upon; (but when the Speaker owing to the urgency of the matter has so directed, adjournment motions of this type will be moved at 7 p.m. on the day on which the leave of the House is obtained (*see* ADJOURNMENT OF THE HOUSE, MOTION FOR)).

The orders of the day, interspersed, it may be, with government motions, come next (although the House sometimes agrees to a motion for its adjournment before they are reached) and, as a rule, the main business of the day is taken on these orders. Once begun, they are liable to interruption at 7 p.m. by private business set down by direction of the Chairman of Ways and Means (*see* PRIVATE BUSINESS) and, in cases of special urgency, by private members' motions for the adjournment of the House. The orders of the day are also liable to interruption at 10 p.m., when a motion may be moved to exempt the business under

BUSINESS, ORDER OF—*continued*
discussion or other business from the provisions of the standing order which would otherwise preclude debate after that hour. Apart from interruptions for these classes of business, the orders of the day and notices of motion are disposed of in succession in the order in which they stand on the order paper. The right is, however, reserved to the Government of moving the adjournment between two orders of the day; and any member may move the adjournment while an order of the day is under consideration. (For the arrangements for bringing the sitting to an end, *see* ADJOURNMENT OF THE HOUSE; SITTINGS OF THE HOUSE OF COMMONS).

The order of business in the House of Lords is somewhat different from that in the Commons. The House sits for public business on Tuesdays and Wednesdays at 2.30 p.m. and on Thursdays generally at 3 p.m.; sittings may also take place on Mondays and on Fridays, if need be. Judicial business may be taken on any of these days from 10 a.m. to 1 p.m., and, if there is no other business, in the afternoon. The sitting begins each day with prayers, which are read by a bishop if one is present; after the judicial business is finished, on days when there is legislative and other business to be done in the afternoon, the House adjourns "during pleasure" until the time for public business.

When the time for public business arrives (*i.e.* in the afternoon), bishops and peers who have not sat before may first take their seats. Then come (1) messages from the Queen (as in the House of Commons), (2) notification to the House of the Royal Assent to bills (although this may take place at any time during the sitting if the Assent is given to a bill on the same day as the final stage of the bill is taken), (3) tributes to deceased peers and similar formal speeches, (4) private business, (5) starred questions (*see* QUESTIONS TO MINISTERS), (6) business of which notice is not given, which includes (among other things) business and ministerial statements, private notice questions, matters of privilege, and the introduction and first readings of bills. After these preliminaries, motions of which notice has been given and orders of the day are proceeded with. "Business" motions are taken first, followed by motions for addresses of congratulation or sympathy. After this provisional order bills and hybrid bills are considered. Other business, including public bills, measures, motions and unstarred questions, follows in the order in which notice regarding each item has been received at the Table; but on Tuesdays and Thursdays public bills and measures are given precedence of motions and questions. It should be observed that the House of Lords often sits only on three days and seldom on more than four days each week, according to the requirements of business.

A sitting of the House of Lords is only brought to an end by a motion "That this House do now adjourn" being agreed to;

there is no provision for the interruption of business at a fixed hour, as in the Commons. This was also the rule in the lower House until 1888.

BUSINESS COMMITTEE

A select committee of the House of Commons appointed by standing order. When an order has been made by the House allotting a certain number of days to the committee and report stages of a bill (*see* GUILLOTINE), it becomes the duty of this Committee to apportion the time so allotted between the various clauses, etc., of the bill. The Committee is also given power, if it thinks fit, to perform similar functions in cases where a general agreement has been reached regarding the number of days to be devoted to proceedings in a committee of the whole House or on the report stage of a bill. The Committee reports its recommendations to the House. When the report is considered by the House the Speaker puts the question " that this House doth agree with the Committee in the said report " at once without allowing any debate. If the question is resolved in the affirmative, the Committee's recommendations have effect as if they were orders of the House. The Committee consists of the members of the Chairmen's Panel (*q.v.*) together with five other members appointed *ad hoc* by the Speaker. The quorum is seven.

A similar task is performed by a sub-committee of a standing committee where an order has been made by the House allocating time to the proceedings of a standing committee on a bill. This order stands referred to a sub-committee of the standing committee called the Business Sub-Committee, which is nominated by the Speaker and consists of the chairman (who is chairman of the sub-committee) and seven members of the standing committee. The resolutions of the sub-committee are reported to the committee at its next meeting and the procedure thereon is similar to that governing the resolutions of the Business Committee in the House itself.

The Business Committee may also be required to act in the absence of an express order of the House imposing a guillotine on a bill where either the Speaker has been informed that no general agreement exists for the allocation of days to the committee and report stages of a bill or any such agreement is, in the opinion of a minister of the Crown, working ineffectively. In such a case a Minister may move that the committee on the bill shall report the bill by a specified day, and that the Business Committee shall draw up a time table for the proceedings in committee, on report and on third reading; and the debate on this motion may not continue for more than two hours. The procedure of the House on the Committee's recommendation is as described above. It may be observed that the Business Committee is given considerably more latitude in drawing up the time table in this case

BUSINESS COMMITTEE—*continued*

than where a guillotine order has been made by the House, since, the date for the report of the bill having been decided by order of the House, the number of days allotted to the various stages remains at the discretion of the Business Committee.

CATCHING THE SPEAKER'S EYE

In the House of Commons a member who wishes to speak must rise in his place and either merely present himself to the notice of the Speaker or address him by his title, as " Mr. Speaker ". If two or more members rise at the same time the Speaker, in theory, calls upon the member whom he first observes to rise. In practice, he decides which shall speak. Members who wish to speak may submit their names in advance to the Speaker, who is thereby assisted, though his discretion is in no way limited, in deciding whom he shall call.

CHAIRMAN

Every committee appointed by the House of Commons is presided over by a chairman, whose duties are, in general, to call upon members to speak, to put the question, to preserve order in debate and to secure the due observance of the rules of the House.

The chairman of all committees of the whole House is the Chairman of Ways and Means, whose place may at any time be taken by the Deputy Chairman. In the absence of both, the chair may be taken by one of the panel of temporary chairmen appointed by the Speaker at the beginning of the session. All chairmen of committees of the whole House may exercise in the committee the powers, given to the Speaker in the House, to check irrelevance or repetition on the part of a member, to order a disorderly member to withdraw from the House or to name him, and to deal with a dilatory motion which he thinks is an abuse of the rules of the House either by putting the question forthwith or by declining to propose it at all, together with the power to disallow debate on the question that a clause stand part of a bill; but only the Chairman and Deputy Chairman of Ways and Means may accept a motion for the closure or select which amendments and new clauses or schedules shall be proposed. The substitution of one chairman for another takes place informally in the committee, without interruption of the business in progress. Like the Speaker, the chairman has only a casting vote.

The Speaker appoints one or more chairmen to every standing committee in respect of each bill allocated to it. The chairmen of standing committees are chosen by the Speaker from the Chairmen's Panel. A Chairman's powers are similar to those of the chairman in a committee of the whole House, including those of the Chairman and Deputy Chairman of Ways and Means with regard to the closure and the selection of amendments. He may not, however, order a disorderly member to withdraw from the committee. He has only a casting vote. Where more than one chairman is appointed any of these powers may be exercised by any of them.

The chairman of a standing committee is chosen by the Speaker from the Chairmen's Panel, a new appointment being made for each bill considered. The Speaker may from time to time change the chairman so appointed. He also has the power to appoint more than one member to be chairman of the same committee, in which case the members so appointed divide the duties between them, and each of them has full powers while actually in the chair.

The chairman of a select committee is chosen by the committee from among its members, who may have to vote on alternative candidates if more than one is proposed. In the absence of the elected chairman another member is chosen to act in his place for the occasion. The chairman calls upon members to speak and puts the question, but he has not the other powers possessed by the chairman of a committee of the whole House. He usually takes the main part in the examination of witnesses. The committee usually leaves it to the chairman to prepare a draft report for its consideration, though in fact the actual work of drafting is often done by the committee clerk on the chairman's behalf and under his instructions. By custom and for the sake of convenience, most of the initiative in the arrangement of a select committee's work is left to the chairman. He has only a casting vote.

Where a select committee has been given power to appoint sub-committees the chairmen of such sub-committees are usually appointed by the committee.

In a joint committee of both Houses the chairman is chosen in the same way as in a select committee ; he is usually a peer. His powers are those of a chairman of a select committee in the House of Lords ; accordingly he has an ordinary vote, and if the votes are equal on a division the question is decided in the manner described in the article EQUALITY OF VOTES.

The chairman of a committee on a private bill is nominated by the Committee of Selection which also appoints the other members of the committee. His powers are similar to those of a chairman of a select committee, but he may vote in a division, having a casting vote in addition.

The chairman of a committee in the House of Commons (including a committee of the whole House) is addressed by name, thus, " Mr. Irving " or "Mrs. Butler ", as the case may be, and not as " Mr. Chairman ".

CHAIRMAN OF COMMITTEES OF THE HOUSE OF LORDS

This officer (often referred to as the Lord Chairman) takes the chair in all committees of the whole House and in all select

CHAIRMAN OF COMMITTEES OF THE HOUSE OF LORDS—*continued*

committees (other than select committees on opposed private bills) which are not expressly given power to choose their chairmen. He discharges many duties in connection with private bills. He and the Chairman of Ways and Means decide which House the various private bills, petitions for which have been deposited at the beginning of the session, shall begin in. He moves the second and third readings of private bills except in cases where the second or third reading is going to be opposed by another peer. He is himself the committee on unopposed private bills. He also considers *unopposed* clauses in *opposed* private bills. Amendments made to private bills on third reading are normally moved by the Chairman of Committees. All amendments made by the Commons to Lords private bills or to amendments made by the Lords to Commons private bills are submitted to him for approval before being agreed to by the Lords. His permission is required for the deposit of a late petition for a private bill. He is chairman of the Committee of Selection and of the Personal Bills, Special Orders and Standing Orders Committees (*q.v.*). (In unopposed cases he can sit alone in the Standing Orders Committee and the Special Orders Committee.) With the tacit consent of the House he exercises considerable authority in relation to private bills. In fact he virtually determines whether provisions contained in such bills which are not opposed by petitioners shall be enacted and, if so, in what form. Under the Private Legislation Procedure (Scotland) Act 1936 and the Statutory Orders (Special Procedure) Acts 1945 and 1965, important functions are assigned to him and the Chairman of Ways and Means (*q.v.*) jointly with regard to legislation for private purposes in Scotland and to petitions against, or for the amendment of, special procedure orders (*q.v.*).

CHAIRMAN OF WAYS AND MEANS

The Chairman of Ways and Means is elected at the beginning of every Parliament, to act as the chairman ex-officio of all committees of the whole House. Although he is elected, on a motion by a member of the Government, from among the Government's supporters, and remains a member of his party, he does not speak in the House or in committee otherwise than in his official capacity, nor does he vote in divisions. On ceasing to hold the office he resumes full freedom of action as a party member. He sometimes (*e.g.* in 1931 and in 1945), but not always, resigns his office when his party goes into opposition otherwise than at a general election.

The Chairman of Ways and Means acts as Deputy Speaker when requested by the Speaker to take his place in the chair; the change takes place informally, without interrupting the business in progress. When thus acting, the Chairman has all the powers of the Speaker, except that he may not accept a motion for the closure or select amendments (he may, however, exercise the Speaker's power with regard to the closure during proceedings on the business of Supply or on the report stage of a bill). If, however, the House has been expressly informed of the absence of the Speaker (for example, if the Speaker is ill, or has obtained the leave of the House to absent himself for some special reason, such as to receive an honorary degree), the Deputy Speaker may exercise these powers as well (*see* SPEAKER).

The Chairman of Ways and Means has certain duties in connexion with private bills, provisional order bills, Scottish private legislation and special procedure orders (*q.v.*).

A Deputy Chairman of Ways and Means is elected at the same time and in the same way as the Chairman; he has the same duties and powers, including the power to act as Deputy Speaker. Like the Chairman, he remains a member of his party, but ceases to act as such while Deputy Chairman.

It may be observed that the Chairman of Ways and Means is often, but erroneously, referred to as the Chairman of Committees, a title that more properly belongs to the peer who holds the corresponding office in the House of Lords.

CHAIRMEN'S PANEL

A body of members from whom the Speaker appoints the chairmen of standing committees. It consists of the Chairman and Deputy Chairman of Ways and Means, together with the members whom the Speaker at the beginning of the session nominates to act as temporary chairmen of committees of the whole House when requested by the Chairman of Ways and Means.

CHAPLAIN, SPEAKER'S

It is the duty of the Speaker's Chaplain to read prayers at the beginning of every sitting of the House of Commons. If he preaches to the House, as he was formerly required from time to time to do, he does so in the parish church of St. Margaret. When the House attends the church for a service of thanksgiving (the last occasion was on August 15, 1945) he usually takes the service. When, in the past, the House has attended church to hear a sermon, it has usually agreed to a resolution thanking the preacher and desiring him to print his sermon.

CHILTERN HUNDREDS

The popular designation of an ancient office which, because it is technically an "office of profit under the Crown" and has not been exempted by statute from the disabilities attaching to such an office, may not be held by a member of the House of Commons.

CHILTERN HUNDREDS—*continued*

Its acceptance, therefore, by a member disqualifies him from further membership and vacates his seat. Since a member may not resign his seat, he must apply for an office of this kind if he wishes to cease to be a member, and the appointment is used purely as a device for enabling members to vacate their seats. In this case the member " asks for the Chiltern Hundreds ", that is, he applies to the Chancellor of the Exchequer for the appointment, and, if there is no reason for its refusal, a notice of the appointment appears in the " London Gazette ", and the seat thereupon becomes vacant. The full title of the office is " Steward or Bailiff of Her Majesty's three Chiltern Hundreds of Stoke, Desborough and Burnham ". The office is a sinecure, and the fees and duties purely nominal. The appointment lasts until another member asks for it. A similar office, which is sometimes used for the same purpose, is that of " Steward or Bailiff of Her Majesty's Manor of Northstead ".

CITATION CLAUSE

A clause in a bill enacting a name by which the intended Act may be cited, thus: " This Act may be cited as the Finance Act 1969." The clause is sometimes called the short title clause.

CIVIL CONTINGENCIES FUND

This fund is used for making, at the discretion of the Treasury, grants to enable departments to undertake urgent and unforeseen expenditure not yet approved by Parliament. Money is voted annually to keep the fund at the required level; the expenditure must in due course be included in the estimates and authorised in the ordinary way, after which the spending department repays to the fund the sum advanced.

CLAUSE

A subdivision of a bill. In committee each clause is considered by itself and amendments may be proposed to it. When any amendments that are proposed to the clause have been disposed of, the committee decides whether the clause (as amended) shall " stand part of the bill ". No motion to this effect is made. If notice has not been given of any amendment, or the chairman has decided not to select any of the amendments of which notice has been given, he proposes the question " that the clause stand part of the bill " directly after calling the number of the clause. If any amendment is moved, the chairman proposes the question " that the clause (as amended) stand part of the bill " when all proposed amendments have been disposed of. If the chairman thinks that the clause has been adequately discussed on the amendments, he may put the question at once, without allowing it to be debated. After this question has been proposed from the chair no further amendment can be moved to the clause.

The consideration of a clause or a number of consecutive clauses may, on motion, be postponed. A motion for postponing a clause cannot be moved after a decision has been come to on an amendment to that clause. If, therefore, it is desired to postpone a clause to which an amendment has been *moved*, the amendment must be withdrawn. A postponed clause is considered after the remaining clauses of the bill have been disposed of unless the motion for its postponement provides otherwise. Subject to this, the clauses of a bill are considered in the order in which they stand in the bill.

It is not in order *in committee* to move to leave out a clause. Notice of an amendment to this effect is sometimes given by members as an indication that they propose speaking against the question that the clause " stand part of the bill ".

New clauses may be added to a bill provided they are relevant to the subject matter of the bill and not inconsistent with a previous decision of the committee, *e.g.* it would be out of order to propose a new clause substantially the same as a clause which the committee had previously decided should not stand part of the bill. In the House of Lords a proposed new clause is moved when that point in the bill at which the clause is proposed to be inserted is reached. In the House of Commons, however, proposed new clauses are not considered until after the original clauses of the bill have been disposed of. A new clause is not proposed to be inserted at any specific point in the bill. If it is agreed to, the place where it shall be inserted is settled after the conclusion of the proceedings by the Public Bill Office (*q.v.*) after consultation with the draftsman or, in the case of a private member's bill, with the member who is in charge of it. The Chairman and Deputy Chairman of Ways and Means have power to select which of the proposed new clauses shall be considered, as also have the chairmen of standing committees. Subject to this, proposed new clauses are considered in the order in which they stand on the amendment paper. Proposed new clauses of which notice has been given are arranged on the amendment paper in the order in which the notices were handed in, except that clauses of which notice is given by the minister or other member in charge of the bill are given priority over those proposed by other members.

If the chairman selects a proposed new clause, he calls on the member who has given notice of the clause, and when the member has concluded his speech in support of the proposed clause, the clerk reads out the marginal note to the clause. The clause is then deemed to have been read a first time and the chairman proposes the question " that the clause be read a second time ". If this question is agreed to, amendments may be moved to the proposed clause. If no amendment is moved, or when all proposed amendments have been disposed of, the chairman proposes the question " that the clause (as amended) be added to the bill ".

CLAUSE—*continued*

New clauses may be proposed at the report stage also; they are considered before amendments to the bill itself, otherwise the procedure is the same as in committee. A new clause may not be moved without notice. The Speaker has power to select which of the proposed new clauses shall be considered. In the case of a bill which has been considered by a standing committee, the mover of a new clause may speak more than once.

CLERK OF THE HOUSE OF COMMONS

The chief of the permanent officers of the House. His office is of great antiquity, being not less old than the Speakership; officially he is entitled the "Under Clerk of the Parliaments to attend upon the Commons"; the Clerk of the Parliaments being the holder of a similar office in the House of Lords. The Clerk of the House of Commons is appointed for life by the Queen under Letters Patent, on the advice of the Prime Minister, the office being usually given, on a vacancy occurring, to the Clerk Assistant. The Clerk's principal duties are to sign addresses, votes of thanks and orders of the House, to endorse and sign bills sent to the Lords, to read whatever is required to be read in the House and to advise the Speaker and members about the rules and procedure of the House. He is responsible for the Clerk's Department which serves the House, as described below, and he also acts as accounting officer for the House of Commons vote. He sits at the Table during the sittings of the House, together with the Clerk Assistant and the Second Clerk Assistant. When the House goes into committee the Clerk's chair is occupied by the Chairman and the Clerk Assistant acts as clerk to the Committee. The Clerks Assistant, who are appointed by the Crown under the Sign Manual, on the recommendation of the Speaker, make a record of all proceedings in the House and Committees of the whole House, and also accept and examine (on behalf of the Speaker) notices of motions and questions handed in at the Table (*see* TABLE OF THE HOUSE).

In recognition of the great increase in recent years in the volume and importance of committee work the Second Clerk Assistant is now also Clerk of Committees, and consequently spends little of his time at the Table. His place there is now mostly taken by the Principal Clerk of the Table Office, who has a special responsibility for the scrutiny of notices of Questions to Ministers. The duty of sitting at the Table is also shared by Deputy Principal Clerks; all Clerks who sit at the table wear barristers' wigs and silk gowns when performing this duty.

The Department of the Clerk of the House of Commons is divided into six offices, viz., the Public Bill Office, the Journal Office, the Committee Office, the Private Bill Office, the Table Office and the Overseas Office.

CLERK OF THE PARLIAMENTS

The title of the officer of the House of Lords who performs functions substantially the same as those of the Clerk of the House of Commons. He is appointed by the Queen by letters patent. He retires on reaching the age of sixty-five. Subject to this he can be removed from office only by the House of Lords voting an address to the Queen praying for his removal. He sits at the table of the House, and reads the orders of the day. If a peer has given notice of a motion or question, the Clerk calls on him by name. He also reads messages from the Queen under the sign manual and messages from the Commons. He advises the Lord Chancellor and other members of the House on questions of order and matters of procedure. He endorses and signs bills sent to the Commons. He carries messages to the House of Commons and receives messages from that House at the bar of the House of Lords. He has the custody of all bills which have been passed by both Houses and are awaiting the royal assent, except money bills which are returned to the House of Commons. He signifies the royal assent to bills when this is given by commission (*see* ROYAL ASSENT).

When the royal assent is to be given by royal commission to a money bill the Clerk of the Parliaments goes to the bar to receive the bill from the Speaker of the House of Commons. He endorses every Act of Parliament with the date on which it received the royal assent. He authenticates by his signature all orders of the House for the attendance of persons, or for their attachment or commitment. He has the custody of the records of, and documents presented to, the House of Lords. He appoints the clerks in the several offices under his control and may remove them at his pleasure. He is the accounting officer for the vote for the House of Lords.

The Clerk of the Parliaments is assisted by the Clerk Assistant and the Reading Clerk, who sit with him at the Table of the House. They are appointed by the Lord Chancellor subject to the approval of the House, and can be suspended or removed from their offices only by the House. The Clerk Assistant takes minutes of all the proceedings, orders and judgments of the House and prepares the order paper. The Reading Clerk records the names of the peers who attend sittings of the House, reads the letters patent and the writs of summons when a newly created peer is introduced and administers the oath to him. He also reads the commission when the royal assent is to be given to bills or when Parliament is to be prorogued. The Clerk Assistant and the Reading Clerk also carry messages to the House of Commons and receive messages from that House at the bar of the House of Lords.

CLOSURE

A method of procedure which brings debate to a conclusion and enables the House to decide upon the matter under discussion.

CLOSURE—*continued*

A motion " That the question be now put " may be moved by any member at any time after a question has been proposed from the chair, even though he has already spoken to the question. It may be moved even whilst another member is speaking. The mover does not make a speech. He says merely " I move that the question be now put ".

When such a motion is made, the Speaker, unless he considers that the motion is an abuse of the rules of the House (*q.v.*) or an infringement of the rights of the minority, must immediately put the question " That the question be now put ". If the motion is carried, the Speaker puts the question under debate without permitting any further discussion. (Even though a majority of the members voting support it, the closure is not carried unless at least 100 members vote for it.) If the closure is carried, it deprives the mover of the motion closured of any right of reply which he would otherwise have had. If the closure is not carried, the debate on the motion is resumed at the point where it was interrupted.

As soon as the question upon which closure was moved and carried has been put, any member may *claim* that any further question, which may be requisite to bring to a decision any question that has already been proposed from the chair, be put. It should be noted that the member does not *move* that the question be now put ; he merely *claims* that it be put. The Speaker has an absolute discretion in conceding or refusing such a claim ; if he concedes the claim, he puts the question which is the subject of the claim without permitting any further debate. Thus, supposing that an amendment has been moved to a proposed amendment to a motion and the closure is moved on the question " That the amendment (*i.e. the amendment to the proposed amendment*) be made " and carried ; and that the House resolves that the proposed amendment should be so amended ; any member may then claim first that the question " That the amendment, as amended, be made " be put, and afterwards " That the main question, as amended, " be put.

When the House is in committee and a clause is under consideration any member may move " That the question that (*certain specified words*) stand part of the clause be now put " or " That the question that the clause stand part of (or be added to) the bill be now put ". The object of such a motion is to stop any further amendments being moved to the clause or to that part of it. The chairman need not accept the motion, but if he does, he must put the question on it forthwith. As the mere calling of a clause by the chairman brings it under consideration, a motion that the question, " That certain words stand part of the clause (or that the clause stand part of or be added to the bill) be now put ", may be moved before the clause has been discussed at all. But it cannot be moved while an amendment or a motion for the postponement of a clause is under discussion. Similar motions may be moved on the report stage of a bill. The power conferred by standing order upon the Speaker, the Chairman and Deputy Chairman of Ways and Means and chairmen of standing committees of selecting which of the proposed amendments shall be moved has made it unnecessary, except in special circumstances, to employ this type of closure.

The Chairman of Ways and Means, when acting as Deputy Speaker, can accept a motion "That the question be now put" only if that question has arisen during any proceedings relating to the business of supply or on the report stage of a bill, unless the Clerk has previously announced that the Speaker is unavoidably absent. Similarly the Deputy Chairman of Ways and Means when acting as Deputy Speaker also has power at any time to accept such a motion on questions arising on the business of supply or on the report stage of a bill; but he cannot accept such a motion in the House on any other question unless the unavoidable absence of the Chairman of Ways and Means as well as that of the Speaker has been formally announced to the House. When the House is in committee, closure cannot be accepted by a temporary chairman.

The closure may be moved when the Speaker or the chairman interrupts the business; and if the motion for the closure is accepted and carried, any member, as soon as the question to which closure was applied has been decided, may claim that any further questions requisite to bring to a decision any question which has already been proposed from the chair shall be put forthwith, and any such questions may, at the discretion of the occupant of the chair, be put forthwith.

Motions for the closure may be moved in a standing committee and the chairman has the same powers in relation to them (and to claims for the putting of questions already proposed) as the Chairman of Ways and Means has in a committee of the whole House. In a standing committee the closure is not carried unless the members voting in the majority number at least as many as the quorum of the committee.

COMMAND PAPER

A paper presented to Parliament or laid upon the table of either House, not in pursuance of an Act of Parliament, but on the initiative of the Minister responsible. It is so called because it is, in theory, presented "by Her Majesty's command". Each paper, if it is printed, receives a number, and may be quoted by this number preceded by the letters Cmnd., *e.g.* Cmnd. 1234. Most "white papers" and many "blue books" are technically command papers (*see* PAPERS, PARLIAMENTARY).

COMMITTEE, JOINT

A committee composed of members of both Houses, normally in equal numbers. It may be appointed to consider either a particular subject or a particular bill or bills or to consider all bills of a particular description. A joint committee may be appointed to consider a particular subject at the instance of either House, but a proposal that a particular bill should be committed to a joint committee must come from the House in which the bill has originated.

If either House considers that it is expedient that a joint committee should be appointed to consider a particular subject, or that a particular bill or bills should be committed to a joint committee, it passes a resolution to that effect, and sends a message to the other House informing it of the resolution and desiring its concurrence. If the other House concurs in the resolution it sends back a message to that effect. The House which proposed the appointment of the joint committee then appoints a select committee consisting of a certain number of members to join with a committee to be appointed by the other House to consider the matter (or commits the bill to a select committee consisting of a certain number of members to be joined with a committee to be appointed by the other House) and sends a message to the other House informing it that it has done so and requesting the other House to appoint an equal number of its members to join with the committee appointed by the first House. The other House then appoints a select committee to join with the committee appointed by the first House and sends a message to that House to inform it that it has done so. (Petitions against special procedure orders (*q.v.*) by statute stand referred to joint committees, unless either House orders otherwise; accordingly no resolution is necessary to enable joint committees on such petitions to be set up.)

The members of a joint committee are usually chosen by the respective Houses except in the case of joint committees on petitions against special procedure orders where the duty is frequently entrusted to the respective Committees of Selection.

When the House of Commons appoints a select committee to join with a committee which has been or is to be appointed by the House of Lords, it usually fixes a quorum and gives the committee power to send for persons, papers and records and any other powers that may be considered necessary.

A joint committee has only such authority as both Houses have concurred in giving it. If, therefore, one House gives the committee appointed by it a power or an instruction which the other House has not given to its committee, the joint committee cannot exercise the power or be bound by the instruction unless by the practice of the other House the power in question is considered to be incidental to, or impliedly conferred on, select committees. For example, although a joint committee may sit on a day on which the House of Lords is not sitting, provided that the House of Commons is sitting on that day, it cannot sit on a day on which the House of Commons is not sitting without obtaining leave to do so from the House unless, of course, power to sit notwithstanding any adjournment of the House has been conferred by the House of Commons on its committee.

A mandatory instruction can be given to a joint committee with the concurrence of both Houses. (A mandatory instruction given by one House to its committee would, of course, not be binding on the joint committee.) A permissive instruction, other than an instruction empowering the committee to divide a bill into two or more bills or to consolidate two or more bills, or to extend a bill which is limited by its title to a part of the United Kingdom to another part or to the whole of the Kingdom, would be nugatory unless both Houses concurred in giving it.

The time and place of meeting of a joint committee are fixed by agreement between the two Houses. The initiative is taken by the House of Lords, which sends a message to the House of Commons proposing that the joint committee shall meet at such and such a time and place. Before such a message is sent steps are usually taken by the Commons clerk who is to attend the committee to ascertain whether the time and place proposed for the meeting will meet the convenience of the Commons members of the committee. The result of this inquiry is communicated to the Clerks at the Table ; if they are satisfied that the time and place proposed will meet the convenience of all or most of the members, an order directing the committee appointed by the Commons to meet the committee appointed by the Lords at the time and place proposed is entered in the " Votes and Proceedings ", and a message is sent to the Lords informing them that the Commons have directed their committee to meet the Lords' committee at the time and place proposed.

A joint committee cannot proceed to business unless a quorum of the members of each House is present, and if at any time during a sitting the number of Commons members present is reduced below the quorum fixed by the House of Commons when the committee was appointed, or the number of peers present is reduced below three, either the proceedings must be suspended until the requisite number of members is present or the chairman must adjourn the committee.

The chairman of a joint committee is chosen by the committee. He may be chosen from among the members appointed by either House, but he is usually a peer.

The procedure in a joint committee is the same as in a Lords select committee, *e.g.* the chairman votes like any other member

COMMITTEE, JOINT—*continued*

and if the votes are equal the question is generally decided in the negative (*see* EQUALITY OF VOTES).

The report of a joint committee on a matter is presented to both Houses. It is presented by the chairman to the House of which he is a member and by a member selected for the purpose by the committee to the other House. A bill is reported to the House in which it is pending and a member is directed to report "accordingly" to the other House except in cases where the committee, in addition to reporting the bill, with or without amendment, makes a report on the matters dealt with in the bill, or a report recommending that the bill should not be further proceeded with or stating that the committee has been unable to complete its consideration of the bill.

COMMITTEE OF THE WHOLE HOUSE

For the transaction of certain kinds of business the House of Commons resolves itself into a committee, presided over by a chairman instead of the Speaker (in colloquial language it "goes into committee"). A committee of the whole House, like a select committee, is appointed for a specific purpose and with limited powers; it can only consider whatever is referred to it by the House and, when it has completed its consideration, must make a report to the House. In other respects, however, it is quite unlike a committee in the ordinary sense of the word. First, it is not a smaller body formed out of a larger, but, as its name implies, is composed of all the members of the House. Secondly, being composed of all the members of the House, it cannot sit while the House is itself sitting. On the other hand, it cannot sit during the intervals between the sittings of the House. The sittings of a committee of the whole House are inseparably connected with, and dependent upon, those of the House; it cannot begin to sit unless the House has met and is sitting. Thirdly, it cannot adjourn its sittings or the debate to a future day.

Since, as a result of recent changes in procedure, financial business is no longer required to originate in a committee of the whole House, the work of these committees is now in practice confined to the detailed consideration of public bills and it is therefore with committees of the whole House on bills that this article is concerned (*see* BILL, PUBLIC).

On an order of the day for a committee of the whole House being read by the Clerk, the Speaker leaves the chair. In former times he used to speak and vote in committees of the whole House, but nowadays he never does so, and invariably leaves the chamber if the committee lasts more than a few minutes. At the same time the Serjeant at Arms approaches the Table and moves the mace from its position on the Table to brackets just below the end of the table top, facing the bar. Then the chairman seats himself in the chair of the Clerk of the House, who has also retired (although he may reappear to take the place of one of the Clerks Assistant, in the latter's temporary absence). The office of chairman of a committee of the whole House is filled by either the Chairman of Ways and Means or the Deputy Chairman; in the absence of both, the chair may be taken by any member of the panel of temporary chairmen. The chairman of a committee of the whole House has the same powers as the Speaker in the regulation of debate (except that a temporary chairman may not exercise those with regard to the closure and the selection of amendments); but if he finds it necessary to "name" a member he must thereupon leave the chair of the committee. The Speaker then takes the chair of the House again, the sitting of the House is resumed and the chairman reports the matter to the House (*see* ORDER IN THE HOUSE). The chairman of a committee of the whole House has no power, in the event of grave disorder arising, to suspend the proceedings.

The procedure in a committee of the whole House is the same as in the House itself, except that a member may speak more than once to a question. As already mentioned, a committee of the whole House cannot adjourn its sittings or the debate to a future day. It can, however, at any time direct the chairman to "report progress and ask leave to sit again". This brings the sitting of the committee to a close. The chairman leaves the chair of the committee; the Speaker resumes the chair of the House; the chairman reports that the committee has made progress and has directed him to ask leave that it may sit again; and a day is then named for its next sitting. (Theoretically the chairman moves "that this House will, upon such and such a day, again resolve itself into the committee"; in practice the Speaker asks: "Committee to sit again, what day?" and the member in charge of the business names a day.) If the committee has not completed its consideration of the bill by the time for the interruption of business (*see* SITTINGS OF THE HOUSE OF COMMONS) the committee must report progress, in the same way. If the committee's proceedings are exempted by order of the House (*see* EXEMPTED BUSINESS), the House will again resolve itself into the committee after the order has been made. If necessary progress is reported at the end of each sitting, until the consideration of the bill is finished, when the chairman reports either that the committee has gone through the bill and made amendments thereto or that it has gone through the bill and directed him to report it without amendment.

A committee's proceedings are liable to interruption in certain cases. (1) When a member is "named" for disregarding the authority of the chair. This has been already mentioned. (2) When a messenger from the Queen or the Lords Commissioners comes to summon the House to the House of Lords to hear the

COMMITTEE OF THE WHOLE HOUSE—*continued*

royal assent given to bills (a rare event since the passing of the Royal Assent Act 1967), the House is immediately formed to receive him. The committee is not resumed until the House has returned from the other House and heard the Speaker give his account of the proceedings there. (3) A committee may also be interrupted at 7 p.m. when a member has obtained leave to move the adjournment under Standing Order No. 9 (and the Speaker has directed that the motion should be moved at that hour) (*see* ADJOURNMENT OF THE HOUSE, MOTION FOR), or when opposed private business is set down for consideration at this hour by direction of the Chairman of Ways and Means (*see* BUSINESS, ORDER OF). (4) The proceedings may be suspended by a resolution to that effect (*see* SUSPENSION OF SITTING). In any of these cases the chairman simply rises at the appropriate moment, says " Order, order ", and immediately leaves his place at the Table; on which the Speaker resumes the chair of the House.

COMMITTEE OFFICE

One of the five offices into which the Department of the Clerk of the House of Commons is divided. From among the clerks in this office, with some exceptions, are appointed all clerks attending select committees (including committees on private bills and joint committees of both Houses). The clerks may also be required to act as clerks to standing committees, when sufficient clerks cannot be provided from the Public Bill Office.

COMMITTEE, SECOND READING

A standing committee appointed to consider a public bill after the first reading. A motion to refer a bill to a second reading committee may be made at the commencement of public business by a minister of the Crown, provided that ten days' notice has been given after the bill has been printed. The question on the motion is put immediately, without amendment or debate. If at that moment not less than twenty members rise and object, the motion is not carried. The committee consists of not less than sixteen or more than fifty members; it must report whether or not it recommends that the bill ought to be read a second time. If the committee's recommendation is unfavourable, it may state its reasons in the report. After the committee has made its report, the bill is appointed for second reading; the question " that the bill be now read a second time " is then decided without amendment or debate.

COMMITTEE, SELECT

Strictly speaking, any committee composed of a certain number of members specially named, as distinguished from one which consists of all the members of the House, is a select committee. In practice, however, the term is not applied either to the committees by which private bills (*see* BILL, PRIVATE) are usually considered in the House of Commons or to the standing committees (*see* COMMITTEE, STANDING) to which in that House public bills (with certain exceptions) stand committed after second reading unless the House otherwise orders. The usual purpose for which a select committee is appointed is that of taking evidence on some subject and reporting its opinion on it for the information of the House. Select committees are, however, appointed for a great variety of other purposes which it would be impossible to set out in detail. Hybrid bills (*see* BILL, HYBRID) are regularly, and other public bills are sometimes, committed to select committees.

Appointment. Select committees are usually appointed when the occasion for such an appointment occurs. They are, however, sometimes appointed to consider all subjects of a particular class which may arise during the session. The standing orders of both Houses provide for the appointment of a number of select committees, *e.g.* the Committee of Public Accounts in the Commons and the Special Orders Committee in the Lords. A number of select committees are reappointed at the beginning of each session, *e.g.* the Select Committee on Nationalised Industries in the House of Commons and the Committee on House of Lords Offices in the House of Lords. These committees are known as sessional committees. Committees known as "specialist" select committees are sometimes set up with an order of reference merely to consider a subject (such as science and technology) or the activities of a particular Government department. The special features of sessional committees and specialist select committees are described under those headings.

Select committees are almost always appointed on the motion of a government whip. A motion for the appointment of a select committee requires notice.

Nomination. The members of a select committee are usually appointed by the House on a motion moved by the member who moved for the appointment of the committee. Where the inquiry is of a judicial or quasi-judicial nature, the selection of all or some of the members is, however, sometimes entrusted to the Committee of Selection. Important committees were formerly often chosen by ballot, *i.e.* by secret voting. This method was last resorted to by the House of Commons in 1819 when the Committee on the State of the Bank of England was so chosen.

In the House of Commons at least one day's notice must be given of the names of members intended to be proposed as members of a select committee. In practice notice of the names of the members who are to compose the committee is usually given at the same time as notice of the motion for the appointment of the committee, and the members of the committee are

COMMITTEE, SELECT—*continued*

appointed immediately after the motion for the appointment of the committee has been agreed to. Not more than fifteen members may be appointed to serve on a select committee unless the House has previously made an order that the committee " do consist of " a larger number of members. A motion to this effect requires notice. Select committees are usually constituted on a party basis, the various parties being represented on the committee in proportion to their strength in the House.

The whips of each party ascertain which members of their party would be best qualified and willing to serve on the committee, and the Government Chief Whip, after consulting, if necessary, the Leader of the House, then selects the majority of the committee, and the Opposition Chief Whip and the chief whips of the other parties, after consulting, if necessary, their leaders, select the minority.

The names of the members proposed as members of a select committee are usually put to the House *en bloc* and agreed to without any debate. If, however, when the Speaker is reading the names, a member objects to one of them, the Speaker proposes the question that the member objected to " be a member (or another member) of the committee "—any members whose names have passed unchallenged being considered to have been appointed to serve on the committee—and when this question has been decided, puts the remaining names to the House *en bloc*. If notice has been given of an amendment to substitute the name of another member for one of the names proposed, the Speaker puts any names which precede that of the member for whom it is proposed to substitute another member to the House *en bloc*. He then proposes the question that that member "be another member of the committee", and, when this question has been agreed to, with or without amendment, puts the remaining names to the House *en bloc*.

Motions for the appointment of the members of select committees may also be made " at the commencement of public business " (*see* BUSINESS, ORDER OF) on Mondays and Thursdays by a member of the Government, and on Tuesdays and Wednesdays by any member. If, when the question on the motion is proposed from the chair, objection is made to one of the names, the Speaker puts the question, either that the member objected to be a member (or another member) of the committee, or that the debate be now adjourned, without allowing any debate except a brief speech from the objector and a brief reply from the mover.

The membership of a committee may subsequently be altered or enlarged. A member of a select committee cannot resign; he must himself move, or induce some other member to move, that he " be discharged from " the committee. Such a motion, and all other motions to alter the composition of a select committee, or to fill up vacancies on it caused by the death of a member or by his having ceased to be a member of the House, require notice.

Authority of Select Committee. A select committee has no power but what it derives from the House which appoints it. The functions of a select committee are set forth in the order appointing it, termed the " order of reference ", and the committee must not consider any motion or embark upon any inquiry which does not come directly within the purposes of its appointment as expressed or clearly implied in the order of reference, unless those purposes have been widened by an instruction (*q.v.*). Nor may it, in the performance of its functions, exercise any power which has not been conferred upon it by the House either expressly or by necessary implication. (The power, constantly exercised by select committees, of adjourning their sittings from time to time is an example of a power which is held to be conferred upon them by necessary implication.) No power will be held to have been impliedly conferred upon a committee unless it can fairly be said to be obviously necessary to the achievement of the purpose for which the committee was appointed. So rigorously is this principle adhered to in the House of Commons that a select committee may not take evidence unless it has been empowered by the House to do so, even though the committee has been appointed to inquire into a matter and the evidence is voluntarily tendered. Moreover, as a select committee has only a *delegated* authority, it cannot appoint a sub-committee for any purpose which would involve a delegation of the authority conferred upon the committee by the House, *e.g.* to examine witnesses, unless it has been given the power to do so by the House.

Select committees appointed by the House of Commons are usually given power " to send for persons, papers, and records ", *i.e.* to summon witnesses to attend to give evidence or to produce documents. The House of Lords, however, does not give its committees authority to require the attendance of witnesses or the production of documents. In both Houses select committees appointed to investigate the conduct of persons, or to inquire into matters in which their private rights and interests, or those of corporate bodies, are concerned, are usually given a discretionary power of hearing counsel on behalf of such persons or bodies. In some instances select committees have been authorised to call in the aid of experts or to confer with other persons.

Time of Sitting. The time of the first meeting of a House of Lords select committee is fixed by the House ; but the time of the first meeting of a House of Commons select committee is fixed by the senior member. A select committee may adjourn itself from time to time. If the inquiry is likely to last some time the committee usually passes a resolution to sit on such and such a

COMMITTEE, SELECT—*continued*

day each week. The passing of such a resolution does not preclude the committee at any time from altering the date of the next meeting. Where it is inconvenient to fix the date of the next meeting this is sometimes left to the chairman. This, however, is, strictly speaking, irregular and may be done only with the unanimous consent of the members. A select committee may meet or continue to sit after the House has met and even after it has risen. Select committees of the House of Lords can sit even on days when the House is not sitting, but Commons select committees cannot do so without express authority. A select committee cannot continue to sit after Parliament is prorogued.

Place of Meeting. The meetings of a select committee are usually held in one of the committee rooms within the Palace of Westminster. If a committee wishes to meet beyond the precincts of Parliament, it must obtain leave to do so, unless it has been previously authorised to " adjourn from place to place ".

It was formerly questioned whether the House could authorise a committee to meet outside the United Kingdom. But from 1966 onwards the House has either formally given leave to committees and their sub-committees to hold meetings abroad, or has authorised special provision in the annual Estimates to meet the expenses involved.

Quorum. A Commons select committee cannot proceed to business unless a quorum of the members is present, and if after the committee has proceeded to business the number of members present falls below the quorum it is the duty of the committee clerk to draw the attention of the chairman to the fact, whereupon the chairman must either suspend the proceedings till a quorum is present or adjourn the committee to a future time. The quorum of a committee is fixed by the House either when it appoints the committee or when it chooses the members. If no quorum is fixed, the committee cannot function unless all the members are present.

The quorum of a select committee of the House of Lords is three.

Election of Chairman. The first proceeding of a Commons committee is to elect a chairman. Usually one member only is proposed and he is called to the chair with the general consent of the members present. Should more than one member be proposed as chairman the procedure is similar to the procedure in the House when there is a contest for the Speakership, the committee clerk putting the question and, if necessary, directing the committee to divide. If the chairman is absent from any meeting, another member is elected chairman *pro tempore*. A select committee may not appoint a deputy chairman.

A select committee of the House of Lords is usually given power to appoint its chairman. When a committee is not invested with this power, the Chairman of Committees (whether he has been appointed a member of the committee or not) is its chairman.

Procedure in Select Committees. The rules of procedure are generally speaking the same for a select committee as in the House by which it is appointed. But (1) a member may speak more than once to the same question; (2) members speak sitting and may refer to other members by name; (3) the chairman may take part in the proceedings; (4) the previous question (*q.v.*) cannot be moved; and (5) the chairman of a select committee has not the powers with which the Speaker in the House, and the Chairman and the Deputy Chairman of Ways and Means in committees of the whole House, are invested of accepting the closure, of dealing with persistent irrelevance or tedious repetition of arguments, and with dilatory motions, and of selecting the new clauses or the amendments which are to be proposed to bills or motions.

The chairman of a Commons select committee votes only when the votes are equal. In a select committee of the House of Lords the chairman votes like any other member, but has no casting vote, and if the votes are equal the question is generally decided in the negative (*see* EQUALITY OF VOTES).

On March 23, 1693, the House resolved "That no member of the House do presume to take tobacco, at the table, sitting at committees". The rule against smoking is not enforced while a select committee is deliberating, but it applies whenever witnesses are under examination.

Divisions. When a Commons select committee divides, the committee clerk calls the names of the members in alphabetical order, each member, as his name is called, answering aye or no, or stating that he does not vote. The clerk notes the answers on his list and, when he has called all the names, counts the numbers and hands the list to the chairman, who states the numbers and declares the decision of the committee. Members are allowed to abstain from voting. The procedure in a Lords committee is the same except that the committee clerk calls the names of the members in order of seniority and that the members answer "content" or "not content".

Admission of Public. The House of Commons sometimes gives its committees power to admit strangers (*i.e.*, members of the public, including the press) during the examination of witnesses, unless the committee otherwise order. If a committee is given this power strangers are excluded only by a majority decision of the committee. If no such power is given, strangers, if admitted at all, must withdraw at the desire of any individual member of the committee; and some committees, notably the Committee of Public Accounts, never admit strangers. In both Houses the public are never allowed to be present while a select committee is deliberating. Members of the House of Commons who are not members of the committee cannot be excluded

COMMITTEE, SELECT—*continued*
from select committees of the House of Commons unless the House has ordered that the committee shall be a " committee of secrecy " (no committee of secrecy has been appointed since 1857), but they usually withdraw out of courtesy whenever the committee is about to deliberate. They are, however, not allowed to address the committee, put questions to witnesses or take part in the proceedings. Any lord is entitled to attend a select committee of the House of Lords and may speak. He is, however, not allowed to vote.

Report. When all the evidence has been taken the chairman usually prepares a draft report which is circulated amongst the members of the committee. A meeting is then held for the purpose of considering the chairman's draft report and any draft reports that may be submitted by other members. If no alternative draft report is submitted to the committee, the chairman's draft report is taken as read, and the chairman puts the question that it " be read a second time, paragraph by paragraph ". If this question is decided in the affirmative, the committee goes through the report, paragraph by paragraph. Every paragraph is open to amendment. If no amendment is proposed, or when all the proposed amendments have been disposed of, the chairman puts the question that the paragraph, or the paragraph as amended, " stand part of the report ". New paragraphs may be inserted between paragraphs or added at the end of the report. The procedure on a new paragraph is similar to the procedure on a new clause (*see* CLAUSE). When the consideration of the draft report and any proposed additional paragraphs is finished, the chairman puts the question, " That this report (or this report as amended) be the report of the committee to the House ", and, on this being decided in the affirmative, the question, " That I do report the minutes of the evidence taken before the committee to the House ".

If more than one report is submitted to the committee, some member moves that one of the rival reports, usually the one submitted by the chairman, be read a second time, paragraph by paragraph. To this motion an amendment may be moved with the object of substituting the other draft report, or one of the other reports if there are more than two. When the committee has decided which of the rival draft reports shall be considered, the report selected is considered in the manner already described. Members of the committee who object to particular paragraphs in the report, or to the whole report, can put their dissent on record by dividing against the paragraphs to which they object or against the whole report, but cannot present a minority report. If more than one draft report is submitted to the committee, all the draft reports are printed in full in the minutes which are published with the report.

The report is presented to the House by the committee clerk handing a paper representing the report to one of the Clerks at the Table during a sitting of the House. The report is then considered to have been ordered to lie on the table and to be printed. No discussion can take place on the presentation of the report nor can a day be then appointed for considering it.

When a committee finds that it will not be able to complete the inquiry before the end of the session, it usually makes a special report to that effect, at the same time recommending that a committee should be appointed in the following session to continue the inquiry. It is usual also to report any evidence that has been taken.

A select committee sometimes wishes to make an interim report or a report on a particular branch of the subject which has been referred to its consideration. It is important to remember that the presentation of a report of any kind will automatically bring the existence of the committee to a close unless it has been previously authorised or obtains leave " to report from time to time ". But this rule does not apply to what is known as a special report, viz. a report made in reference to some matter relating to the powers, functions or proceedings of the committee, which has arisen incidentally, *e.g.* a report that a person summoned as a witness has failed to attend, refused to answer a question or produce a document, or prevaricated.

Consideration of Report. Reports of select committees are not as a rule considered by the House. The report of a committee may be brought under the consideration of the House, on motion, after notice, that the report " be now considered ". If the motion is carried, any motion may be made which is relevant to the subject matter of the report or necessary to give effect to the recommendations of the committee. The motion usually made is " that this House do agree with the committee in their report ". A report of a committee cannot be amended by the House. It may, however, be recommitted, *i.e.* referred back to the committee.

Select Committees on Public Bills. What has been said above regarding select committees on matters applies to select committees on public bills also, with such modifications as are necessarily involved in the substitution of a bill as the subject of inquiry. The bill itself is the order of reference to the committee and the deliberations (and, if the committee is authorised to take evidence, the inquiries) of the committee must be confined to the bill and relevant amendments. Evidence may be taken if the committee is empowered to send for persons, papers and records. When the evidence, if any, has been concluded, the committee goes through the bill, clause by clause, in the same way as a committee of the whole House or a standing committee does, making whatever amendments it thinks fit. The chairman has

COMMITTEE, SELECT—*continued*

not, however, power to select which amendments or new clauses shall be proposed. If the committee, in addition to reporting the bill with or without amendment, wishes to express its views on the matters dealt with in the bill, it makes a special report, which is drawn up in the same way as the report of a select committee on a matter. In some cases a select committee, after taking evidence, has come to the conclusion that it is inexpedient that the bill should pass into law, and has made a special report to that effect and reported the bill without amendment.

Committee Clerk. Each select committee is attended by a clerk who keeps the minutes, conducts the correspondence of the committee, makes arrangements for the attendance of witnesses (subject, of course, to such directions as he receives from the chairman), examines corrections made by witnesses in the proof sheets of their evidence and checks their claims for payments of expenses. He advises the chairman and the committee on question of order and procedure. It is now usual for the clerk to assist the chairman in the preparation of his draft report and even to write it for him.

COMMITTEE, SESSIONAL

A term applied to two types of select committee:

(1) A select committee which is permanent in the sense that, being appointed by standing order, it does not have to be re-appointed each session, though the members have to be nominated.

(2) A select committee which is appointed session after session.

In the House of Commons there are five sessional committees of the first type, viz., the Committee of Selection, the Standing Orders Committee, the Committee of Public Accounts, the Estimates Committee and the Business Committee.

Committees of Privileges and Committees on Public Petitions have been appointed every session for more than a century, and accordingly beyond doubt are committees of the second type. Committees with the same orders of reference (or with orders of reference not materially different) have also sat to consider the following subjects in every session from that given until 1969–70, viz., Statutory Instruments (1943–44), Nationalised Industries (1956–57), Procedure (1961–62), House of Commons (Services) (1965–66), Science and Technology (1966–67) and Parliamentary Commissioner for Administration (1967–68).

In the House of Lords there are four sessional committees of the first type, viz., the Standing Orders Committee, the Committee of Selection, the Special Orders Committee and the Personal Bills Committee, and eight sessional committees of the second type, viz., two Appeal Committees, two Appellate Committees, the House of Lords Offices Committee, the Leave of Absence Committee, the Select Committee on the Procedure of the House and the Committee for the Journals. There is also a sessional joint committee of the second type on Consolidation, &c., Bills.

COMMITTEE, SPECIALIST SELECT

A term applied to a select committee of the House of Commons appointed with wide terms of reference to consider policy and administration in a particular field. Since 1966 select committees of this type have been appointed in one or more sessions to consider Science and Technology, Agriculture, Education and Science, Race Relations and Immigration, Scottish Affairs and Overseas Aid.

The intention with " specialist " select committees has been that they should consist wholly or mainly of members who already have special knowledge of the subject which the committees are to consider.

These committees have all been given the power to admit strangers during the examination of witnesses " unless the Committee otherwise order ". This power has been interpreted to mean that strangers can be excluded during the examination of witnesses only by the decision of the committee, and not at the desire of a single member, as is the case when the power is not given. All the Committees mentioned have regularly heard evidence in public.

COMMITTEE, STANDING

In the House of Commons the term " standing committee " is usually applied to committees set up to examine in detail all public bills which, after receiving a second reading, are not committed to committees of the whole House, select committees and joint committees ; but second reading committees, committees to consider bills on report, the Scottish Grand Committee and the Welsh Grand Committee (all of which are described under separate headings), are in fact standing committees as defined in the standing order. Accordingly while it may be said that the main purpose of standing committees is to enable the committee stage of public bills to be taken otherwise than on the floor of the House, their functions also extend in certain circumstances to providing alternative methods of debating bills on second reading (second reading committees and the Scottish Grand Committee), and of considering them on report (committees to consider bills on report), to debating estimates (Scottish Grand Committee*) and to debating other matters referred to them (Scottish and Welsh Grand Committees).

* The standing order in fact contemplate that other business in addition to public bills should be referred to other standing committees, and in fact certain estimates were so referred in 1919.

COMMITTEE, STANDING—*continued*

There is no limit to the number of standing committees that may be appointed, but in practice the largest number of committees set up to consider bills at the committee stage that has ever been appointed in one session is twelve, including two Scottish Standing Committees. The only bills which are considered by the Scottish Standing Committees are those relating exclusively to Scotland; with that exception standing committes set up to consider bills at the committee stage are not appointed to consider bills of a particular class and have no distinctive names, being referred to simply as Standing Committees A, B, C, etc. Bills committed to a Standing Committee which have been certified by the Speaker as relating exclusively to Scotland are allocated by him to one or other Scottish Standing Committee; other bills are distributed among the remaining standing committees by the Speaker. Private members' bills are usually allocated to the standing committee previously designated by the Committee of Selection as the committee in which government bills are *not* to have precedence.

Constitution of Standing Committees. The numbers of members on the Scottish and Welsh Grand Committees, Scottish Standing Committees, second reading committees and committees to consider bills on report, are specially provided for in standing orders. Otherwise each standing committee consists of a chairman and not less than sixteen nor more than fifty members appointed in respect of each bill allocated to the committee, who serve on the committee only while it is considering that particular bill. The members of a standing committee other than the chairman are appointed by the Committee of Selection, which is directed by standing order, in choosing the members to "have regard to their qualifications and the composition of the House". The object of this provision is to ensure that the balance of parties in the committee shall be similar to that in the House as a whole, but that, subject to this, special knowledge of, or interest in, the bill which they are to consider shall be the criterion in appointing members to serve on the committee.

The Committee of Selection is empowered to discharge members from standing committees and to appoint others in their stead, but it will not entertain applications for changes in the membership of a standing committee as constituted in respect of a particular bill after the committee has begun to consider the bill, except in cases of illness or where ministers concerned with a bill take, change or give up their offices during the time when the committee is proceeding with the bill. A standing committee is thus constituted differently in the case of practically every bill that comes before it. Indeed, the changes which take place in the membership of a standing committee in the course of a session may be so kaleidoscopic as to make the term "standing committee" somewhat of a misnomer.

The Scottish Grand Committee consists of all the members for Scottish constituencies together with from ten to fifteen additional members appointed from time to time by the Committee of Selection to serve on the committee while it is considering estimates or a particular bill or matter. These members are drawn from the various parties in such proportions as will ensure that the proportions of party representation in the committee shall reflect those in the House.

Under the standing order not more than two Scottish Standing Committees may be appointed to consider bills at the committee stage. The first of these consists of thirty members for Scottish constituencies appointed by the Committee of Selection to serve on the committee while a particular bill is under consideration, to whom the Committee of Selection may add not more than twenty other members; the second consists of not less than sixteen nor more than fifty members, appointed in respect of each bill, with a minimum of sixteen members representing Scottish constituencies.

Analogous provision is made for Welsh business under the Standing orders. A committee, known as the Welsh Grand Committee, is appointed for the purpose of considering specific matters relating to Wales and Monmouthshire which may be referred to it by the House. It consists of all the members for those areas together with not more than five additional members chosen by the Committee of Selection. However, the Welsh Grand Committee has power only to consider matters and, unlike the Scottish Grand Committee, has no power to consider bills or estimates.

There is no standing committee with the exclusive duty to consider Welsh bills at the committee stage; however, in the rare case when a bill relating exclusively to Wales and Monmouthshire is committed to a Standing Committee, the Standing Orders provide that all members for constituencies in those areas must be included in the membership of the committee. This provision has been put into effect on three occasions, viz. in 1962 in the case of the Marriage (Wales and Monmouthshire) Bill, in 1964 in the case of the Elections (Welsh Forms) Bill and in 1967 in the case of the International Eisteddfod Bill.

Law Officers are allowed to speak in a standing committee of which they are not members, but not to move motions or amendments or vote. They are not counted in determining whether a quorum is present.

Chairmen. Chairmen of standing committees are appointed by the Speaker from a panel consisting of the Chairman of Ways and Means, the Deputy Chairman of Ways and Means and the

COMMITTEE, STANDING—*continued*

members appointed by the Speaker to act as temporary chairmen of committees of the whole House. The Speaker has the power to appoint more than one member to be chairman of the same committee, in which case the members so appointed divide the duties between them, and each of them has the full powers invested in the chairman of a standing committee (*see below*) while he is actually in the chair. (In addition any member of a standing committee may, at the request of a chairman, act as chairman temporarily, but not for longer than a quarter of an hour; but the full powers of the chairman are not given to any temporary chairman.) The Speaker may from time to time change the chairmen so appointed. It is the Speaker's practice, when appointing members as chairmen of a particular standing committee, to appoint them chairmen of the committee in respect of a particular bill or bills only.

Sittings. The day on and the hour at which a standing committee is to meet to begin the consideration of a particular bill or matter are fixed by the member who has been appointed chairman of the committee.

If a division is called in the House, the chairman must suspend the proceedings temporarily so that the members can vote in the division.

No standing committee may sit between 1 p.m. and 3.30 p.m. This ensures that there shall be an interval for lunch and allows members to be present in the House at question time.

If the committee has not previously adjourned, the chairman adjourns it at 1 p.m. If, however, he thinks that the consideration of the bill, etc., could be concluded if the committee were to continue sitting for a short time, he may defer adjourning the committee until 1.15 p.m. If the closure has been moved and the resulting proceedings are still in progress at the time when the chairman is required to adjourn the committee, he must not adjourn it until the question for closing the debate, the question on which closure was moved and any questions requisite to bring to a decision any question already proposed from the chair have been decided.

Except in cases where it is clear that the consideration of the bill will be completed before 1 p.m., a standing committee, before it begins to consider a bill, decides on what days of the week it will sit and the hour of meeting. The passing of such a resolution does not, however, preclude the committee at any time from altering the date of its next sitting or the hour of meeting.

The sitting of a standing committee cannot be suspended until a later hour the same day without the unanimous consent of the members unless oral notice of a motion to that effect has been given at a previous sitting. When it is desired that the committee shall meet in the afternoon as well as in the morning until the consideration of the bill in hand is completed or during any shorter period, a resolution to that effect must be passed. It is usual to give previous notice of a motion that the committee do meet in the afternoon as well as in the morning.

Generally speaking, once a committee has met to consider a bill, it must dispose of that bill before it can proceed with any other business. Where, however, a committee on two successive occasions has to be adjourned by reason of the failure of a quorum to assemble within twenty minutes of the time of meeting, the chairman instructs the clerk to place the bill at the bottom of the list of bills awaiting consideration by the committee, and the committee is summoned to consider the next bill on the list. At the beginning of each session the Chairmen's Panel passes a resolution "that if during the consideration of a bill before one of the standing committees it shall appear that the business would be expedited by postponing the further consideration of the bill in hand until the bill next on the list has been reported, and if the member in charge of the bill rises and makes a motion to that effect, the chairman will be in order in proposing such a question". But this resolution has never been acted on.

Procedure. The procedure in a standing committee is much the same as in a committee of the whole House. The chief differences are :—

(1) that motions for the adjournment of the debate or of further consideration of the bill are made use of to dispose of the business before the committee, instead of motions "that the chairman do report progress and ask leave to sit again",

(2) that a motion for the closure is not carried unless at least seventeen members or one-third of the membership of the committee (excluding the chairman), whichever is the less, vote in the majority, and

(3) if the number of members present falls below that required to form a quorum (*see below*) it is the duty of the clerk to inform the chairman who must immediately take notice of the fact and not (as in the House) allow the proceedings to continue until a member draws his attention to the deficiency.

A question is put only once from the chair, and if the chairman's statement that he thinks the ayes (or the noes) have it is challenged, the committee must proceed to a division.

When a division takes place the names of the members are called in alphabetical order by one of the clerks, and each member, as his name is called, answers "aye" or "no" or states that he is not voting. The doors of the committee room are locked during a division.

COMMITTEE, STANDING—*continued*

Powers of Chairman. The chairman of a standing committee has the same powers as the Chairman of Ways and Means exercises in a committee of the whole House of—

(1) directing a member who persists in irrelevance or tedious repetition of his own or other members' arguments to discontinue his speech,
(2) putting the question on a dilatory motion, *i.e.* a motion for the adjournment of the committee or of the debate, etc., forthwith or refusing to accept it,
(3) accepting or refusing motions for the closure,
(4) selecting which amendments, if any, shall be proposed to bills or motions,
(5) putting the question "that the clause (or the clause as amended) stand part of the bill" forthwith.

But he cannot direct a member who is guilty of grossly disorderly conduct to withdraw from the committee room. None of the above-mentioned powers can be exercised by a member who is acting as chairman temporarily at the request of the chairman.

Quorum. The quorum of a standing committee is seventeen, or one-third of the membership of the committee, excluding the chairman, whichever is the less.

Except in special circumstances, if a quorum is not present within twenty minutes from the time of meeting, the chairman adjourns the committee to the day, if any, appointed for the next sitting unless the committee has previously decided to sit in the afternoon as well as in the morning, in which case he suspends the sitting until the hour at which the committee is to meet that afternoon.

If during the sitting of a standing committee the number of members present falls below a quorum, the chairman must either suspend the proceedings until the requisite number of members is present or adjourn the committee. If the committee has previously decided to meet in the afternoon as well as in the morning, the chairman suspends the sitting until the time at which the committee is to meet that afternoon. It is not usual to allow more than twenty minutes for a quorum to reassemble.

Admission of Public. The public are admitted to meetings of a standing committee unless the committee decides to exclude them.

Official Report of Debates. A shorthand note of the debates in a standing committee is taken by the official reporters. An official report of the debates is published daily.

Report of Bill before its consideration has been completed. In special circumstances (*e.g.* when the Committee has disagreed to the sole effective clause) a standing committee has resolved to proceed no further with a bill and has reported it, without amendment, or with such amendments only as have been made, together with a special report explaining the committee's reasons for not completing the consideration of the bill. A motion " that the committee do not proceed further with the consideration of the bill " will not, as a general rule, be accepted by the chairman from a member who is not in charge of the bill. In one or two cases the member in charge of a bill has been allowed to move " That the committee do not proceed with the consideration of the bill " before its consideration has been begun.

Application of Guillotine to Proceedings in a Standing Committee. When the guillotine (*q.v.*) is applied to a bill which has been committed to a standing committee the committee may be required to report the bill by a certain date. In such cases a body, known as the Business Sub-committee of the committee, is set up to make recommendations to the committee as to how many sittings shall be allotted to the consideration of the bill, what proceedings shall be taken at each sitting, and the time at which proceedings, if not previously brought to a conclusion, shall be concluded. The Business Sub-committee consists of the chairman of the committee in respect of the bill and seven other members of the committee as constituted in respect of the bill chosen by the Speaker. The quorum is four. The sub-committee's recommendations, which take the form of resolutions, are reported to the committee at the beginning of the next sitting. On the recommendations being reported to the committee, the member in charge of the bill may forthwith move " that this committee doth agree with the sub-committee in the said resolution(s) ". This motion does not require notice, may not be debated or amended and must be put forthwith. If it is carried, the resolution or resolutions operate as if they had formed part of the order of the House. If, however, the motion is defeated, the resolution or resolutions stand re-committed to the Business Sub-committee.

COMMITTEE TO CONSIDER A BILL ON REPORT

A standing committee appointed to consider a public bill, after the bill has been reported from committee, as an alternative to the more usual procedure of the House itself considering the bill at the report stage. A motion to refer a bill to such a committee may be made, after notice, by a minister of the Crown at the commencement of public business, provided that the bill has been considered by a second reading committee or by the Scottish Grand Committee (*q.v.*) " in relation to the principle of the bill ". (Bills which have been considered in relation to their principle by the Scottish Grand Committee are referred to that Committee for their report stage if that stage is taken in a committee.) The question must be put immediately, without amendment or debate, and if not less than twenty members rise and object, the motion is not carried. The committee consists

COMMITTEE TO CONSIDER A BILL ON REPORT— *continued*

of not less than twenty nor more than eighty members; it must report to the House that it has considered the bill and made amendments, or has made no amendment, as the case may be. After the committee has reported, the bill is appointed for third reading on a future day.

COMPTROLLER AND AUDITOR GENERAL

The head of the Exchequer and Audit Department. He is appointed by the Crown by letters patent, his office being independent of the Treasury. He controls all issues of money from the Consolidated Fund and is also responsible for auditing all appropriation accounts (*q.v.*) as well as many other accounts of public expenditure where the statutes so provide. He makes regular reports to the House on the result of his investigations. His reports are considered by the Committee of Public Accounts, which he assists in its work; he is present at all the Committee's meetings. Though he is not a Civil Servant, the appointment to the office of Comptroller and Auditor General is usually made from among the senior officials at the Treasury.

CONFERENCE

A procedure formerly used as a means of communication between the two Houses, *e.g.* when one House disagreed to the amendments made by the other to a bill which it had passed. In such cases a conference was arranged, at a time and place named by the Lords, between managers appointed by each House. At the conference the reasons for disagreement were communicated to the other House. The Commons always appointed twice as many managers as the Lords. The proceedings at the conference were formal. The managers merely read and delivered a message from their House and no discussion took place. The Lords sat, wearing their hats, at the conference, and rose uncovered to speak. The Commons stood hatless. The conference over, the managers retired and reported the proceedings to their respective Houses.

If the reasons given for disagreement failed to satisfy the other House, a second conference was held, at which the reasons for disagreeing to the reasons were in turn given. If the second conference also failed to secure agreement, a "free" conference was held, at which the managers had authority to use arguments of their own choosing in order to convince the other party, their instructions limiting their discretion in the matter of concessions. If the free conference did not solve the difficulty, the bill was lost.

The last conference was held in 1860, the last free conference in 1836.

CONSOLIDATED FUND

The fund into which are paid all proceeds of taxes and other revenues of the State and out of which all governmental expenditure is made. It is an imaginary fund represented in fact by the account kept by Her Majesty's Government at the Bank of England. For practical purposes the Consolidated Fund and the Exchequer are one and the same thing.

Services which are financed by money paid out of the Consolidated Fund in accordance with the Acts founded on Supply resolutions, to meet the expenditure contained in the Estimates, are known as Supply Services. Certain payments are also made regularly from the Fund under statutory authority to meet expenditure which does not require the annual approval of Parliament. Examples of such payments, for what are known as the Consolidated Fund Services, are the salaries of the Lord Chancellor, the Speaker of the House of Commons, and Her Majesty's Judges, and the interest on the National Debt.

CONSOLIDATED FUND BILL

A bill to authorise the issue of sums out of the Consolidated Fund to meet the costs of government services within the financial limits set out in the bill. The bill covers grants of money already approved by the House of Commons by resolutions come to during the business of Supply. Several such bills may be passed during a session to authorise issues of sums to meet expenditure covered by supplementary estimates and excess votes, in addition to the annual Consolidated Fund (Appropriation) Bill which is passed every year in late July or early August to authorise the issue of sums to meet expenditure covered by the main annual estimates. (This latter bill passes into law as the Appropriation Act, and provides that the sums authorised to be issued are to be spent in accordance with the sums approved in the votes contained in the annual estimates (*i.e.*, appropriated).)

Consolidated Fund Bills are founded on Supply resolutions, and debate on second reading is expressly exempted from interruption at 10 p.m. On second reading any subject may be raised which arises out of any of the expenditure covered by the bill, and in recent years the Speaker has held unofficial ballots to decide the order in which individual private members are called to raise the numerous and varied subjects which they wish to debate.

After second reading a Consolidated Fund Bill is automatically committed to a Committee of the whole House. It cannot be amended in substance in committee, and the question for third reading must be put without amendment or debate. By standing order the House may not be counted during proceedings on a Consolidated Fund Bill.

CONSOLIDATION BILL

A bill the purpose of which is to throw together, into a single Act, several previous Acts relating to the same subject. The consolidation of the statute law has been greatly facilitated by the enactment in 1949 of the Consolidation of Enactments (Procedure) Act which enables " corrections and minor improvements " to be made in the Acts which are to be consolidated without at the same time opening the door to all sorts of other amendments.

Under this Act any " corrections and minor improvements " of the existing law which the Lord Chancellor thinks expedient are embodied in the consolidation bill. Before, or at the same time as, the bill is introduced a memorandum of the changes proposed is laid before Parliament, a notice having previously been published in the Gazette saying where copies may be obtained and where representations regarding the proposed changes in the law should be sent. The Joint Committee on Consolidation, &c., Bills, after considering any representations that have been received, informs the Lord Chancellor and the Speaker which of the proposals it is prepared to approve. If both of these officers concur with the Committee in its approval, the Committee makes any amendments that are necessary to give effect to the alterations made by the Committee in the original proposals and makes a report to both Houses stating that the bill re-enacts the existing law with such corrections and minor improvements only as have been approved by the Committee with the concurrence of the Lord Chancellor and the Speaker. These corrections and minor improvements are deemed, for the purposes of further proceedings on the bill, " to have become law in like manner as if made by an Act ". No further amendments can, therefore, be made to the bill in either House, though it can be rejected.

CONSOLIDATION, &c., BILLS, JOINT COMMITTEE ON

A joint committee appointed each session to consider all consolidation bills, statute law revision bills and bills presented under the Consolidation of Enactments (Procedure) Act 1949. It consists of twenty-four members, twelve from each House, and is empowered to send for persons, papers, and records and to sit notwithstanding any adjournment of the House. The quorum is six, three from each House.

CONTEMPT OF EITHER HOUSE OF PARLIAMENT

Any act or omission which either directly obstructs the due proceeding of that House or has a tendency to produce that effect by bringing its authority into contempt, *e.g.* the publication of reflections on the character or conduct of a member in his capacity as a member. Such acts are usually described as breaches of privilege, but this is not strictly correct. All breaches of privilege are contempts of the House whose privileges are violated, but a person may be guilty of a contempt of one or other House without violating any privilege properly so called of that House, *e.g.* by disobeying an order to attend a committee.

COSTS

The Parliamentary Costs Act 1865 gives a committee on an opposed private bill power to award costs to a petitioner against a bill, but only if (*a*) the preamble is not proved or the committee inserts some provision in the bill for the protection of the petitioner, or for his protection strikes out or alters some provision in the bill, and (*b*) the committee unanimously reports that the petitioner has been " unreasonably or vexatiously subjected to expense in defending his rights ". The Act also gives the committee power to award costs *against* a petitioner opposing the bill, but only if (*a*) the preamble is proved, and (*b*) the committee unanimously reports that the promoters have been " vexatiously subjected to expense " by his opposition.

Costs may not be awarded against a landowner who *bona fide* at his own risk and charge opposes a bill which proposes to take any part of his property. Committees have very rarely exercised their power to award costs.

The Parliamentary Costs Act 1871 gives a committee on an opposed provisional order bill a similar power of awarding costs. In certain cases under the Allotments (Scotland) Act 1892, the Public Health (Scotland) Act 1897 and the Ancient Monuments Consolidation and Amendment Act 1913, and also in the case of a joint committee under the Private Legislation Procedure (Scotland) Act 1936, costs may be awarded by a majority of the committee.

Under the Statutory Orders (Special Procedure) Act 1945 a joint committee on a special procedure petition has the same power of awarding costs as a committee on a provisional order bill. If costs were awarded to a petitioner against a special procedure order, they would be paid by the Government unless the minister had transferred his right of audience to the person whc had applied for the order.

COUNSEL

Promoters and opponents of private bills and provisional order bills, petitioners against special procedure orders whose petitions stand referred to joint committees and the ministers who made the orders are given by standing order the right to be heard before the committee on the bill or the petition " by themselves, their counsel or agents ". A similar right is given to promoters and opponents of hybrid bills when such bills are committed to select committees. In other cases counsel are not allowed to appear before select committees of either House unless that

COUNSEL—*continued*

House either has given the parties for whom they appear a right to be heard by counsel or has given the committee a discretionary power of hearing parties by counsel. Formerly it was the practice when a select committee was appointed to investigate the conduct of some person, or to inquire into matters in which the private rights or interests of particular persons or corporate bodies, as distinct from those of the general public, were concerned, to give the parties a right to be heard by counsel. In recent years, however, the tendency has been to leave the hearing of counsel to the discretion of the committee. The last instance of a party's being given a right to appear by counsel occurred in 1940 when a member whose conduct was being investigated by a select committee was given the right to be heard by himself or his counsel, if he thought fit. Counsel appearing before a select committee wear their wigs and gowns.

COUNSEL TO THE CHAIRMAN OF COMMITTEES

An officer of the House of Lords who performs functions similar to those performed by the Counsel to Mr. Speaker (*see* SPEAKER'S COUNSEL). He also acts as legal adviser to the Special Orders Committee (*q.v.*).

COUNT

If during a sitting of the House of Commons less than forty members (*i.e.* a quorum) are present, including the Speaker, any member may call his attention to the fact ; whereupon the Speaker orders strangers to withdraw, and the proceedings are suspended. The division bells are rung* and four minutes are allowed for members to reach the chamber. When enough members have entered the Chamber to make a quorum the Speaker calls the member previously in possession of the House and the proceedings are resumed. If less than forty are present at the end of four minutes, he adjourns the House till the next sitting day.

A count may also take place in the same way in a committee of the whole House. If the required number is not reached, the chairman leaves the chair of the committee, and the Speaker resumes the chair of the House; the chairman reports that a quorum has not been present in the committee and the Speaker then follows the same procedure as when the deficiency is brought to his notice as described above. If forty members are present before four minutes have expired, he leaves the chair, the chairman returns to the chair of the committee, and the proceedings in committee are resumed.

When once the Speaker has satisfied himself that a quorum is present he does not allow the proceedings again to be interrupted

* Intermittently for a period of one minute.

for a count (even though his attention is called to the lack of a quorum) before a reasonable time (say an hour) has elapsed ; this also applies to the case where the deficiency of numbers has been revealed by a division. A similar practice is followed by the chairman of a committee of the whole House.

The House may not be counted (1) on Mondays, Tuesdays, Wednesdays and Thursdays between 7.30 and 8.30 p.m. or after 10 p.m., (2) on Fridays between 1.15 and 2.15 p.m., (3) during proceedings in the course of which the Speaker is directed forthwith to put any question—such as, for example, on consideration of a report from the Business Committee or on a motion for the closure of debate, or (4) during proceedings on any Consolidated Fund or Appropriation Bill (*see* QUORUM).

If the House, on being counted, is adjourned for the lack of a quorum, it is said to be " counted out ".

DEBATE

May only take place in the House of Commons when a motion has been made and a question has been proposed from the chair (*see* MOTION). It excludes, therefore, the asking and answering of parliamentary questions, ministerial statements (such as are made after " question time ") and personal explanations by members. None of these come in the category of debate, which consists of speeches in the parliamentary sense. The rules of debate, except in so far as is explained below, are the same in a committee of the whole House as in the House itself.

A member who wishes to speak in a debate must rise at the conclusion of another's speech and try to " catch the Speaker's eye ". If he is successful, the Speaker calls on him by name, and he proceeds to make his speech. While he is thus on his feet, he is said to be " in possession of the House ", and he need not give way except to the Speaker, who will only interrupt him if it is necessary to call him to order or to allow another member to raise a point of order. If the Speaker rises, the member must immediately sit down, and if he fails to do so, he will quickly be reminded by loud cries of " Order " from other members. Although a member making a speech need not give way to others who seek to interrupt him, he will often do so for a moment to allow a fellow-member to correct him or put a question for him to answer in his speech.

The member must address his remarks to the chair, and not to the House at large or to individual members. The occupant of the chair is addressed as " Mr. Speaker " or " Mr. Deputy Speaker " as the case may be ; in committee, the chairman is addressed by name. Other members must never be referred to by name, but as " the honourable member for so-and-so (the member's constituency) ", or " the right honourable gentleman the Secretary of State for (such and such a department of state) ",

DEBATE—*continued*
or some other descriptive phrase. A barrister is always " honourable and learned " and an officer of the armed forces of the Crown (if he chooses to be known by his rank) is " honourable and gallant ". A privy counsellor is " right honourable ". A member who is an Irish peer or a peer's son having a courtesy title is referred to as " the noble lord ".

Except in committee, no member may speak more than once to a question. This rule does not apply in the case of a member who has moved a substantive motion, or, on consideration of a bill reported from a standing committee, to the mover of an amendment or new clause ; it is also relaxed when it is obviously convenient for a reply to be given at the end of a debate by a minister, who is expected, however, to claim the indulgence of the House in so doing. In the case of an amendment, a motion for the adjournment of the debate or a motion for the adjournment of the House (made during a debate), the mover is speaking to the main question (the question on the amendment or adjournment motion not having yet been proposed from the chair) and his speech therefore counts as such, but once the question on the amendment or adjournment motion has been proposed, a member who has spoken on the main question may speak again ; likewise a member who has spoken only on the amendment may speak again in the debate on the main question if that is continued after the amendment has been disposed of. In committee there is no restriction on the number of speeches which a member may make to a question (*see* REPLY, RIGHT OF).

With regard to the content of speeches, the first and most important rule (and that most often violated) is that a speech must be relevant to the question before the House. In certain cases this allows debate to range over all the activities of government, as, for example, on the motion for an address of thanks to the Queen for her speech at the opening of Parliament (because the speech announces the policy of the Government in the session just opened), and on the second reading of the annual Consolidated Fund Bills (which give authority for the expenditure required by the estimates of the various departments of state, including the fighting services). In the former case reference to legislation is in order, since the speech mentions the bills which the Government proposes to introduce ; in the latter, anything involving legislation must be avoided, since the actual subject matter of the bill prescribes the limits of the debate, and it is necessarily not concerned with the question of further legislation. On the second reading of a bill, debate covers the whole subject matter of the bill, and reference may also be made to matters which would involve amendment ; but on third reading the scope of the debate is narrower, since the bill is now before the House in its final form, there being no further opportunity for amendment.

On an amendment, the debate is restricted to the subject matter of the amendment itself. When an estimate is debated in Supply, the whole activities of the department concerned can be discussed, but no reference may be made to anything involving legislation ; on a supplementary estimate, debate is restricted to the matter for which the extra expenditure is needed, and may therefore be very narrow indeed. A motion for the adjournment of the House may, by custom, provide the occasion for a debate on any subject which does not involve legislation, so long as the Government are to some extent responsible.

Some motions are by their terms confined to so narrow a point, that in spite of the importance or complexity of their subject matter debate on them is virtually impossible. The standing orders prescribe that certain motions, whose form must be strictly adhered to, must be decided without debate (*e.g.* closure and " business " motions), and in other cases give the chair the discretionary power to put the question forthwith, *i.e.* without debate, for example in the case of dilatory motions.

An ancient rule protects the impartiality of the Crown by decreeing that the Sovereign's name may not be introduced to influence debate. Likewise, other organs of the state and persons in authority must not be criticised, unless a motion has been made with the express object of calling their conduct in question. This rule applies to the judges (down to county court level), the Speaker, the Chairman of Ways and Means and other chairmen of committees of the House, members of statutory commissions and similar persons, but not such persons as ambassadors, officers of the fighting services and civil servants, for whom a minister is responsible. Reference to matters which are " sub judice ", awaiting the decision of a court of law, is out of order as liable to prejudice the course of justice.

No reference may be made in debate to the debates or proceedings of the other House. This rule, which is based on the principle that the House has no knowledge, until formally apprised by message, of what goes on in the other House, and which ensures that members of either House shall not indulge in mutual recrimination or other such undignified proceedings, is responsible for the convention by which members refer to the other House as " another place ", and does not (as many people seem to think) prevent the House of Lords being spoken of as such when a direct reference would be appropriate.

Members are expected to observe moderation of language in debate, and a number of words and expressions have at various times been decided by the Speaker to be " unparliamentary ". Among them are such abusive words as " liar ", " traitor ", etc., and many others which reflect on another member's motives, honesty or sincerity (*see* UNPARLIAMENTARY LANGUAGE).

DEBATE—*continued*

Treasonable and seditious language is out of order, as are reflections on either House or any of its committees; from this it follows that a contemptuous or otherwise disrespectful reference to an Act of Parliament or any decision of the House is also forbidden. The use of unparliamentary language in any of the categories mentioned above leads to an immediate demand by the chair for a withdrawal; and a refusal on the part of the member to comply with such a demand is a serious breach of order (*see* ORDER IN THE HOUSE).

DELEGATED LEGISLATION

Under many Acts of Parliament the Queen in Council, ministers and certain statutory bodies have power to make orders, regulations, rules and similar instruments having the force of laws, the power to legislate or make law being thus delegated by Parliament to the authorities or persons making the instruments (*see* STATUTORY INSTRUMENTS; PAPERS, PARLIAMENTARY).

DEMISE OF THE CROWN

The passing of the Crown to his or her successor.

The death of the Sovereign formerly brought about the dissolution of Parliament. By section 51 of the Representation of the People Act 1867 Parliament is no longer automatically dissolved by the demise of the Crown and its life is in no way affected by it; but the Meeting of Parliament Act 1797 provides that if the demise should occur between the dissolution of one Parliament and the constitution of the next, the members of the dissolved Parliament are to "convene and sit at Westminster and be a Parliament" again for a period not exceeding six months.

If Parliament is sitting when the Sovereign dies, the business is immediately interrupted; and no ordinary business is done again until after the funeral has taken place. The first duty to be performed by members of both Houses is the taking of the oath of allegiance to the new Sovereign. In the House of Commons the sitting is suspended until the new Sovereign has been proclaimed, and, on its resumption, the Speaker proceeds to take the oath, followed by the other members. If Parliament is not sitting at the time of the demise, both Houses must meet again as soon as possible after the proclamation of the new Sovereign, so that their members may take the oath without delay. During one of the following days a message respecting the late Sovereign is received by each House from the new Sovereign. An address expressing the sorrow of the House and assuring the new Sovereign of the peers' or members' loyalty is forthwith agreed to, and this provides an opportunity for tributes to be paid by the leader of each House, leaders of the Opposition, and a few other prominent members. Similar messages are sent to the late Sovereign's consort and mother, if surviving. Each House then adjourns until after the funeral, when ordinary business is resumed.

DILATORY MOTION

A generic name for motions the object of which is to put off further consideration of the business in hand for the time being, including motions for the adjournment of the House moved while another question is under discussion, motions for the adjournment of a debate, of further consideration of a bill, or of further consideration of Lords amendments, motions that the chairman do report progress and ask leave to sit again, and motions that the chairman do leave the chair.

In the House of Commons, debate on a dilatory motion must be confined to the matter of such motion, *i.e.* to the reasons why the House should or should not adjourn, or as the case may be, and a member who has moved a dilatory motion may not move a similar motion during the same debate. If the Speaker or the chairman thinks that a dilatory motion is an abuse of the rules of the House (*q.v.*), he may either refuse to accept the motion or accept it and put the question on it forthwith, *i.e.* without allowing it to be debated.

DISSOLUTION

Parliament may at any time be dissolved by proclamation of the Queen. This power is, however, only exercised by Her Majesty on the advice of the Prime Minister. On being dissolved, Parliament ceases to exist; but the proclamation, which is usually issued at a time when Parliament is already prorogued*, nowadays invariably announces that the Lord Chancellor has been directed to issue writs for the return of a new Parliament.

The maximum duration of a Parliament being fixed by the Parliament Act of 1911 at five years, it ceases to exist five years after the date of its first meeting. Parliament was formerly dissolved automatically by the death of the Sovereign, but is now no longer affected thereby. On the other hand, if the Sovereign should die after Parliament has been dissolved, it must come together again and continue to exist for not more than six months (*see* DEMISE OF THE CROWN; ELECTIONS). Parliament was last dissolved by the Sovereign in person in 1681, by Charles II; it was, however, so dissolved by the Prince Regent in 1818. Both William IV and Victoria announced, in their prorogation speeches in 1831 and 1847 respectively, their intention to dissolve Parliament immediately afterwards.

* The proclamation dissolving Parliament in 1964 was issued during an adjournment.

DIVISION (*see also* QUESTION, PUTTING THE)

When a question has been put by the Speaker, and his opinion that " the Ayes (or the Noes) have it " is challenged, the House must divide, so that the exact balance of opinion may be discovered. The signal for this is given by the Speaker's command " Clear the lobby " (*i.e.* the Members' Lobby). On this members begin to leave the chamber and make their way into the division lobbies, while the electric " division bells " are rung all over the building to announce that a division is about to take place. The two division lobbies are long narrow rooms which extend for the full length of the chamber on either side. Two minutes after giving the order to clear the lobby the Speaker puts the question again, and if his opinion is still challenged, he proceeds to " name the tellers ", *i.e.* to read out the names, which have been meanwhile supplied to him, of the members, two for each side, who have been appointed to " tell " or count the members as they emerge from the lobbies. The tellers take their places, one from each side, at the exit doors of each lobby, these doors having been locked soon after the ringing of the division bells. These doors are now unlocked, and members file out past the division clerks, two of whom sit at desks in each lobby and mark off the members' names on the printed division lists from which the published record of divisions is taken. As each member passes the tellers he bows, and one of the tellers counts out loud, so that his opposition colleague can check the figure.

When four minutes have elapsed from the naming of the tellers, the Speaker orders " Lock the doors ". The entrance doors of the lobbies are then locked, and as soon as the members already in the lobbies have passed out, the division is finished and the tellers can return to the House to announce the numbers. This they do in formal manner, the tellers for the majority on the Speaker's left, having taken up their position facing the Speaker and bowing before they approach the Table. As they stand before the Table the senior teller for the majority says, " The Ayes to the right were 350, the Noes to the left were 150 " (or as the case may be). The Speaker repeats the numbers to the House, saying " So the Ayes (or the Noes) have it ". A division usually takes between seven and twelve minutes to complete. If the tellers cannot agree on the correct numbers in a division, they must report the fact at the Table, and the division must then take place again ; the same course is followed if a mistake is discovered in the telling. Such mishaps are, however, rare. If a member votes in the wrong lobby by mistake, he cannot alter his vote afterwards ; but if he discovers his mistake in time he may vote in the other lobby as well, and afterwards state in the House which way he should have voted, on which the numbers can be corrected. They can also be corrected in the Journal if a mistake is subsequently discovered and reported to the House. A member's vote, however "must agree with his voice"; *i.e.* if he has called "Aye" or "No" when the question was put, he must not vote in a contrary manner.

In order that the House may not be forced to divide on trivial occasions, the Speaker has the power, if he thinks a division unnecessarily claimed, to call upon the members who support, and those who challenge his decision, successively to stand up, and thereupon, as he thinks fit, to declare that "the Ayes (or Noes) have it", or to name tellers for a division; nevertheless, there have occasionally been divisions on which one side could muster no votes at all, its only supporters have been nominated tellers. If the requisite two members are not found willing to act as tellers for one side, the Speaker declares that the other side have it. No member is obliged to vote, and members may, and often do, vote without having heard the question put from the chair.

If a member wishes to raise a point of order during a division, instead of rising to his feet in the ordinary way, he must speak "seated and covered". In so doing he makes it clear that he is speaking informally and is not attempting to raise a debate, which cannot take place at a time when the question is fully put and is no longer before the House. A lady member, however, is not required to wear a hat on this occasion.

A division in a committee of the whole House takes place in exactly the same way as in the House itself; in other committees, however, members remain seated while the committee clerk reads out their names in alphabetical order, each member saying "Aye" or "No" in his turn.

DROPPED ORDER

When an order of the day is read by the Clerk it must be either proceeded with or deferred. If the order is not proceeded with, an instruction must be given by the member in charge of the bill or other business to which the order relates. For example, if the order is for the second reading of a bill, the Clerk reads out the short title of the bill, followed by the words "second reading", and the member in charge must say "now", if he wishes it to be proceeded with at once, or name another day. If he says nothing, the bill becomes a "dropped order" and disappears from the order paper and order book.* It may, however, be reinstated at

* In practice in the case of private members' bills, until the stage of the session is reached after which no bill not having already been read a second time can hope to make further progress (about Whitsuntide), it is assumed, in the absence of any instruction to the contrary from the member in charge of the bill, that he wishes it to be deferred until the next day reserved for private members' bills.

DROPPED ORDER—*continued*

any time, by the member's giving instructions at the Table for it to be put down for a particular day.

An order may also become " dropped " if, although it has been proceeded with, it is superseded by the adjournment of the House, or the House is counted out during the proceedings, or at their conclusion the member in charge omits to name a day for the further consideration of the business, or if, during the proceedings in committee, a motion " that the chairman do leave the chair " is carried.

An item of *government* business which has become a " dropped order " can be reinstated only if a motion to that effect (of which notice is required) is carried.

DUMMY

This word is used in the parliamentary vocabulary to denote a piece of paper which represents a document formally laid upon the Table or presented to the House. Thus, when a bill is introduced in the House of Commons, the member who brings it in goes beforehand to the Public Bill Office and obtains there a piece of paper inscribed with the long and short titles of the bill, and his name and those of his supporters. When his name is called by the Speaker he hands the dummy to the Clerk, who reads the short title, and the bill is then considered to have been presented and read a first time (*see* BILL, PUBLIC). If the bill is a government bill, the dummy is laid on the Table beforehand and it is sufficient for the minister to nod when his name is called.

Dummies are also used by government departments to represent the papers which they present to either House. Their chief use here is to represent white papers which it is not yet possible or convenient to publish, estimates and accounts. A paper which has thus been presented by the delivery of a dummy bearing its title is regarded as having been duly laid before the House on that date ; but if a dummy is used for a statutory instrument or other enactment which is liable to annulment within a specified number of days, the period only begins to be reckoned from the day on which a full copy has been received by the House.

EARLY DAY MOTION

A motion for which no day has been fixed and for which notice is therefore given simply " for an early day ". The member giving such notice may hope to secure the promise of time for his motion from the leader of the House ; or he may intend the notice merely as an expression of his own views and perhaps as a means of testing opinion in the House by inviting other members to add their names to his own.

ECCLESIASTICAL COMMITTEE

A body set up under the Church of England Assembly (Powers) Act 1919. Its function is to consider measures passed by the General Synod (formerly the National Assembly) of the Church of England and to report to both Houses of Parliament on the nature and legal effect of the measures and on their expediency, especially with regard to the constitutional rights of all Her Majesty's subjects. No motion directing that a measure be presented to the Queen for her royal assent may be made in either House until the report of the committee has been presented. The committee consists of fifteen peers and fifteen members of the House of Commons nominated at the beginning of each Parliament by the Lord Chancellor and the Speaker of the House of Commons respectively. It continues in existence until Parliament is dissolved. Twelve members form a quorum irrespective of whether they are peers or members of the House of Commons. The Ecclesiastical Committee may sit even though Parliament is not sitting.

ELECTIONS

Under the Parliament Act 1911 the duration of a Parliament is limited to five years; that is, it ceases to exist five years after the day on which it was directed to meet, unless it has been previously dissolved by proclamation. Since 1911, no Parliament has reached the full term of its existence. On the other hand, the Parliaments of 1911 and 1935 prolonged their own existence, by statute, during the two great wars, till 1918 and 1945 respectively. In former times Parliament was automatically dissolved by the death of the Sovereign, but the Representation of the People Act 1867 provided that its existence should no longer be affected thereby. If the Sovereign should die while Parliament is dissolved, the old Parliament must come together again and sit for not more than six months.

A new Parliament is summoned by the royal proclamation which dissolves its predecessor. This proclamation discharges peers and members from their duty of attendance, and announces that the Lord Chancellor has been directed to issue writs for the attendance of the Lords Spiritual and Temporal and Commons in a new Parliament. The writs for the election of the Commons are addressed to the returning officer in each constituency, who must then within two days give public notice of the election.

The returning officer may receive nominations of candidates up till the eighth day after the day of the proclamation. If only one candidate is nominated in a constituency, he is declared elected, when the time for nomination has expired; if more than one candidate has been nominated, a poll must be held on the ninth day after the day of election (that is, the final day of the nomination period). Voting takes place in booths at polling

ELECTIONS—*continued*

stations (usually schools, town halls or other public buildings engaged for the occasion), by secret ballot, between the hours of seven in the morning and ten in the evening. The successful candidate's name is announced as soon as conveniently practicable after the conclusion of the poll. A recount is allowed at the returning officer's discretion, and if the numbers are found to be equal, the returning officer must decide the election by lot. Provision is made for assistance to be given to blind persons, and absent electors are allowed in certain cases to vote by proxy or by post.

When a seat becomes vacant during the existence of a Parliament, a by-election must be held to fill it. A motion is made (usually by the chief whip of the party to which the late member belonged) ordering the Speaker to issue his warrant to the Clerk of the Crown to make out a new writ for the election. This motion is usually agreed to without debate or division, but the occasion has sometimes been used in recent years for a debate; the desirability of a revision of the electoral register and the unsuitability of the date chosen for the poll are among the subjects which have been raised. As the issue of the Speaker's warrant is a matter of privilege, the motion has precedence of other business, and is usually taken at the beginning of the sitting and immediately after Prayers. If a debate arises on such a motion, the motion is usually withdrawn and moved again at the commencement of public business.

When the vacancy occurs during a recess or adjournment* the Speaker issues his warrant for a new writ if he receives a certificate, signed by two members, of the vacancy; such a notice is usually sent only at the instance of the chief whip of the party to which the late member belonged. If the Speaker issues his warrant in these circumstances he informs the House of the fact when it meets again.

The returning officer must give notice of the day of election (that is, the final day for receiving nominations) within two days of receiving the writ. The day of election must be not later than the ninth day after the receipt of the writ in a county constituency and not later than the seventh day in a borough. The poll must then be not earlier than the seventh nor later than the ninth day after the day of election, and takes place in the manner described above. In reckoning periods for the purpose of elections, Sundays, Christmas Day, Good Friday and public fast and thanksgiving days are excluded.

After a general election has taken place, the Clerk of the Crown delivers to the Clerk of the House of Commons a book containing a list of all the constituencies, with the names of the members

* This does not apply to vacancies caused by the acceptance of the Chiltern Hundreds or the Manor of Northstead.

returned for each. This book, which is written in manuscript and bound in white vellum, is known as the Return Book, and provides the evidence of the election of members, which is necessary before the oath is administered to them at the Table.

After a by-election the Clerk of the Crown sends a certificate of the new member's return to the Public Bill Office whither the member must, on his arrival, go and there obtain another certificate that the first certificate has been received. He must present this to the Clerk of the House when he goes to the Table to be sworn.

The right to vote at parliamentary elections now belongs to all British subjects (with certain exceptions) aged eighteen and over. The principal exceptions are peers,* persons of unsound mind, convicted persons while detained in a penal institution in pursuance of sentence, and those convicted of corrupt practices at a parliamentary election (in which case the disqualification lasts for seven years). Certain persons who are not British subjects, such as citizens of the Irish Republic, may also acquire by residence in the United Kingdom the right to vote. The right to vote in a particular constituency is conferred by residence in that constituency for a qualifying period. No person may vote more than once at an election, apart from proxies, the university and business franchises having been abolished in 1948.

ENACTING WORDS

A short formal statement in a bill of the authority by which the proposed Act is to be made. It follows immediately after the title of the bill or, if the bill has a preamble, immediately after the preamble. In the case of a public bill the usual formula is :—

> " Be it enacted by the Queen's Most Excellent Majesty, by and with the advice and consent of the Lords Spiritual and Temporal and Commons, in this present Parliament assembled, and by the authority of the same."

These words are preceded in the case of a bill granting money to the Crown by the words :

> " Most Gracious Sovereign, we, Your Majesty's most dutiful and loyal subjects the Commons of the United Kingdom in Parliament assembled, towards making good the supply† which we have cheerfully granted to Your Majesty in this Session of Parliament, have resolved to grant unto Your

* Other than Irish peers.

† When the grant is not of supply, the formula is varied, *e.g.* in the Civil List Bill of 1952 the words used were: " We, Your Majesty's most dutiful and loyal subjects, the Commons of the United Kingdom in Parliament assembled, have freely and voluntarily resolved to make such provision as hereinafter appears for the purpose aforesaid (set out in the preamble) and we do most humbly beseech Your Majesty that it may be enacted and ".

ENACTING WORDS—*continued*

> Majesty the sums hereinafter mentioned ; and do therefore most humbly beseech Your Majesty that it may be enacted and "

and in the case of the Finance Bill, by the words :

> " Most Gracious Sovereign, we, Your Majesty's most dutiful and loyal subjects, the Commons of the United Kingdom in Parliament assembled, towards raising the necessary supplies to defray Your Majesty's public expenses, and making an addition to the public revenue, have freely and voluntarily resolved to give and grant unto Your Majesty the several duties hereinafter mentioned; and do therefore most humbly beseech Your Majesty that it may be enacted, and ".

No question is put upon the enacting words nor can they be amended.

EQUALITY OF VOTES

In the House of Commons and its committees, when the votes are equal, the Speaker or the chairman gives the casting vote. (The Speaker and, except in committees on opposed private or provisional order bills, the chairmen of committees never vote save when the votes are equal.) When the Speaker or a chairman has to give a casting vote, he may, if he chooses, give his vote on the merits of the question as he sees them; but usually he gives it in accordance with a formula: he gives it, if possible, in such a manner as to afford the House a further opportunity of considering the question. In the case of amendments to bills, he gives his casting vote for the bill as read a second time and against the amendment. If the votes are equal on the question whether a particular clause shall " stand part of " a bill, the chairman votes " Aye ". In committees on opposed private or provisional order bills the practice is different, because the chairman has a casting vote in addition to his ordinary vote.

In the House of Lords and its committees it was formerly the general rule that in case of an equality of votes the question was decided in the negative. In 1951, however, the Lords adopted a standing order which provides that no proposal to reject or amend a bill or a statutory instrument shall be agreed to unless there is a majority in favour of such rejection or amendment ; and that no proposal to reject or amend a motion relating to the stages of a bill, *e.g.* a motion that the bill be read a second (or third) time, or that the bill be committed, or that the House do now resolve itself into a committee on the bill, shall be agreed to unless there is a majority in favour of such rejection or amendment. As regards other questions, *e.g.* proposed resolutions, the rule remains as before. If, therefore, on a division on the question that a bill be read a second or a third time now, or that the House do agree to an amendment made by the Commons to a Lords bill, the " contents " and " not contents " were equal, the question would be resolved in the affirmative. Similarly, in case of an equality of votes a motion that certain regulations be approved would be carried. On the other hand, if the House was equally divided on the question that it " do insist on " an amendment made by the Lords to a Commons bill or on a motion for presenting an address to the Queen, praying that certain regulations should be annulled, the question would be decided in the negative.

ERSKINE MAY

The name popularly given to "A Treatise on the Law, Privileges, Proceedings and Usage of Parliament ", by Sir Thomas Erskine May, Clerk of the House of Commons from 1871 to 1886. This work, the most authoritative book on parliamentary procedure, was first published in 1844. The 18th edition is due for publication in 1971.

ESTATE BILL

A bill the object of which is to enable settled land or other property to be dealt with in a manner which is not authorised by the will, deed or other instrument creating the settlement, *e.g.* to free settled estates from a statutory entail. (For the procedure on an estate bill, *see* PERSONAL BILL).

ESTIMATES (*see also* FINANCE ; SUPPLY)

Annual detailed statements of the public expenditure proposed to be undertaken by the Government. They relate to the financial year, which runs from April 1 to March 31, and are arranged in two groups, the Civil Estimates and the Defence Estimates. The Civil Estimates are divided into eleven classes. Each class of the Civil Estimates is divided into a number of Votes, which are again divided into sub-heads. The Defence Estimates include, in respect of the Navy, Army and Air Force, three Votes authorising the number of men and women to be employed in each service. Of the numbered votes, three are concerned with the pay and allowances of the three services, while the remainder provide the money needed for the services common to all three.

The Estimates are presented by the Government to the House of Commons, which considers them as a part of the business of Supply and, if it thinks fit, approves them in the form of Supply resolutions. The Consolidated Fund (Appropriation) Bill is then brought in to give statutory sanction to the payment of the necessary sums out of the Consolidated Fund and to their appropriation in the form set out in the Estimates. This bill receives the royal assent as the Appropriation Act.

ESTIMATES—*continued*

Supplementary estimates, for expenditure over and above that in the main Estimates, are also presented, and dealt with in the same way as the Estimates. They are arranged under the same headings as the main Estimates.

It is usual for some or all of the Estimates relating to Scotland to be referred to the Scottish Grand Committee before they are considered by the House. The Committee debates but has no power to reject or amend the Estimates; it can only report to the House that it has considered them, after which the House deals with them in the ordinary way.

ESTIMATES COMMITTEE

A select committee of the House of Commons appointed by standing order. Its functions are (1) to examine such of the estimates presented to the House as may seem fit to the committee and to report how, if at all, the policy implied in those estimates may be carried out more economically and, (2) if the Committee thinks fit, to consider the principal variations between the estimates and those relating to the previous financial year and the form in which the estimates are presented to the House. Accordingly it is the principal function of the Committee to report on any field of government expenditure that it chooses; its reports are mainly directed to the questions of how services could be conducted to show better value for money, whether by improving the administration of the service concerned, or by modifying the scope of the service. But while the intention is that the Committee should suggest ways of obtaining better value for money spent, it is expected that any savings will be reflected in the estimates of future years rather than by changes in the estimates actually before the House at the time of the Committee's inquiry.

Under the standing order the Committee is to consist of forty-three Members, but that number has been varied by sessional orders. The quorum is seven. The Committee has power to send for persons, papers and records; to sit notwithstanding any adjournment of the House; to adjourn from place to place; and to report from time to time. It has power to appoint sub-committees and to refer to such sub-committees any of the matters referred to the Committee. The quorum of each sub-committee is fixed at three. Each sub-committee has the same powers as the parent committee except, of course, that it cannot report to the House but only to the parent committee. The Committee has power to report from time to time the minutes of evidence taken before the sub-committees.

The Estimates Committee does not as a rule itself take evidence (experience having shown that it is too large a body for this purpose). The inquiries are conducted by sub-committees, the reports of the Committee being founded on reports made to it by these sub-committees. When forty-three members have been nominated to the Committee, seven sub-committees have been appointed, six to conduct inquiries and the seventh to make recommendations as to the composition of the investigating sub-committees and the estimates referred to them for examination. In recent sessions, however, the number of sub-committees has been reduced to match the number of members nominated to the Committee by the House under sessional orders.

Reports of the Committee may be considered on an allotted day (*q.v.*) if the opposition wishes.

EVIDENCE

The evidence given before a select committee is taken down in shorthand and is printed or duplicated daily for the use of the members of the committee. Proofs of his evidence are sent to each witness for correction. Uncorrected proof copies of evidence already given before a select committee of the House of Commons may be sent to prospective witnesses and, with the Speaker's permission, to other persons. In the House of Lords, however, a somewhat wider distribution of the minutes of evidence is permitted on condition that it is not made public.

When the public are not admitted to the sittings of the committee at which evidence is taken, the committee does not usually report the evidence to the House until the inquiry has been completed and the report agreed upon; and it is a breach of privilege for a member or any other person to publish evidence given before, or documents presented to, a select committee until such evidence or documents have been reported to the House. When the public are admitted to a sitting it is usual to report the evidence taken at the sitting shortly after its conclusion; and printed copies of the evidence are made publicly available as soon as the witnesses have had an opportunity to correct any errors of reporting or printing. But no committee may report any evidence except at the end of an inqury unless it has the leave of the House to report the minutes of the evidence from time to time.

A shorthand note must be taken of all the evidence given before a select committee. It would be out of order for a committee to instruct the shorthand writer not to take down a question and the answer or to accede to requests by members or witnesses that questions and the answers thereto shall not be taken down. If a committee considers it inadvisable that a part of the evidence should be published, the proper course is to refrain from reporting that part of the evidence to the House.

EXAMINERS OF PETITIONS FOR PRIVATE BILLS

Officers (not members) of both Houses of Parliament, whose duty it is to ascertain and report whether the standing orders

EXAMINERS OF PETITIONS FOR PRIVATE BILLS—*continued*

have been complied with by the promoters of private bills. The standing orders referred to are those which require certain notices to be given and documents deposited and other preliminary steps to be taken before, or in certain cases after, a private bill is introduced. One of the Examiners is appointed by the Speaker, the other by the House of Lords. Except in the case of bills which are referred to them after first or second reading, the Examiners report their findings to both Houses.

The Examiners are from time to time ordered to examine particular public bills with respect to the applicability thereto of the standing orders relating to private bills. If the Examiner who hears the case reports that the standing orders are applicable, the bill is proceeded with as a hybrid bill (*q.v.*). The Examiners of Petitions for Private Bills also perform duties with regard to provisional orders under the Private Legislation Procedure (Scotland) Act 1936 (*see* SCOTTISH PRIVATE LEGISLATION), analogous to those which they perform with regard to private bills.

EXCESS VOTE

When a department has spent more than the amount authorised on a vote, a statement of the excess must be presented to the House of Commons in a subsequent session. The amount required to make good the excess is voted by resolution of the House in the same way as an estimate, and the necessary provision is made in the next Appropriation Act. The question that the necessary amount be granted may be included in those questions which are required to be put, under the guillotine, without amendment or debate (*see* SUPPLY) but only if the Committee of Public Accounts have reported that they see no objection to the sums necessary being provided by excess vote. An excess is usually authorised some two years after the money has been spent.

EXCHEQUER

The Exchequer was originally the department responsible for managing the royal accounts, for receiving revenues and for making payments on behalf of the Crown. The name is derived from the chess or chequer board which mediaeval officials used in doing their accounts. In the nineteenth century the Exchequer was amalgamated with the Audit Office; the combined department is now the Exchequer and Audit Department (*see* COMPTROLLER AND AUDITOR GENERAL). In modern usage, the word "Exchequer" is practically synonymous with the Consolidated Fund (*q.v.*).

EXEMPTED BUSINESS

Certain business may be entered upon and proceeded with after 10 p.m. (4 p.m. on Fridays), though opposed, and is exempted from interruption at that hour (whence its name) except for the purpose of moving a motion for the exemption of business as explained below. Exemption may either be for an unlimited period (which allows the sitting to continue indefinitely so far as the exempted business is concerned and ensures that it shall not fail to be completed for lack of time) or for a limited period. Business exempted by standing order consists, in the first category, of proceedings on any bill brought in on a Ways and Means resolution or any Consolidated Fund or Appropriation Bill (that is, broadly speaking, any bill authorising taxation, such as a Finance Bill, or a bill sanctioning the payment of money from the Consolidated Fund to meet Government expenditure) and proceedings in pursuance of any standing order when the order so provides (as, for example, a motion to approve a resolution of the Business Committee); in the second category it includes (*a*) proceedings in pursuance of an Act of Parliament and (*b*) proceedings on a motion authorising expenditure in connection with a bill (*i.e.* a " money resolution "). The application of the rule under (*a*) depends on the nature of the proceeding. If it is a motion (commonly called a " prayer " by Members) having as its object the annulment of a statutory instrument, whether by address or by simple resolution that the instrument be annulled or be not made, no such proceedings may be entered upon at or after 11.30 p.m.; if the motion is under consideration at that hour, the Speaker must forthwith put any question for its decision, or, if he thinks that the time for debate has not been adequate, adjourn the debate till the next sitting other than a Friday. A debate which has been so adjourned may not be resumed after 11 p.m. but must be further adjourned till the next sitting other than a Friday. In the case of any other proceedings in this category, the Speaker must put any question not later than 11.30 p.m. or one and a half hours after the commencement of the proceedings, whichever is the later; though here too, he may in his discretion adjourn the debate till the next sitting other than a Friday; and the rule that the debate may not be resumed after 11 p.m. does not apply. In the case (*b*) of proceedings for a " money resolution " the Speaker must put any question for their disposal at 10.45 p.m. or at the end of three-quarters of an hour, whichever is the later.

Any specified business may be exempted from interruption at a particular sitting by order of the House. A notice of motion to this effect must appear in the name of a minister at the commencement of public business on that day. It is not however taken at that point but stands over till 10 p.m., and is then taken after the business which is under consideration at that hour has been disposed of. It sometimes happens that the business which is interrupted is the subject of the motion and in that case the House resumes the business as soon as the motion has been agreed to. It may also happen that business which is itself

EXEMPTED BUSINESS—*continued*

exempted under standing order must be interrupted in order to allow a motion exempting other business to be moved and in that case also the House may return to the interrupted business as soon as the exemption motion has been disposed of. The motion may be for the unlimited exemption of the business named, or for its exemption for a stated period (usually from one to two hours), or it may include business in both categories. In the case of a limited exemption the period runs from 10 p.m. or from the time at which the business is entered upon, whichever is the later. (*See also* SITTINGS OF THE HOUSE OF COMMONS).

EXPIRING LAWS CONTINUANCE BILL

A bill passed every year for the purpose of continuing (generally for a year) a considerable number of temporary Acts which would otherwise expire. The Acts to be continued are specified in a schedule to the bill. The advisability of continuing a particular Act must be discussed in committee when the appropriate point in the schedule is reached, and not on the operative *clause*, *i.e.* the one which provides that the Acts mentioned in the schedule shall be continued until a specific date.

It is out of order by way of amendment to the bill to propose either that the provisions of an Act proposed to be continued shall be amended or that the Act shall be made permanent, but an amendment extending or shortening the period for which the Act is to be continued, or omitting one of the Acts proposed to be continued, or excepting from continuance particular provisions of one of such Acts, or inserting another Act or particular provisions of another Act in the schedule of Acts to be continued, is in order.

EXPLANATORY MEMORANDUM

The member introducing a bill may have printed with it, at the beginning, a memorandum explaining its purposes, or its financial proposals. This is known as an explanatory or a financial memorandum, as the case may be. It must be strictly confined to explanation, without argument, or advocating the bill in any way.

FATHER OF THE HOUSE

The member who has sat in the House of Commons without a break for the longest period irrespective of whether he has sat for the same constituency or for different ones.

FEES

In both Houses the promoters of, and petitioners against, private bills, applicants for provisional orders other than orders issued under the Private Legislation Procedure (Scotland) Act

1936, petitioners against bills for confirming provisional orders, petitioners against hybrid bills, petitioners against special procedure orders (*q.v.*), counter-petitioners and, in certain circumstances, applicants for such orders are charged certain fees, for details of which reference should be made to the tables of fees appended to the standing orders of the respective Houses. The promoters of a provisional order bill, being a government department, are not charged fees, and the promoters of a hybrid bill are charged fees only in cases where the bill is not promoted by a government department. The fees are appropriated in aid of the votes for the respective Houses, *i.e.* they are set off against the expenses of the two Houses.

FINANCE

The importance attached by the House of Commons to the granting of money to the Crown is shown by certain rules which must be observed in all proceedings involving the authorisation of public expenditure.

The first of these is that any business which has in view the expenditure of money from the Exchequer may only be entered upon when the Queen's recommendation has been signified to the House by a Minister of the Crown. This rule has the effect of preventing the discussion of any proposal for initiating or increasing any expenditure which the Government are not prepared to support, and in practice precludes private members from taking the initiative in such matters. The rule even extends to petitions asking for the grant of public money (*see* PETITION).

Secondly, any such proceedings must begin with a resolution of the House (which, since 1967, is no longer preceded by a resolution of a committee of the whole House) authorising the expenditure; and the bill, or part of a bill, involving or authorising the expenditure may then be proceeded with (*see* BILL, PUBLIC). In the case of the regular expenditure of the year, which is contained in the annual Estimates, the Queen's recommendation is held to be given by the relevant passage in her Speech at the opening of the Session.

Thirdly, when the House votes money for any purpose, it does so only for one year. Any sums outstanding at the end of the year must be returned to the Exchequer; they cannot be carried over to the next year (except where the sum voted takes the form of a grant in aid). Similarly, all money voted is appropriated to particular votes, and no money so voted may be diverted to any other vote.

The year's ordinary expenditure on the public services is contained in the annual Estimates (divided into those for Civil Departments, grouped by classes, and those for the Ministry of Defence, which cover the armed forces). These estimates are presented to the House in the early months of the year and their

FINANCE—*continued*
consideration forms part of the business of supply. The standing orders provide that twenty-nine days shall be allotted to the business of supply during the session ("allotted days"); additional time is given for this purpose if necessary. Any supplementary estimates which may be needed to complete departmental expenditure during the financial year which is nearing its end are considered during the early months of the session, the final ones being agreed to in February and March, together with any Excess Votes, which are necessary to make good excesses on the authorised expenditure of the last completed year. Sufficient money must also be voted to make provision for the year which is about to begin, until the full amount can be authorised. This is done by means of Votes on Account, which include a separate item for each vote in the services for which they make provision equal in amount to about five-twelfths of the total amount in the estimates, the period for which they are needed being roughly that between the beginning of April and the beginning of August. Two votes on account are required, one for the civil estimates and one for the Ministry of Defence. All estimates are now voted in the House in the form of simple resolutions of the House, known as " Supply resolutions " ; these also authorise the expenditure of money " from the Consolidated Fund " and thus contain the authority formerly given separately by resolutions originating in the Committee of Ways and Means. Consolidated Fund Bills, founded on the Supply resolutions, are brought in to set the legislative seal upon the expenditure thus approved in resolutions by the House. These must receive the royal assent before the end of March, in order that the government of the country may be carried on without a break, and punctually paid for with money duly authorised by Parliament.

The most important task of the House in the early part of the financial year is to provide for the raising of the revenue to meet the expenditure foreseen in the Estimates which will be authorised by Supply resolutions. For this purpose the House agrees to Ways and Means resolutions which determine the level of income tax, surtax and customs, excise and other duties, and provide for the amendment of the law relating thereto. These resolutions are the occasion for the budget statement which the Chancellor of the Exchequer makes each year. In this he reviews the national economy and finances, and announces the changes in taxation which he proposes to recommend (*see* BUDGET). At the conclusion of the statement he moves a preliminary motion, which gives provisional authority to those of his proposals which require new rates of tax to be put into effect immediately (*see* TAXES, PROVISIONAL COLLECTION OF). This is followed by a debate extending over several days (the " budget debate "). When the resolutions have been reported and agreed to, the Finance Bill, which is concerned entirely with taxation, is brought in. This provides further occasions for debate on national finance and, in particular, in committee and on report, for proposals for altered or reduced taxation.

Since the Committee of Supply was abolished in 1967, few of the " days allotted to the business of Supply " are in fact used for the consideration of the estimates (*see* ALLOTTED DAYS), but on three days of each financial year the estimates must actually be voted on, even if they are not discussed; these are the three days on which provision is made by the standing orders for a guillotine to ensure that certain estimates are duly approved. On the first occasion (not later than the 6th February) the Speaker is directed to put the question in respect of all outstanding supplementary estimates and on the civil vote on account. On the second occasion (before the 25th March) the Speaker must put a similar question on the vote on account for the Ministry of Defence and on all outstanding supplementary estimates for the current financial year and, finally, on any excess vote for the last completed year, provided that the Committee of Public Accounts have reported that they see no objection to the necessary sums being provided by excess vote. On the third occasion, on the last of the allotted days, questions must be put similarly on all outstanding votes, whether on the main estimates or on supplementary estimates which may by then have been found necessary for the new financial year. The resolutions on this last allotted day cover all the remaining expenditure which is required (so far as can be foreseen) for the current financial year; any further supplementary estimates will be dealt with in the following session. The Consolidated Fund (Appropriation) Bill is brought in on these resolutions. This authorises and appropriates the expenditure contained in the estimates and gives the authority for payment of the necessary money out of the Consolidated Fund. The bill receives the royal assent as the Appropriation Act.

FINANCE BILL

A Finance Bill is introduced after every budget to give legislative effect to the proposals contained therein. It is, therefore, a bill to impose or alter taxes. Under the Provisional Collection of Taxes Act 1968 a resolution of the House imposing or altering a tax has full legal force for four months from the date when it takes effect (or till the 5th August in the case of a resolution passed in March or April), provided that the bill giving effect to the resolutions (in this case the Finance Bill) is read a second time within twenty-five sitting days. The Finance Bill is always one of the most important and keenly contested bills of the year (*see* FINANCE; BUDGET; TAXES, PROVISIONAL COLLECTION OF).

FRONT BENCH

The two benches nearest the Table in the House of Commons are known as the front benches. They are occupied by ministers and by the principal members of the Opposition respectively.

GANGWAY

The benches which face each other across the floor of the House of Commons chamber are divided into two sections by a gangway which crosses the chamber about half-way down. A seat "below the gangway", *i.e.* in the part further from the Speaker, is held to indicate a rather greater degree of independence of the party point of view than one in the nearer part.

GREEN PAPER

A Command Paper setting out proposals for future government policy, but with the express intention that the proposals should serve as a basis for discussion rather than a commitment of the government to a particular course of action. Such a Command Paper is presented to the House in the same way as any other Command Paper, whether a "White Paper" or a "Blue Book" (*q.v.*).

GUILLOTINE

A colloquial term for an order made by the House of Commons fixing the amount of time which may be spent in discussing a particular bill or a particular section of a bill at various stages. Such orders are technically termed "allocation of time orders". An order of this kind provides that on the expiration of the time allowed for the debate on the second or third reading of the bill, or for the consideration of a particular portion of the bill in committee or on report, any question then under discussion shall be put without further debate, and that whatever questions are necessary to dispose of the bill at that stage or to complete the consideration of that particular portion of the bill shall then be put *seriatim* without any debate. It also provides that after the arrival of the hour at which discussion on a particular portion of the bill is to cease, only amendments of which notice has been given by a member of the Government may be moved. The questions on such amendments are put without being debated.

An order of this kind usually forbids the moving of dilatory motions or of motions for the recommittal of the bill or for the postponement of a clause except by a member of the Government. It also as a rule provides that any opposed private business set down by direction of the Chairman of Ways and Means on a day allotted for the discussion of the bill, and any motion for the adjournment of the House for the purpose of discussing a specific and important matter that should have urgent consideration, shall be taken when the proceeding on, or the consideration of the particular portion of, the bill which is to be completed that day has been finished, instead of at 7 p.m.

A guillotine is also provided by standing order to ensure that the business is completed on three of the supply days (*see* ALLOTTED DAYS; SUPPLY).

HANSARD

A colloquial term for the official report (*q.v.*) of the debates in the two Houses of Parliament. In 1812 Thomas Curson Hansard, eldest son of Luke Hansard, printer to the House of Commons for many years, took over the publication of Cobbett's Parliamentary Debates, first issued in 1803. These reports were not verbatim reports, but were compiled chiefly from the reports in "The Times" and other newspapers. They were published not daily but at intervals. From 1829 they were published under the title "Hansard's Parliamentary Debates". After T. C. Hansard's death, the publication was continued by his son, who bore the same name, until 1889, when he sold the undertaking. The publication, however, continued to be referred to as "Hansard" even after the name disappeared from the title page in 1891, and when an official report of the debates appeared in 1909 the name was applied to it also.

HOUSE OF COMMONS OFFICES COMMISSION

A body established by the House of Commons Offices Act **1812**, the function of which is to regulate the pay, pensions and conditions of service of the officers and officials of the House of Commons. It is composed of the Speaker of the House of Commons and such of the following as are members of the House of Commons: The Secretaries of State, the Chancellor of the Exchequer, the Attorney General and the Solicitor General. (The Master of the Rolls, who was originally a member of the Commission, is no longer eligible for election to the House of Commons.) Three commissioners, of whom the Speaker must be one, form a quorum. Proposals relating to the conditions of service of the officers and officials which come before the Commission have normally already been considered by the Select Committee on House of Commons (Services) (*see* HOUSE OF COMMONS (SERVICES), SELECT COMMITTEE ON).

HOUSE OF COMMONS (SERVICES), SELECT COMMITTEE ON

A Committee appointed every session to advise the Speaker on the control of the accommodation and services in the House of Commons and its precincts, and to report to the House.

The Palace of Westminster is a royal palace which is made available to Parliament by the Sovereign. Formerly control of

HOUSE OF COMMONS (SERVICES), SELECT COMMITTEE ON—*continued*

the whole building rested ultimately with the Lord Great Chamberlain, but in 1965 the Queen signified her pleasure that control of that part of the building which is occupied by or on behalf of the House of Commons should rest with the Speaker.

The " Services Committee " advises the Speaker on how to exercise that control and on many other matters of administration of the House of Commons. In recent sessions the Committee has consisted of sixteen members and has appointed sub-committees to report to it on (i) accommodation and administration, (ii) catering and (iii) the Library. The allocation of accommodation was formerly undertaken directly by the Serjeant at Arms, as were the general functions of " house-keeping " in the House of Commons, but those functions are now administered by the Serjeant at Arms under the direction of the Speaker who in turn is advised by the Committee. Similarly the Clerk of the House now administers his department in the light of any directions of the Speaker based on advice from the Committee, and the Speaker's own department, which includes the Library, is also administered in the light of the Committee's advice to him.

The Committee has superseded two former sessional select committees, viz., the Select Committee on Kitchen and Refreshment Rooms (House of Commons), generally known as the Kitchen Committee, and the Select Committee on Publications and Debates Reports, which advised the Speaker on the arrangements for the official reports of debates and inquired into the expenditure on stationery and printing for the House and the public service generally.

HOUSE OF LORDS OFFICES COMMITTEE

A select committee appointed by the House of Lords at the beginning of every session. Its functions are to consider and report on all matters relating to the Clerk of the Parliaments, the Clerk Assistant and the Reading Clerk, and the staff of the Clerk of the Parliaments, including their duties, salaries, retirements and superannuations ; and all matters relating to the Offices of the Lord Great Chamberlain and the Gentleman Usher of the Black Rod, the preparation of the annual estimate of the House of Lords, the accommodation provided for the House and its committees, and, in short, all the domestic affairs of the House. It consists of some fifty peers. The Lord Chancellor, the Lord President (if a peer), the Lord Privy Seal (if a peer) and the Chairman of Committees are always members of the committee. The Committee appoints sub-committees on Administration, the House of Lords Estimates, the Library and the Refreshment Department.

HOUSES OF PARLIAMENT

The Lords (from the earliest times) and the Commons (since about the year 1550) have occupied the ancient royal palace of Westminster. This building, which was largely destroyed by fire in 1834 and rebuilt afterwards, is known indifferently as the Palace of Westminster or the Houses of Parliament. Both names are slightly misleading; it has not been used as a royal residence since its use for its present purpose began in 1550, and its present form is entirely unsuited to any other purpose; at the same time it incorporates buildings (such as Westminster Hall) and houses officials (such as certain members of the Lord Chancellor's Department) whose functions are in no sense parliamentary. Its status as a royal palace is, nevertheless, unquestionable, and is marked, among other things, by the fact that much of it remains subject to the authority of the Lord Great Chamberlain, one of the hereditary officers of state; but the parts used by the House of Commons were made subject to the control of the Speaker and the parts used by the House of Lords were made subject to the control of the Lord Chancellor by an expression of the Queen's pleasure in 1965.

The present buildings are roughly oblong, though irregular, in shape, lying between Bridge Street on the north, the River Thames on the east, Victoria Tower Gardens on the south, and Abingdon Street, Old Palace Yard, Saint Margaret's Street and Parliament Square on the west. The total area covered and enclosed by buildings is some eight acres. The precincts include the space occupied by New Palace Yard at the north-west corner, and enclosed north and west by railings, and a succession of courts which run north and south and divide the buildings into three main blocks, linked by connecting halls, stairways and corridors. It is possible for a car to pass into New Palace Yard through the carriage gates, thence through the Speaker's Court, and southwards through the whole length of the building at a level below the main floor as far as the Victoria Tower, then westwards again into Abingdon Street by the Chancellor's Gate.

With the exception of Westminster Hall, which dates from 1098, the chapel of Saint Mary in the crypt below Saint Stephen's Hall (1327), a part of the cloisters in the Star Court, and the Commons' debating chamber, the present buildings were erected in the years following the fire of 1834, to the design of Charles Barry. The Commons' debating chamber and its surrounding lobbies, which formed a part of this building, were hit by bombs and totally destroyed by fire in the air raid of May 10, 1941; they have now been rebuilt in the same form with certain minor alterations and additions. While their own chamber was out of use, the Commons used the Peers' debating chamber, and the Lords the room at the south end of the building known as the Queen's Robing Room, which was altered for their convenience.

HOUSES OF PARLIAMENT—*continued*

The central point of the building is a large circular hall, covered by a dome surmounted by a lantern, and known as the Central Lobby. This is the general meeting place where members of the public come to see their parliamentary representatives and is crowded before and during the sittings of the House of Commons with visitors, journalists, parliamentary agents, officials and the friends and guests of members of both Houses. It is approached from the public entrance opposite Westminster Abbey, across the dais at the south end of Westminster Hall, and through Saint Stephen's Hall, which occupies the site of the chapel used up till 1834 as the debating chamber of the House of Commons and is now used as a waiting place for visitors to the public galleries. North of the Central Lobby is a passage leading to the Commons' Lobby and Chamber; south of it a similar passage leads to the Peers' lobby and debating chamber, properly called the Parliament Chamber. North of the Commons' chamber are ministers' rooms and above it are various offices and conference rooms. South of the Peers' chamber is the Prince's Chamber, a lobby or waiting hall notable for the pictures and statues which adorn its walls, leading to the lofty and spacious Royal Gallery, now used only on special occasions. It was, for example, specially fitted up for the last trial of a peer by his peers (Lord de Clifford was so tried for manslaughter and acquitted in 1937); and meetings of members of both Houses to hear addresses by General Smuts and Mr. Mackenzie King were held here in 1942 and 1944 respectively. Recently it was used for the same purpose in 1967 when Mr. Brezhnev addressed a similar meeting (but Westminster Hall has also been used for similar purposes, notably when President de Gaulle addressed a meeting in 1960). Beyond the Royal Gallery lies the Queen's Robing Room.

The west side of the building contains offices on both main and first floors, and extra accommodation on six floors has recently (1965–66) been constructed beside the east side of Westminster Hall; this accommodation is divided mainly into small offices which have been allocated to the individual use of ministers, leading members of the opposition and some private members. The press also have some accommodation there. On the east side the libraries, dining- and tea-rooms and smoking-rooms of both Houses occupy the main floor, while further dining-rooms, two cafeterias (one for the use of members, the other for the use of non-members) and various offices occupy the floor below. The latter rooms look out on the terrace which runs for most of the length of the building on the east side, and, overlooking the river, provides a pleasant retreat where peers and members can enjoy a breath of fresh air without leaving the precincts, and entertain guests to tea or other refreshments in hot weather. The floor immediately above the main floor is occupied, on the east side, by committee rooms, and above those is a floor mainly partitioned into smaller rooms suitable for the use of one or more individuals ; these are allocated to chairmen of committees and some other private members. A flat for the residence of the Clerk of the House of Commons is situated at the north end of this accommodation. The north end of the building contains the residences of the Speaker and Serjeant at Arms, the former including a number of fine rooms in which receptions are regularly held ; the Clock Tower surmounted by the famous " Big Ben " is at the north-west corner of the block. The Victoria Tower similarly crowns the southern end ; the Record Office of the House of Lords is here situated.

Numerous rooms used by the representatives of the press occupy much of the space in the north end of the building other than the residences of the Speaker and the Serjeant at Arms. At various points scattered all over the building are to be found the offices and other rooms used by the Clerks and other officers of the two Houses, the party whips, the Post Office (including the telephone exchange and engineers), the two refreshment departments, members' secretaries, civil servants and the police. Among other amenities which are to be found in the building may be mentioned a television room, a barber's shop, bathrooms, a gymnasium, a chess room and a miniature rifle range.

IMPEACHMENT

The trial of a person, usually a minister of the Crown, before the House of Lords, on an accusation of treason or other crimes and misdemeanours brought by the House of Commons. The prosecution must be initiated by the House of Commons and is conducted on their behalf by managers appointed out of their own body. The last instance of an impeachment was that of Lord Melville, First Lord of the Admiralty, in 1805 for alleged malversation in his office. He was acquitted. In 1816 Lord Cochrane presented articles against Lord Ellenborough, Lord Chief Justice of the Court of King's Bench, and moved that they should be referred to the consideration of a committee of the whole House, but the motion was defeated by eighty-nine votes to none. In 1848 Mr. Anstey moved that an address should be presented to the Queen for papers concerning certain transactions and for the names of the ministers or councillors who had advised Her Majesty concerning these transactions, with a view to moving a motion for the impeachment of Lord Palmerston. But after the motion had been debated on several days he abandoned the attempt.

INSTRUCTION

An order empowering or directing a committee to do something which is not within the scope of the authority already conferred on it, or directing it to do or not to do something which otherwise it could do or not do as it pleased.

INSTRUCTION—*continued*

In the House of Commons an instruction to a committee of the whole House or to a standing committee must not be mandatory in form, *i.e.* it must not direct the committee to do the particular act which forms the subject of the instruction, but only empower the committee to do it. Mandatory instructions may, however, be given to select committees or, with the concurrence of both Houses, to joint committees. They may also be given to committees on private bills.

An instruction empowering a committee of the whole House or a standing committee to make amendments in a bill which are not relevant to the subject matter of the bill as defined by its contents is not in order unless the objects to which it is desired to extend the provisions of the bill are cognate to its general purposes.

No instruction may be moved to a committee on a private bill requiring or authorising the committee to make an amendment in the bill which could not be proposed by the promoters unless they had previously presented a petition for additional provision to the House.

Generally speaking, in the House of Commons an instruction to a committee of the whole House on a bill must be moved after the order of the day for going into the committee has been read and before the House resolves itself into the committee for the first time. But when a bill has been partly considered in committee and progress has been reported, no instruction can be moved when the order of the day for the committee is read. Instructions authorising charges are, however, moved when the resolutions upon which they are founded have been agreed to by the House.

An instruction to a standing committee may be moved either immediately after the second reading of the bill or at any time before the bill is reported from the committee.

An instruction to a select committee on a bill or to a committee on a private bill may be moved immediately after the committal of the bill or at any time before the bill is reported from the committee.

An instruction to a select committee on a matter may be moved at any time after its appointment and before it has made its report.

The Speaker is empowered to select which, if any, of the instructions of which notice has been given may be moved, but, subject to this, there is no limit to the number which may be moved in succession. A member cannot however move more than one instruction to the same committee.

The mover of an instruction has not the right of reply.

A proposed instruction is open to amendment, but any amendments moved to an instruction must be so drawn that if carried the amended motion would retain the form of an instruction.

Notice must be given of an amendment to a proposed instruction which would widen its scope or materially alter its character.

INTERRUPTIONS

Members must not interrupt a member's speech, except to call the attention of the House to a point of order (*q.v.*). In practice, if the member interrupting is only seeking to correct a mistake on the part of the member speaking, or endeavouring to secure an explanation, he is allowed to do so; but the member speaking, being "in possession of the House", need not give way unless he so wishes. Attempts to convert an interruption into a speech are soon met by cries of "Order!" from other members, and, if necessary, by a reproof from the Speaker or the chairman.

IRREGULARITIES IN PROCEDURE

If the House of Commons inadvertently transgresses its own rules of procedure, it subsequently, on the error being discovered, agrees to a resolution that the proceedings relating to the business in question shall be null and void; after which it proceeds with the business in the normal and proper manner. If a committee has exceeded its powers or failed to observe the rules of the House in any way, as, for instance, by amending a bill in a manner inconsistent with its purpose, or by conducting its business without a quorum, the House, on being made aware of the fact, recommits the bill, report or other matter to the committee, in order that the task may be properly carried out. It sometimes happens that one House sends to the other a bill which has not been read the third time; in that case, when the mistake is discovered, a message is sent, requesting that the bill be returned and stating the reason. If it should be discovered that a bill has received the royal assent without having duly passed through all its stages, nothing can be done to make good the omission; but the act, once it has received the royal assent, has the full force of law and its validity cannot be questioned.

JOURNAL OFFICE

An office of the House of Commons, the clerks in which are responsible for compiling the Journals and examining public petitions presented to the House. They also undertake research into precedents and, in addition, supply clerks to certain committees. The Clerk of the Journals is Clerk to the Committee of Privileges. Clerks in this office also form the staff of the Votes and Proceedings Office.

The clerks in the Journal Office of the House of Lords prepare the Journals of that House and receive and examine all the papers presented to the House.

JOURNALS

The Journals of the House of Commons are the authentic record of the proceedings of the House, prepared in the Clerk's department under the authority of the Speaker. The earliest known Journal begins with the first Parliament of Edward VI in 1547, and consists of little more than a record of readings of bills. The Journals were gradually expanded in subsequent sessions, and often included references to the arguments used by members in their speeches; but this was forbidden by the House in 1628 and the practice ceased accordingly. The manuscript Journals are complete from 1547, with the exception of a period from 1584 to 1601, until 1800, although the regular printing and publication of the Journals began in 1762. The period from 1584 to 1601 is covered by the Journals of Sir Simonds D'Ewes, who had access to contemporary records—possibly the missing Journals themselves—which are now denied to us.

In 1742 the extant Journals were printed by order of the House and published. Indexes to each session were prepared; general indexes, each covering a number of sessions, began to be published in 1785. The surviving manuscript Journals for the period from 1547 to 1800 are preserved in the Record Office of the House of Lords.

A single volume of the Journals now covers, as a rule, one session. The original material from which it is compiled is supplied by the notes made by the Clerks at the Table in their minute books. From these, and from certain other sources (such as the Parliamentary Papers), the Votes and Proceedings are prepared by the Clerks in the Votes and Proceedings Office during each sitting, printed during the night and published on the following morning. The Journal is then compiled in the Journal Office from the same sources, checked with the Votes and Proceedings, printed in instalments during the session, and published, together with its own index, as soon as possible after the end of it.

The Journal and the Votes and Proceedings (*q.v.*) are now once again (after an interval of more than 150 years) written in the same narrative style, which is a somewhat abbreviated form of that used in the Journal up till 1969. No reference is made to the contents of speeches, except those of the Sovereign, and, on special occasions, of the Speaker. In addition to the index covering the proceedings of each session, and included in that session's volume, a general index is also published in a separate volume covering each period of roughly ten years; this includes most of the material found in the sessional indexes, and, as well, a collection of digests or analyses of the different kinds of procedure. The record contained in the Journals is regarded as *prima facie* evidence of a proceeding in Parliament, and the production of the relevant volume is accepted by the courts of law in proof.

The Journals of the House of Lords, which date from 1510, are generally similar in form to those of the Commons. They also are provided with general indexes, each of which covers several sessions, as well as an index accompanying each sessional volume. Unlike the Commons' Journals, they record the names of all those Lords who attend each sitting.

JOURNALS, COMMITTEE FOR THE

A committee appointed by the House of Lords at the beginning of every session " to peruse and perfect the Journals of this and former sessions of Parliament ". It consists of all the lords who have been or shall be present during the session. The quorum is three. The Committee has not met for many years.

KITCHEN COMMITTEE

The colloquial name for a select committee formerly appointed by the House of Commons at the beginning of each session to control the arrangements for the kitchen and refreshment rooms in the department of the Serjeant at Arms. This function is now carried out by the Catering Sub-Committee of the Select Committee on House of Commons (Services) (*see* HOUSE OF COMMONS (SERVICES), SELECT COMMITTEE ON).

LAW LORDS

The Lord Chancellor, the nine Lords of Appeal in Ordinary (*q.v.*), ex-Lord Chancellors, and other peers who have held high judicial office. At the present time (1970) the number of Law Lords is twenty-three.

LEADER OF THE HOUSE

The term " Leader of the House " was originally applied to the chief spokesman for the Government in the House of Commons when the Prime Minister was a member of the House of Lords. (When the Prime Minister was a member of the House of Commons he led the House himself.) The last Leader of the House in this sense of the term was Mr. Balfour who led the House of Commons from 1895 to 1902 when Lord Salisbury was Prime Minister. In order that he might be enabled to devote the whole of his energies to the prosecution of the war, Mr. Lloyd George, on becoming Prime Minister in 1916, confided the leadership of the House of Commons to Mr. Bonar Law and, when failing health caused Mr. Law to withdraw from active politics in 1921, Mr. Austen Chamberlain succeeded him as Leader of the House. When Mr. Law succeeded Mr. Lloyd George as Prime Minister in 1922 he reverted to the former practice and his successors continued to lead the House of Commons until 1940 when Mr.

LEADER OF THE HOUSE—*continued*
Churchill entrusted the leadership of the House to Mr. Attlee. Since then the post of Leader of the House has never been combined with that of Prime Minister. In 1969 a cabinet minister was appointed Deputy Leader of the House.

The leadership of the House is not an office and the Leader of the House receives no salary as such. The leadership is usually entrusted to the holder of an office with few or only nominal duties such as the Lord President of the Council or the Lord Privy Seal, but it has been held by the Home Secretary. His chief responsibility is for planning and supervising the Government's legislative programme, and in particular for the arrangement, in consultation with the Chief Government Whip, of the business of the House. Every Thursday, after question time, in answer to a question usually put to him by the Leader of the Opposition, the Leader of the House announces the business for the following week and deals with any objections made, *e.g.*, that insufficient time has been allotted for a particular item of business, and requests that the Government should provide time for the discussion of certain subjects.

Whenever the authority of the Speaker, the executive of the House, has been disobeyed, it must be supported. Accordingly when a member is named by the Speaker or the Chairman of a Committee of the whole House the Leader of the House invariably moves that the offender be suspended from the service of the House (*see* ORDER IN THE HOUSE).

When any difficulty arises it is for the Leader of the House to advise the House as to the course to be followed. The Leader of the House himself now usually moves that the matter of a complaint be referred to the Committee of Privileges. Formerly the member who made the complaint moved this motion; in that case, if the Leader of the House considered that the House would best consult its own dignity by taking no notice of a breach of privilege of which complaint had been made, he moved the previous question or moved (as an amendment to the motion made by the member who raised the matter) that the House should proceed to the orders or business of the day. Speaking of libels on members, Mr. Gladstone said: "The Leader of the House is the protector of the whole House and every member sitting on these benches (the benches on the Speaker's left, occupied by the Opposition) and on the benches below the gangway has the same right to apply to him as any member who sits behind him." The Leader of the House is usually a member of the Committee of Privileges, in which event he is invariably elected chairman.

The Leader of the House of Lords is the chief spokesman for the Government in that House. His other functions in that House are similar to those of the Leader of the House of Commons.

LEAVE OF ABSENCE COMMITTEE

A committee appointed by the House of Lords at the beginning of every session for the general supervision of the arrangements relating to leave of absence (*see* ABSENCE, LEAVE OF). It consists of the Lord Chairman and the whips of the three major parties.

LEGISLATION BY REFERENCE

A term used in two senses. First, to describe a bill or an Act which provides that the provisions of an existing Act shall apply to matters dealt with by the new bill or Act with the necessary modifications or subject to certain specified modifications. The provisions of the Municipal Corporations Acts with respect to municipal elections were thus applied by the Local Government Act 1888 to county council elections. The term is also applied (though less properly) to a bill or an Act which amends an earlier Act by enacting that certain sections of the earlier Act shall have effect as if other words were substituted for some of the existing words.

LOCUS STANDI

The right of a petitioner against a private, provisional order or hybrid bill or special procedure order to be heard upon his petition. Parties are said to have no *locus standi* when their property or interests are not affected by the bill in such a manner as according to the practice of Parliament entitles them to be heard. The general principle is that, if a petitioner is to have an absolute right to be heard, there must be something in the bill which, if passed into law, will injure him, not as a member of the general public, but in respect of his particular property or interest; in addition the Court of Referees (*q.v.*) have a discretion to admit representatives of amenity and other societies who petition against a private bill to be heard by the committee on the bill. If the right of a petitioner to be heard against a bill is objected to by the promoters, the question is determined in the Commons by the Court of Referees (*q.v.*), but in the Lords by the committee on the bill. The onus is on the promoters to show that the petitioner has no *locus standi*. In the case of petitions against special procedure orders (*q.v.*) questions of *locus standi* are determined by the Lord Chairman and the Chairman of Ways and Means.

LORDS, HOUSE OF

The House of Lords forms, with the Queen and the House of Commons, the High Court of Parliament, which is the supreme legislative authority in the Kingdom. The functions of the House of Lords, which, being superior in degree to the House of Commons, is called the "Upper House", are twofold, legislative and judicial. Though both Houses participate in the making of law, they are

LORDS, HOUSE OF—*continued*
markedly unequal in power ; the exclusive right of the Commons to initiate measures imposing taxes or authorising the expenditure of public money has been virtually unchallenged for more than 250 years. The Parliament Act 1911 practically deprived the Lords of the power either to amend or to reject money bills, and reduced their power in the case of other public bills to that of merely delaying their passage for two years (now one year, by the Act of 1949) (*see* BILL, PUBLIC). In the field of delegated legislation, however, the House of Lords retains rights, equal to those of the House of Commons, to withhold its approval or to procure the annulment of statutory instruments and similar enactments in all cases where the relevant statutes provide that the instruments, etc., concerned are subject to approval or annulment by both Houses. The preponderant function of the Commons, which is due to their representative character, is marked by the fact that it is nowadays considered necessary for most of the ministers of the Crown to be members of the Lower House. The last Prime Minister who sat in the House of Lords was the Marquess of Salisbury, who held that office from 1895 to 1902.

The main judicial function belonging to the House of Lords is that of acting as the highest court of appeal in the kingdom, in both civil and criminal cases. It may also try persons impeached by the Commons, that is, brought to trial by that body for " high crimes and misdemeanours beyond the reach of the law ". (This, however, has not happened since 1805.) It also decides peerage cases, that is, disputed claims to the inheritance of a peerage, when such cases are referred to it by the Crown. Until the Criminal Justice Act 1948 abolished the privilege, a peer accused of treason or felony, or of misprision of either, was tried by his peers ; the last such trial took place in December 1937, when Lord de Clifford was charged with manslaughter as the result of a motor accident and was acquitted.

The House of Lords usually meets only three or four times a week for legislative business, at half past two (three on Thursdays). Judicial sittings may be held in the morning on all week-days except Saturday. Any peer may attend a sitting of the House to consider an appeal, but not less than three Lords of Appeal must be present. The Lords of Appeal consist of the Lord Chancellor, such peers as have held high judicial office, and the Lords of Appeal in Ordinary, who are life peers (*see* p. 121).

The members of the House of Lords fall into two categories ; Lords temporal and Lords spiritual. The temporal peerages are of two kinds, those which are hereditary and those which are for the holder's life only. Peers of England, of Scotland, of Great Britain (created after the Union with Scotland in 1707), and of the United Kingdom (created after the Union with Ireland in 1800) are entitled to sit as members of the House of Lords by hereditary right. Until the Peerage Act 1963 put peers of Scotland in the same position as those of England, Great Britain and the United Kingdom, the peers of Scotland elected at every general election sixteen of their number to represent them as members of the House of Lords. By the same Act peers of Ireland, who had been represented since the Union in 1800 by twenty-eight of their number elected for life, ceased to be in any way disqualified by reason of their peerages from being elected to the House of Commons or voting in elections thereto ; rights which had up till then belonged only to non-representative peers (for seats other than Irish). No election of Irish representative peers has in fact taken place since the creation of the Irish Free State in 1922 (when the Lord Chancellorship of Ireland and the Clerkship of the Crown and Hanaper were abolished) ; the last of the representative peers (the fourth Earl of Kilmorey) died in 1961. Among the Irish peers who sat in the House of Commons Viscount Palmerston (who was Prime Minister from 1855 to 1858 and from 1859 to 1865) and the sixth Earl Winterton (who represented Horsham from 1904 to 1951) may be mentioned. A number of Scottish and Irish peers were, however, also peers of England, Great Britain or the United Kingdom and were thus entitled to sit in the House of Lords. A person succeeding to a hereditary peerage may disclaim his peerage for his own life and cease to be a peer (*see* PEER).

The Peerage Act 1963 also gave to a woman holding a hereditary peerage in the peerages of England, Scotland, Great Britain or the United Kingdom (a peeress, that is to say, in her own right) the same rights of sitting and voting in the House of Lords as a man in that position, and imposed on her the same disqualifications with regard to election and membership of the House of Commons.

Since 1958 the Crown has had the right to confer peerages for life on either men or women. In addition there are the nine life peers who are created for the special purpose of assisting the House in its judicial business, and who are called Lords of Appeal in Ordinary. At the present time (1970) there are also eleven retired Lords of Appeal in Ordinary who remain members of the House.

The Lords Spiritual are twenty-six in number, comprising the Archbishops of Canterbury and York and twenty-four of the English bishops. The two Archbishops and the Bishops of London, Durham and Winchester have seats as of right, the other bishops in order of the seniority of their consecration. A number of abbots sat in the House of Lords before the Reformation. Irish bishops sat until the disestablishment of the Church of Ireland in 1869, and Welsh bishops till the Church of Wales was

LORDS, HOUSE OF—*continued*
disestablished in 1920. The Bishop of Sodor and Man has no seat.

The chamber occupied by the House of Lords is the " Parliament Chamber ", being the place where the constituent elements of Parliament meet together. The superiority in degree of the House of Lords (referred to above) is marked by the fact that the Commons stand at the bar of the chamber, while the Peers sit.

LORDS OF APPEAL

The Lord Chancellor, the Lords of Appeal in Ordinary (*q.v.*), ex-Lord Chancellors, ex-Lords of Appeal in Ordinary and such peers as are, or have been, members of the Judicial Committee of the Privy Council or Judges of the Superior Courts in Great Britain or Ireland. No appeal can be heard and determined by the House of Lords unless at least three Lords of Appeal are present.

LORDS OF APPEAL IN ORDINARY

Persons appointed by the Queen for the purpose of aiding the House of Lords in the hearing and determination of appeals. To be appointed a Lord of Appeal in Ordinary a man must have held one of certain specified high judicial offices or have practised for at least fifteen years as a barrister in England or Northern Ireland or as an advocate in Scotland. A Lord of Appeal in Ordinary has the rank of a baron for life, but the dignity is not hereditary. He is entitled to sit and vote in the House of Lords when it is acting in its legislative capacity, as well as when it is acting as a court of appeal. There are at present nine Lords of Appeal in Ordinary. By the Administration of Justice Act 1968 the maximum is fixed at eleven. It may be increased by order in council subject to affirmative resolutions by both Houses.

MACE

A silver-gilt ornamented club carried by the Serjeants at Arms, to whom are assigned the duties of attending the Speaker of the House of Commons and the Lord Chancellor respectively. The mace is the symbol of the authority with which all Serjeants at Arms are invested by the Crown, in particular of their power to arrest persons without a warrant.

At each sitting of the House of Commons before prayers are read the Serjeant places the mace on two rests on the table of the House at the end furthest from the Speaker, where it remains (except while the House is in committee) until the end of the sitting. When the House goes into committee and the Speaker leaves the chair, the Serjeant takes the mace off the table and places it on two brackets below the surface of the table. When the chairman leaves the Clerk's chair, the Serjeant places the mace on the table again. On the meeting of a new Parliament the mace is placed, not on the table, but on the two brackets below the table already referred to. When the Speaker has been elected, the Serjeant places the mace on the rests *on* the table. (The practice of placing the mace on the table as soon as the Speaker has been elected, but before he has been approved by the Sovereign, seems to have arisen during the Commonwealth when the Speaker did not require to be approved. In earlier times the mace was not placed on the table until the Speaker had been approved by the Sovereign.) When the House adjourns, after electing a Speaker, the mace is subsequently removed by the Serjeant. Until the Speaker-elect has been approved by the Sovereign, the Serjeant, when attending him, carries the mace on his left arm. When the Commons go up to the House of Lords to hear the speech from the throne or the royal assent given to bills or at the prorogation, the Serjeant does not carry his mace into the House but leaves it outside with one of the Commons doorkeepers. If Parliament is to be prorogued, the doorkeeper carries the mace back to the Commons chamber and thence to the Speaker's office, where he puts the mace in the bag in which it is kept when not in use and returns it to the Lord Chamberlain. During an adjournment of the House, however, the mace is kept in the Speaker's office.

An almost mystical significance has come to be attached to the mace. When it is not on the table, but on the Serjeant's shoulder, no member except the Speaker is allowed to speak. If the Serjeant were sent out of the House with his mace, no business could be done until he returned.

At a sitting of the House of Lords the Serjeant at Arms places his mace on the woolsack before prayers are read, where it remains until the sitting ends. The mace is not removed from the woolsack when the House goes into committee or adjourns "during pleasure" or when a sitting for judicial business terminates provided that the House is to meet for legislative business later the same day.

MAIDEN SPEECH

The first speech which a member makes in the House of Commons. It is the custom for a member to be given precedence on this occasion, that is, he will be called as soon as he stands up, but this privilege is not extended to him after the Parliament to which he is first elected. It is usual for a member on this occasion to express a becoming diffidence and to ask for his fellow members' indulgence. It is also customary for the member who follows

MAIDEN SPEECH—*continued*

him—and who will probably belong to the party opposed to his—to compliment him on his speech.

MARGINAL NOTE

A note printed at the side, and explanatory of the contents, of each clause of a bill. It is not part of the bill.

MEASURE

Under the Church of England Assembly (Powers) Act 1919, as amended by the Synodical Government Measure 1969, the General Synod of the Church of England has the power of legislation with regard to any matter concerning the Church; its enactments, known as measures, become law on receiving the royal assent. A measure may repeal or amend, wholly or partly, any Act of Parliament.

A measure, having been approved separately by the three Houses of the Synod, is submitted by the Synod's Legislative Committee to the Ecclesiastical Committee (*q.v.*), which considers the measure and drafts a report "stating the nature and legal effect of the measure and its views as to the expediency thereof, especially with relation to the constitutional rights of all Her Majesty's subjects". This report, after being communicated to the Legislative Committee, is presented to both Houses of Parliament, if the Legislative Committee so desires. (It can presumably withhold it, and the measure with it.)

A copy of the measure is laid before each House with the report; and if both Houses pass resolutions directing it to be presented to Her Majesty, the measure receives the royal assent in due course in the same manner as an Act of Parliament. A measure cannot be amended by Parliament, but either House can, in effect, reject it by defeating the motion directing the measure to be presented for the royal assent, as happened in the case of the Prayer Book Measures in 1927 and 1928.

The motion for the presentation of a measure is moved in the House of Commons by a member of the Ecclesiastical Committee; it is regarded not as government business but as a non-party matter.

MEMBERS

Any British subject of not less than twenty-one years is qualified to be a candidate for membership of the House of Commons, provided that he does not come within one of the categories mentioned below. Women have been eligible since November 21, 1918, when the Parliament (Qualification of Women) Act 1918 enacted that "A woman shall not be disqualified by sex or marriage for being elected to or sitting or voting as a member of the

Commons House of Parliament ". Certain other persons who have the same status as British subjects (such as citizens of the Irish Republic) are apparently also eligible.

The chief disqualifications are as follows:

Peerage: Peers, other than Irish peers, are disqualified. Among Irish peers elected to the House of Commons, Lord Palmerston and the late Earl Winterton may be mentioned. The receipt by a member of a writ of summons to the House of Lords (either on succeeding his father or on being made a peer by the Queen) at once vacates his seat in the House of Commons; though he may retain his seat if he chooses to disclaim his peerage (*see also* LORDS, HOUSE OF; PEER).

Clergy: Clergy episcopally ordained and ministers of the established Church of Scotland are not eligible for membership. But, by the Clerical Disabilities Act 1870, clergy of the Church of England can render themselves eligible by executing a deed of relinquishment; and ministers of the Church of Scotland can attain the same object by demitting their status if the demission be authorised by the General Assembly or the Presbytery.

Offices of Profit: The Succession to the Crown Act 1705 disqualified from membership the holders of offices under the Crown created after the passing of the Act, and required the holders of previously created offices to seek re-election on the acceptance of office. These requirements have been gradually modified by subsequent legislation, concurrently with the development of the system of cabinet government, until it may be said that they do not now affect the holders of ministerial office (with the exception that the number of holders of certain offices who are at the same time members of the House of Commons is limited). Colonial governors, judges, stipendiary magistrates, sheriffs, civil servants and officers of both Houses are, however, still excluded; as also are returning officers, in respect of the constituencies in which they act in that capacity. Persons holding government contracts are also disqualified; but this does not apply to those who merely own shares in companies holding such contracts.

Treason: A person convicted of treason may not be elected a member; he remains disqualified until he has served his sentence or has been pardoned.

Bankruptcy: A member adjudged bankrupt vacates his seat and remains disqualified until he is discharged, when his disqualification ceases, provided that his bankruptcy has been due to misfortune and not misconduct.

Lunacy: If a member is detained on grounds of mental illness, the Speaker is informed of the fact and must then require confirmation of the member's illness by two suitably qualified medical practitioners. After six months the Speaker requires the member to be re-examined, and if he is reported still to be of unsound

MEMBERS—*continued*

mind the Speaker lays both reports before the House and the member's seat thereupon becomes vacant.

A member is entitled to receive a yearly allowance of £3,250, payable monthly, which he may begin to draw as soon as he has taken the oath after his election. Ministers, officers of the Royal household, the Speaker, the Chairman and Deputy Chairman of Ways and Means, the Leader of the Opposition and the Chief Opposition Whip receive only £1,250 of this allowance in addition to the salaries which they receive in these capacities. A member is also allowed to claim an allowance, up to £500, towards the cost of secretarial assistance in respect of his parliamentary duties. It may be observed that questions to the Chancellor of the Exchequer have at various times elicited the information that a small number of members have chosen not to draw the salary to which they have been entitled. A member may post his correspondence with ministers and their departments, officials of the House and nationalised industries in franked envelopes, and he is entitled to free first-class railway, bus, steamer and air travel, or an allowance for the use of his own car in lieu thereof, between Westminster, his constituency and his home.

A member may not resign his membership, which continues until the dissolution of Parliament, unless he becomes disqualified for any of the reasons given above. If, therefore, he wishes to cease being a member, he must apply for one of the sinecure offices granted by the Crown, which, because they nominally entitle the holder to certain fees or profits, disqualify him from membership. The offices now used for this purpose are those of Steward or Bailiff of Her Majesty's three Chiltern Hundreds of Stoke, Desborough and Burnham, and Steward or Bailiff of the Manor of Northstead. Unless there is some reason to the contrary (such as an uncompleted inquiry into some matter which might lead to disciplinary action being taken against the member by the House), the appointment is duly made by the Chancellor of the Exchequer, and a notice to that effect appears in the " London Gazette ". This immediately renders vacant the member's seat.

MEMORIAL

A written representation of facts unaccompanied by a prayer. A memorial in the strict sense of the word will not be received by either House. Documents headed "memorials ", but containing language equivalent to a prayer, have, however, been received as petitions.

Memorials complaining that the promoters of a private bill have neglected to comply with the standing orders may be addressed to the Examiners of Petitions for Private Bills. Such memorials must be deposited in the Private Bill Office. Memorials objecting to the certification of a special procedure petition (*see* SPECIAL PROCEDURE ORDER) as proper to be received, or, if it is presented as a petition for amendment, objecting that it is a petition of general objection, may be addressed either to the Lord Chairman or to the Chairman of Ways and Means. If addressed to the Lord Chairman they must be deposited in the Committee and Private Bill Office in the House of Lords, but, if addressed to the Chairman of Ways and Means, they must be deposited in the Private Bill Office of the House of Commons.

Memorials are prepared in the same form and are subject to the same general rules as petitions.

MINISTERS OF THE CROWN

The rules of the House of Commons, both written and unwritten, reserve certain duties and privileges to the Ministers of the Crown; the meaning of this term varies, however, according to the context. In its widest sense, with reference to the custom that a minister may move a motion of which notice has been given in the name of another, it means any member of the Government, of whatever rank. (This does not, of course, include parliamentary private secretaries, who have no official status at all.) The Queen's consent may, however, only be signified by a minister who is a privy counsellor; for this purpose the Chairman of Ways and Means, who usually performs this function, when required, for a private bill, is regarded as a minister.

MONEY BILL

A money bill is differently defined (i) for the purpose of its introduction in the House of Commons, and (ii) under the Parliament Act 1911.

In the first category it is defined as a bill the main object of which is the creation of a public charge. If such a bill imposes a tax or authorises the expenditure of money from the Exchequer, it must be founded on a Ways and Means resolution approving the tax or the expenditure. If the bill, though a money bill, does not impose a tax or authorise expenditure from the Exchequer, it may be introduced in the ordinary way and the creation of the charge authorised by a money resolution after the second reading.

In the second category it is defined by the Parliament Act as a bill wholly concerned with certain matters, including the imposition or regulation of taxation, the imposition of charges on the Consolidated Fund or the National Loans Fund or on money provided by Parliament and the appropriation or issue of public money. It is possible therefore that a bill which satisfied the conditions set forth in the first of these definitions might not come within the definition in the Act, through including other matters not directly concerned with finance.

MONEY BILL—*continued*

When a money bill, as defined under the Act, is sent up to the Lords it must be endorsed with a certificate signed by the Speaker declaring that the bill is a money bill within the meaning of the Act (*see* BILL, PUBLIC).

MONK RESOLUTION

The " Monk Resolutions " owe their name to Charles James Monk, on whose motion the House resolved in 1879 that a statement of every case in which a transfer of surplus sums realised on one vote of a defence department's estimate to meet a deficiency incurred on another vote of the same department, should be laid before the House within three weeks. Each transaction had to be approved at the time by the Treasury and sanctioned first by a committee of the whole House, in a " Monk Resolution ", and then by the House itself. This procedure has become obsolete since it has become the practice to agree to a vote on account for the estimates for the defence services in the same was as for the estimates for civil departments.

MOTION

A proposal, made to one or other House by a member, that the House do something, order something to be done or express an opinion with regard to some matter. A motion must be phrased in such a way that, if assented to, it will purport to express the judgment or will of the House. Motions are usually expressed in the affirmative even though their purpose and effect are negative. Thus a motion to dissent from the findings of a committee will take the form " That this House do disagree with the committee in their report " not that the House " do not agree " therewith.

Motions may conveniently be classified as substantive or subsidiary. A *substantive* motion is a self-contained motion made in reference to a subject which the mover wishes to bring forward. A *subsidiary* motion relates to a substantive motion and is made use of to enable the House to dispose of it in the most appropriate manner. The previous question and a motion for the adjournment of the debate are examples of subsidiary motions. (A motion for proceeding with an order of the day or a motion " That this House do now adjourn " made during the debate on another motion, though not subsidiary motions within the above definition, may for practical purposes be regarded as such.)

As a general rule a substantive motion requires notice. With the general consent of the House, however, such a motion may be moved without previous notice. A motion on a matter of privilege does not require notice.

A motion which requires notice can be moved only by the member in whose name it stands on the order paper unless it stands in the name of a member of the Government, in which case it may be moved by any member of the Government.

In the House of Commons a motion does not require to be seconded (*see* SECONDING OF MOTIONS), but it is still customary for motions for the election of the Speaker and for the address in reply to the Queen's Speech at the opening of the session to be seconded. In the House of Lords no motion requires a seconder except the motion for the address in reply to the speech from the Throne.

In the House of Commons when a motion has been moved, the Speaker reads it out, prefacing it with the words " The question is ". This is termed " proposing the question from the chair ".

In the House of Lords, however, the Lord Chancellor (or Lord Speaker) usually reads the motion to the House and says " the question is that this motion (or, when the motion is " that this House do resolve, etc.", " that this resolution ") be agreed to ". In the case of motions for reading bills a second or third time and similar motions, however, he proposes the question in the terms in which the motion was moved.

Until the question on a motion has been proposed from the chair it is not in order for any member to speak to it or move an amendment or any other motion. When it has been so proposed, (1) the motion is in the possession of the House and cannot be withdrawn without its consent, and (2) the motion becomes a question for the decision of the House and must be agreed to, with or without amendment, negatived or disposed of in some other manner, *e.g.*, by the adjournment of the debate, before the House can proceed with any other business. A motion which has been withdrawn, or has been superseded by the adjournment of the House or by the carrying of the previous question, may be moved again on a subsequent day.

No motion may be moved which is substantially the same as one on which the House has already come to a decision during the session or which is still pending. This rule cannot be evaded by merely altering the language of the motion. Similarly, a motion which is inconsistent with a resolution which has been passed by the House is out of order. If a member wishes to move such a motion, he must first move that the resolution be rescinded.

A motion dealing with the subject matter of a bill or other matter already appointed for consideration is out of order. So also is a motion dealing with the subject matter of a bill which a member has given notice of his intention to introduce on a future day, provided that notice of the intended presentation of the bill has been printed and circulated with the Votes and Proceedings (*see* ANTICIPATION, RULE AGAINST). It would, however, be in

MOTION—*continued*

order for a member to move a motion dealing with the subject matter of, or even identical in terms with, a motion of which another member had given notice for a later day.

When the debate on a motion is concluded, the Speaker states or reads the motion to the House, prefacing it with the words " the question is " and directs " as many as are of that opinion " to " say ' aye ' ". After pausing long enough to allow the supporters of the motion to call out " aye ", he directs " as many as are of the contrary opinion " to " say ' no ' ". (This process is termed " collecting the voices ", and when the voices of both the ayes and the noes have been collected, the question is said to be " fully put " and no member may speak to it.) After giving the opponents of the motion time to call out " no ", the Speaker says " I think the ayes (or the noes) have it ", *i.e.* are in the majority. (In theory the Speaker judges by the loudness of the respective cries of " aye " and " no " which side is in the majority. In practice, if the question is a party one, the Speaker takes it for granted that the supporters of the Government are in the majority and phrases his statement accordingly.) Unless some member demands a division by calling out " no " if the Speaker says that he thinks the ayes have it or *vice versa*, the Speaker *declares* that the ayes or the noes, as the case may be, have it. If, however, any member calls for a division, the Speaker directs the lobby to be cleared and, after an interval of two minutes, puts the question a second time, and if the demand for a division is repeated, directs the ayes to go to the right and the noes to the left and names four members, two from each side, to act as tellers.

In the House of Lords (except in the case of motions for reading a bill a second time now and other motions for advancing a bill a stage) the question put for the determination of the House is " that this motion (or that this resolution) be agreed to ", the terms " content " and " not content " are used instead of the terms " aye " and " no " respectively, and the Lord Chancellor (or the Lord Speaker) directs, not the lobby, but the bar, to be cleared. In other respects the procedure is the same as in the House of Commons.

NAMING A MEMBER

A declaration by the Speaker or the chairman of a committee of the whole House that a member has been guilty of some irregular or improper conduct. When the Speaker or the chairman names a member, he says " I name Mr. So-and-so for disregarding the authority of the chair " (or as the case may be).

When the Speaker names a member for disregard of the authority of the chair, persistent and wilful obstruction of the business of the House by abusing the rules of the House or otherwise, or grossly disorderly conduct, the Leader of the House at once moves that the offender " be suspended from the service of the House ". The question on the motion is put forthwith, no debate being allowed. When the chairman of a committee of the whole House names a member, he at once suspends the proceedings of the committee and leaves the chair of the committee. On the Speaker's resuming the chair the chairman reports that he has named the member and proceedings similar to those already described ensue.

NOTICE OF MOTION

Notice of an intended motion is usually given by handing a paper containing the terms of the motion, the name of the mover and the date on which it is to be moved to one of the Clerks at the Table during a sitting or to one of the clerks in the Table Office. But if a member wins a place in one of the periodical ballots for notices of motions, he may, directly his name is called by the Speaker rise and give public notice of the subject of his intended motion and the day on which he proposes to move it ; whether or not the member gives oral notice in this way, he must give notice in writing of the text of his intended motion, not less than nine days before the day for which he has won the right to move the motion. Notice of a motion may be given for " an early day " without specifying any particular day.

Notices of motions received by the Clerks at the Table or in the Table Office are printed and circulated with the Votes and Proceedings and appear in due course on the order paper for the day for which notice has been given.

A member who has given notice of his intention to move a motion on a particular day may put it off to a later day, but he cannot bring it forward to an earlier day. (He may, however, withdraw a notice of motion and give a new notice in identical terms for an earlier day, if that day falls within any time limit for giving notice which is applicable.)

If notice is given of a motion which is couched in unbecoming words or infringes the rules of the House, the Clerks at the Table may correct it. Before correcting such a notice, the Clerks may submit the proposed corrections to the Speaker or to the member who gave notice of the motion.

A member who has given notice of a motion may modify the terms of his motion by handing in an amended notice, so long as the amended notice is given within any time limit which is applicable.

A notice which has been printed and circulated with the Votes and Proceedings holds good until the day after that on which the member who gave it asks one of the Clerks at the Table to remove it from the order book.

NOTICE OF MOTION—*continued*

Notice of an intended motion may be withdrawn by the member who gave it at any time previous to the day fixed for the motion, but it cannot be withdrawn on the day for which notice was given. He is, of course, not obliged to move the motion.

OATH OF ALLEGIANCE

After the Speaker has been chosen no Member of the House of Commons may sit in the House or vote until he has taken the oath of allegiance to the Queen or made an affirmation to that effect and signed the test roll. If he sits or votes without taking the oath or making the affirmation, he is liable to a penalty of £500 for each offence and his seat is vacated as if he were dead. By sitting in the House is meant sitting in any part of the chamber which is technically within the House. An unsworn member may sit in the chamber below the bar. He is entitled to all the privileges (*q.v.*) of a member, and may be appointed a member of a committee, but he cannot present a petition.

The oath must be taken at the Table of the House whilst the House is sitting with the Speaker in the chair. It may be taken either before the orders of the day and notices of motions have been entered on, or after they have been disposed of, but no debate or business may be interrupted for the purpose.

Members returned at a general election usually take the oath on the day on which the Speaker's election receives the royal approval, after the Speaker has reported the fact to the House, and on the two following days. The oath is first taken by the Speaker himself, standing on the upper step of his chair. The other members then come to the Table and are sworn by one of the Clerks Assistant. Ministers, opposition front-benchers and privy counsellors who do not sit on either of the front benches are given precedence. After taking the oath each member signs the test roll and is presented to the Speaker by the Clerk of the House.

A member elected at a by-election cannot take the oath unless he produces a certificate stating that a certificate of his return has been received from the Crown Office. This certificate may be obtained at the Public Bill Office. Nor will such a member be allowed to take the oath unless he is introduced by two other members. Members elected at by-elections are usually introduced and take the oath immediately after questions are over. This is required by the House to be done in the following manner in order that the persons elected may be better known to members. On receiving a summons from the Speaker, the newly elected member, hitherto waiting at the bar, walks up to the Table between two members, bowing three times on the way, takes the oath (or makes affirmation), signs the test roll, and shakes hands with the Speaker. As a rule this proceeding passes without incident; but before alternatives were provided for those whose consciences forbade them to take the prescribed oath, it proved an obstacle to the full membership of a Jew (Baron Lionel de Rothschild in 1894) and a professed atheist (Charles Bradlaugh in 1880). In 1945 a member, Mr. Robert McIntyre, who, as a Scottish Nationalist, preferred to dispense with the sponsorship of members of other parties, was not allowed to come to the Table. He appeared, however, on the following day, with sponsors, and made affirmation in the usual way.

The form of the oath is as follows: "I swear by Almighty God that I will be faithful and bear true allegiance to Her Majesty Queen Elizabeth, her heirs and successors according to law, so help me God." The form of the affirmation is as follows: "I solemnly, sincerely and truly declare and affirm that I will be faithful and bear true allegiance to Her Majesty Queen Elizabeth, her heirs and successors according to law."

A member may, if he wishes, take the oath and then kiss the book, or he may swear in the Scottish form with uplifted hand, no book of any kind being used. But unless he objects, the oath is administered to him in the ordinary manner, *i.e.* he takes the oath holding the New Testament (or, if he is a Jew, the Old Testament) in his uplifted hand. The oath must be taken or the affirmation made in English and not in translation.

A member of the House of Lords must take the oath of allegiance to the Queen or make an affirmation to that effect and sign the test roll before taking his seat in a new Parliament. If he votes or sits during any debate without having taken the oath or made the affirmation, he is liable to a penalty of £500 for each offence. The oath may be taken at any convenient time during a sitting of the House. It may be taken during a sitting for judicial business. Lords of Appeal in Ordinary may take the oath during sittings for hearing appeals held during a prorogation.

In a new Parliament the Lord Chancellor is the first peer to take the oath. He takes it at the Table as soon as prayers have been read on the sitting (which is adjourned as soon as the Commons have left the House) being resumed. Other peers present take the oath after the roll of temporal peers has been delivered in at the Table. With the exception of the royal dukes, peers are sworn in in batches, but not in any particular order. A peer before taking the oath must hand his writ of summons to one of the Clerks at the Table. After taking the oath a peer signs the test roll. A newly created peer takes the oath on being introduced, after his patent and writ of summons have been read by the Clerk.

OBSTRUCTION

The use by a member of his right to speak and to move motions for the purpose of delaying or preventing the passing of some

OBSTRUCTION—*continued*

measure to which he feels strong objection. Mr. Gladstone defined obstruction as " the disposition either of the minority of the House, or of individuals, to resist the prevailing will of the House otherwise than by argument ". Persistent and wilful obstruction of the business of the House by abusing its rules or otherwise is a contempt of the House. Under Standing Order No. 24 a member who is " named " by the Speaker or the chairman of a committee of the whole House as guilty of this offence is liable to punishment by suspension from the service of the House. Obstruction is countered by the closure and the " guillotine ". The Speaker and the chairmen of committees of the whole House and standing committees are given power to deal with various kinds of obstructive conduct. Thus the Speaker is given power to order a member who persists in irrelevance or tedious repetition of his own arguments or of the arguments used by other members in debate to discontinue his speech and to resume his seat ; to put the question on dilatory motions without allowing them to be debated or to refuse to accept them ; to take the vote by calling first on the members who support his decision and then on the members who challenge it to stand up in cases where he thinks that a division is unnecessarily demanded ; and to select which of the amendments shall be moved to bills or motions. All these powers except the last (which is conferred only upon the Chairman and Deputy Chairman of Ways and Means) are given to the chairmen of committees of the whole House ; and all of them except the last but one are given to the chairmen of standing committees also.

OFFICIAL REPORT

A verbatim shorthand note of the debates in each House of Parliament is taken by official reporters and a report is published daily by H. M. Stationery Office, as " Parliamentary Debates, Official Report ". (Since November 1943 the word " Hansard " has been printed on the cover.) The reports are made up to about 10.30 p.m., reports of any subsequent proceedings being printed with the next day's report. Each member is entitled to five free copies of the official report from the Vote Office in addition to one delivered direct from the Stationery Office. The daily parts are bound into five-day sets and are published as the " Weekly Hansard ". Bound volumes each containing the reports of several weeks' debates are issued periodically. These volumes are issued free to such members as ask for them. Members are allowed to make verbal corrections in the reports of their speeches, such corrections being embodied in the reports printed in the bound volumes. Reprints of particular speeches, in leaflet form, may be obtained by members, on application to the

Editor of the Official Report, on payment to the Stationery Office of a fee based on the cost of production.

OPPOSED BUSINESS

Business to the transaction of which a member objects. Private business (*q.v.*), if opposed, cannot be taken at the time of private business. Opposed private business may, at the discretion of the Chairman of Ways and Means, be taken at 7 p.m. on Mondays, Tuesdays, Wednesdays or Thursdays. After the business under consideration at 10 p.m. on Monday, Tuesday, Wednesday or Thursday, or at 4 p.m. on Friday, has been disposed of no opposed business may be transacted unless it falls within the category of exempted business (*q.v.*). A member may object to business being transacted either by rising in his place and saying " I object ", or, if he failed to object before the Speaker put the question, by calling out " aye " or " no " contrary to the Speaker's declaration, made after he has collected the voices, that the ayes or the noes " have it " (*see* DIVISION). Merely speaking to a question does not make it opposed business except in cases where, the business not having been interrupted at the hour fixed by standing order because a question was then in course of being decided, the main, or the original, question, or any further question consequent upon the question which was in course of being decided at the hour appointed for the interruption of business, is proposed from the chair. In such a case a member's offering to speak to the question makes it opposed business and compels the Speaker, or, if the House is in committee, the chairman, to interrupt the business.

ORDER BOOK

The Order Book of the House of Commons is published in the afternoon of each sitting day. It contains a complete list of all the orders, notices and questions appointed for the following and subsequent days up till the end of the session.

ORDER IN THE HOUSE

In the House of Commons order is maintained by the Speaker or, if the House is in committee, by the chairman. If a member who is speaking wanders from the question or breaks any of the rules of debate, the Speaker calls him to order. If the member persists in the course which the Speaker has declared to be out of order, the Speaker orders him to withdraw from the House or names him to the House for disregarding the authority of the chair. If a member speaking in debate uses any unparliamentary language, the Speaker calls upon him to withdraw it and to apologise to the House for using it. The Speaker's demand usually produces the required retraction and apology ; but if the

ORDER IN THE HOUSE—*continued*
offending member refuses to withdraw the offensive expressions, the Speaker either orders him to withdraw from the House or names him to the House for disregarding the authority of the chair.

If a member speaking in debate persists in irrelevance or in tedious repetition of his own arguments or the arguments used by other members, the Speaker, after calling the attention of the House to the member's conduct, may direct him to discontinue his speech. If the member does not at once sit down, the Speaker will either order him to withdraw from the House or name him.

If a member who is present in the House during a debate behaves in a grossly disorderly manner, it is the duty of the Speaker to order him to withdraw from the House unless he thinks the offence calls for punishment, in which event he may name the offending member.

If a member who has been ordered to withdraw from the House refuses to comply with the direction, the Speaker " names " him.

When the Speaker names a member to the House, whether for grossly disorderly conduct, or for disregarding the authority of the chair, the Leader of the House or, if he is absent, some other leading member of the Government, invariably at once moves " That Mr. ——— be suspended from the service of the House ". The question on this motion is put at once, no debate being allowed. As the right of the House to proceed against any member according to ancient usages is expressly preserved by Standing Order No. 24, it would be open to any member, when the Speaker names a member to the House, to move that the offender be committed to the custody of the Serjeant at Arms or to prison, or even that he be expelled the House. Such a motion would be debatable.

Suspension from the service of the House lasts, in the case of a first offence, for five sitting days, in the case of a second offence, for twenty sitting days, and in the case of each further offence, until the House terminates it. (By a first offence is meant the first offence committed during that particular session.)

Only one member may be named at a time, unless several members, present together, have jointly disregarded the authority of the chair.

On a motion for the suspension of a member being carried, the Speaker directs him to withdraw from the House. If he does not do so, the Speaker orders the Serjeant at Arms to summon him to obey the Speaker's direction. If the member still refuses, the Speaker calls the attention of the House to the fact that recourse to force is necessary to compel obedience to his direction, and the recalcitrant member is automatically suspended from the service of the House for the remainder of the session. When resort to force is necessary the Speaker may suspend the sitting during the removal of the member.

Suspension from the service of the House does not exempt a member from serving on any private bill committee to which he has been appointed. Subject to this, a member who is either ordered to withdraw from the House or suspended from its service must at once leave the House and its precincts, and not re-enter them until the next day or, if he has been suspended from the service of the House, until the period of suspension expires.

If grave disorder arises in the House, the Speaker may suspend the sitting for a specified time or even adjourn the House. In over sixty years this power has been exercised only nine times.

When the House is in committee, order is maintained by the chairman who has the same powers as the Speaker (1) of ordering a member who is guilty of grossly disorderly conduct or refuses to obey his directions to leave the House or of naming him, and (2) of directing a member who persists in irrelevance or in tedious repetition of his own or other members' arguments to sit down. If, however, the chairman names a member, he at once leaves the chair of the committee and, when the Speaker has resumed the chair of the House, reports to the House that he has named the member for grossly disorderly conduct or disregarding the authority of the chair, as the case may be. The same proceedings then take place as when the Speaker names a member.

In the House of Lords order is maintained by the House itself. The Lord Chancellor or Lord Speaker has no greater power to preserve order than any other member. A member who breaks any rule may be called to order by any other member. If debate becomes acrimonious, any member may move that the standing order relating to asperity of speech be read by the Clerk. This was last done on May 2, 1950.

ORDER PAPER

A number of papers dealing with the business of the House of Commons are printed by the Stationery Office and published every morning under the authority of the Speaker. Apart from the "Votes and Proceedings" (*q.v.*), most of them (with the exception of the Division Lists) concern forthcoming business; they consist of the following separate publications.

First comes the Order Paper proper (on white paper), containing the public business for the day of publication. Any private business for the day is repeated at the head of this sheet; this is followed by a list of the "Questions for Oral Answer" which are to be put to ministers by members during "Question Time". These may be followed by one or two miscellaneous

ORDER PAPER—*continued*

items which precede the main business of the day, such as motions connected with the business or sittings of the House, or notices of the intended presentation of bills (*see* BILL, PUBLIC). Then come those Orders of the day and notices of motions which it is intended should be proceeded with on this particular day (see ORDERS OF THE DAY). Where the standing orders make provision for a particular procedure to be followed in connection with any order of the day or notice of motion, a note of the procedure required to be followed is added, printed in italics. For example, a notice of motion to refer a matter to the Scottish or Welsh Grand Committees (*q.v.*) will carry the note "To be decided without amendment or debate pursuant to Standing Order No.— ". Some notices of motions are given contingently upon the passing of other motions; for example, when a notice of motion is given relating to the report of a select committee, it is usual to give notice of a motion "That the Report of the Committee be now considered" and secondly of the contingent motion expressing an opinion on the matter of the report. In such cases the notice of the second or contingent motion is printed in italics.

Notices of motions, which appear among the orders of the day in the position in which it is intended to move them, are numbered in one series with the orders; such a notice is however only an intimation of an intention to move, not (like an order of the day) a reminder of business which the House has ordered to be taken on that particular day. A notice of an amendment to a motion is printed immediately after the motion itself, and notices of motions to be moved (or of any amendments thereto) on an order of the day being read, are printed immediately below the order to which they relate.

If there is opposed private business set down for seven o'clock, a reminder to this effect (in addition to the reference to this business which appears at the head of the sheet) is given at the conclusion of the list of items of public business which are expected to be taken; and at this point will also be found the name of the member who has obtained the right to raise a matter on the motion for the adjournment, together with the subject to be raised.

Two more items complete the business for the day, the names of the public committees due to meet on that day, with the hours and places of meeting, and a list of the questions for written answer. (While questions for written answer are deemed to be asked on the day on which they appear in this list, and cannot be subsequently altered or withdrawn, an answer to them is not necessarily provided on the day on which they appear, although every effort is made to avoid undue delay in answering.)

Next come the "remaining Orders of the day and Notices of motions". The remaining Orders of the day are those items of business which the House has ordered as a matter of form to be taken on the day in question, but which the Government do not propose to proceed with on that day, and which will consequently normally be deferred to the next sitting day without being read. The " remaining Orders of the day " also include orders of the day deferred in this way from previous sitting days; and the " remaining notices of motions " include notices of motions which have not been proceeded with on the previous day and have been deemed to be renewed for the day in question.

Next comes the Private Business List (on blue paper), giving the titles of all private and provisional order bills which are to be proceeded with on the day of issue as well as the terms of any motions that are to be moved at the time of private business, *e.g.* amendments to the private business standing orders. The words " by Order " printed after the name of a private bill show that it has been put down by order of the House (after being objected to) and not on the parliamentary agent's notice (*see* BILL, PRIVATE). Bills to be taken at seven o'clock come lower on the page, and notices of committees on private bills come last. On the reverse side of the sheet is printed a list of notices given, and deposits made, in the Private Bill Office by parliamentary agents and others with regard to private business, in compliance with the standing orders.

The next section among the papers (on blue paper) is headed " Notices given on (the day before the day of publication) ". This consists mainly of questions of which notice was given by members on the previous day, but also includes notices of motions. The notices of questions are arranged, according to the days on which each item is to be taken, in the order in which they were given, but with the categories of questions for oral answer and questions for written answer kept separate. Then follow the notices of motion given for particular days, and finally the " early day " motions—so called because no particular day has been specified for them and they are grouped under the heading " an early day ". In the papers published on Saturday mornings, which include the Order Paper proper for the following Monday, there is no section entitled " Notices given on Friday . . . (the previous day) "; instead a complete list is given of all orders, notices and questions for the following Tuesday and for each succeeding day throughout the session. At the end of this list come the " early day " motions of which notice has been given on the previous day, a list of the subjects proposed to be raised by members on motions for the adjournment from the following Tuesday to the next succeeding Monday, and an index to all the " early day " motions which have been put down during the session and have neither been moved nor withdrawn.

After the papers described above come (on white paper) any lists of amendments to bills to be considered in committee or on

ORDER PAPER—*continued*

report on that day, followed by the Supplement to the Vote (on blue paper) which contains notices of amendments to bills which are to be considered in committee or on report on future days. The Supplement is followed by the minutes of proceedings of standing committees on the previous day and lists of members voting in each division in the House on the previous day.

The " Order Book of the House of Commons " (on white paper) is a separate but similar publication which appears in the afternoon of each sitting day. This contains all the orders, notices and questions appointed for the following and subsequent days, arranged in exactly the same form as in the list published every Saturday morning (*see above*), but with the omission of the " early day " motions, the index to them, and the list of subjects proposed to be raised on motions for the adjournment.

ORDER, POINT OF

A member who wishes to raise a point of order, that is, to call the attention of the Speaker or chairman to what he believes is a breach of order and, if necessary, to ask his opinion thereon, may interrupt another member's speech for the purpose ; the other member must sit down. It is undeniable that this right is often abused in order to raise matters that have nothing to do with order ; such attempts are quickly repressed by the occupant of the chair with the words " That is not a point of order ".

ORDERS OF THE DAY

A matter which has been appointed by an order of the House to be considered on a particular day is called an order of the day for the day for which it is appointed. If, as is commonly the case, several items of business are appointed for consideration on the same day, they are referred to collectively as " the orders of the day ". The public business each day consists of a number of orders of the day, together, it may be, with one or more notices of motions, the whole arranged by the Government (subject to the standing orders giving precedence on certain days to private members' business) in whatever order they think best. The number of items of business appointed by the House to be proceeded with on any particular day is usually greater than the number which it is actually desired to proceed with. Accordingly the orders of the day (and notices of motion) which the Government intend to proceed with on the day in question are set out in the order paper (*q.v.*) with a separate list of the " remaining Orders of the day (and notices of motions) ". The implication is that these remaining orders (and notices) will not be proceeded with on the day in question, although, the House having ordered them to be proceeded with that day, it is theoretically possible to proceed with them whether they have been marshalled in the list of orders which it is intended to proceed with or whether they appear among the list of " remaining Orders of the day ". In practice, however, a member of the Government moves the adjournment of the House when, or sometimes before, the orders of the day (and notices of motions) which have been selected to be proceeded with have been disposed of.

A notice of motion is not an order of the day ; it is no more than a notice given by a member of his intention to make a motion on a stated day. When that day comes, if the member is not called by the Speaker, or if on being called he is not there or does not move, no record appears of the motion in the Votes and Proceedings. But once it has been moved and the Speaker has proposed the question upon it, the House must either dispose of it or adjourn the debate to a future day. The order for resuming the adjourned debate is then an order of the day on which the debate has been ordered to be resumed.

When the first order standing on the order paper is reached (*see* BUSINESS, ORDER OF), the Speaker says, " The Clerk will now proceed to read the Orders of the Day ". The Clerk then reads the first order, *e.g.* " Finance Bill, second reading ". Proceedings on the order then begin with the member in charge rising and making the necessary motion. The remaining orders which have been selected for inclusion on the order paper are then normally gone through, with any motions there may be, in the order in which they appear on the paper.

The House is not bound to consider a particular item of business which it has appointed for a certain day, when that day comes. It may decide to adjourn, for example, before that business is reached; or it may defer, *i.e.* postpone consideration of, the business till a later day. But business which has been appointed to be taken as an order of the day in the future cannot be brought forward to an earlier day.

OUTLAWRIES BILL

At the beginning of every session the House of Commons gives a first reading to this bill, which never makes any further progress. This is done when the sitting is resumed in the afternoon after the House has returned from hearing the Queen's speech, between the passing of the sessional resolutions and the reading of the Queen's speech by the Speaker from the chair. The bill, whose title is " A Bill for the more effectual preventing Clandestine Outlawries ", seeks to ensure that persons in danger of being outlawed in personal actions shall receive due information thereof, and deals with matters long obsolete in English law. The Select Vestries Bill (" for the better regulation of Select Vestries ") is similarly read a first time every session in the House of Lords, under a standing order of the House.

OUTLAWRIES BILL—*continued*

The object of this practice of the Commons is generally thought (following Hatsell) to be to demonstrate and preserve their right to decide what business they shall do; but it has also been suggested (by Dwarris) that it is done in order to secure as soon as possible, by means of an ordinary parliamentary proceeding, the privileges appropriate to a Parliament in full session. A third explanation (given by Hakewill) is that it is to give the Speaker "seisin as it were of his place".

OVERSEAS OFFICE

An office of the House of Commons. The clerks are responsible for meeting requests from Commonwealth and other Parliaments for advice on questions of parliamentary procedure. They also make arrangements for the many clerks from overseas parliaments who come to Westminster to spend short periods of attachment to the Clerk's Department. One of the clerks makes arrangements for supplying staff from the Clerk's Department who serve temporarily at the sittings of the various European assemblies and act as secretary to the parliamentary delegations from the United Kingdom to those Assemblies.

PAIRS

If a member wishes to be absent from the House, he may arrange with a member of the opposite party, who also wishes to be absent, that neither shall attend the House, or at least vote in a division, for an agreed time. They are then said to be "paired", each member being the other's "pair". This is a custom of long standing, though not recognised by the rules of the House; the arrangement is usually made through the whips of the party to which each member belongs.

PAPERS, MOVING FOR

An expedient made use of by a member of the House of Lords who wishes to ventilate a subject without asking the House to express any opinion thereon. He either gives notice of his intention on a day named to call attention to the subject "and to move for papers" or gives notice of a question, adding at the end of the question the words "and to move for papers". On the day named he makes his speech when his name is called by the Clerk of the Parliaments or, if he has given notice of a question, after it has been answered, and concludes by moving "that there be laid before the House papers relating to the subject". A debate may then ensue. The mover has a right of reply. Motions for papers are usually withdrawn.

PAPERS, PARLIAMENTARY

Accounts and papers are delivered in large numbers every session to the House of Commons for the information and use of members. These " papers ", as they are generally comprehensively called, are in theory, as they were actually in former times, presented by ministers, who are supposed to bring them into the House and deliver them to the Clerk ; in cases where no minister is responsible, a paper is sent to the Clerk, who is supposed to lay it on the Table himself. Formerly, such papers were delivered at the bar by officers of the departments. After a paper has been presented it is ordered to lie upon the Table (for the information of members).

For convenience sake, all papers are now sent direct, either by hand or by post, to the Votes and Proceedings Office in the House of Commons ; there they are examined, and their presentation is recorded in the Votes and Proceedings and subsequently in the Journal. On the day following presentation, they are sent to the Library, where they are kept for the use of members. The majority, however, are printed by the Stationery Office and copies can be obtained by members at the Vote Office and by the public through the Stationery Office.

The papers may be divided broadly into four categories. First there are the estimates, including main and supplementary estimates, and votes of credit ; with these may be classed statements of excess on votes in the previous year.

Secondly, there are accounts. Among these are the national accounts—that is, the Finance Accounts and the Appropriation Accounts—and also numerous accounts of particular funds whose expenditure is not provided for in the annual estimates but under permanent statutory authority. These include accounts of government loans to foreign countries, of subsidies to home industries (such as the shipbuilding industry), of nationalised industries and semi-public bodies such as the General Medical Council and the Thames Conservancy. In many cases they are accompanied by a report from the Comptroller and Auditor General ; and they may be appended to the annual reports which the administering authority is under statutory obligation to make to Parliament concerning its activities.

Thirdly, there is a variety of reports, memoranda and statements of government policy. Some of these are annual reports, like those mentioned in the last paragraph, presented under statutory authority ; others are reports of Royal Commissions or departmental committees, presented by command of Her Majesty as " blue books " or " white papers " ; others again are memoranda in which the Government puts before members, also in the form of white papers, information which has been asked for in the House, or statements of future policy on particular subjects; a recent development in this field is the issue, in the form of

PAPERS, PARLIAMENTARY—*continued*
"green papers," of Government memoranda which are intended to form the basis for discussion rather than definitive statements of policy. In former times, much of the information thus supplied by government departments was furnished in the form of returns to addresses or orders moved by the members interested; nowadays, this is more usually done by command papers prepared at the direction of the minister concerned.

Finally, there is the most numerous class of all, the rules, orders in council, schemes, etc., which are made by, or by the Queen on the advice of, the various ministers or other branches of the executive* in exercise of legislative authority delegated to them by Acts of Parliament, and presented to the House in pursuance of those Acts. In most cases the authority is given by the Act itself, but it is sometimes supplied by a regulation or order, itself made under statute, or by a measure under the Church of England Assembly (Powers) Act 1919. The majority of these orders, etc., deal with comparatively minor matters, and, once made, they come immediately into force. They are presented to both Houses and, when once they have been ordered to lie upon the Table, no further action is taken upon them in Parliament. There are, however, two classes of such orders, etc., which deal with more important matters. The first class consists of those which need to be confirmed by resolution of one or both Houses, either before they come into force, or within a certain period after they are made. Examples of this are to be found in orders imposing or increasing import duties and purchase tax, and orders fixing rates of agricultural guarantees and subsidies.

In the other class are those which, though they come into force when made, are liable to be annulled as a result of the passing of a resolution by either House within a specified period after presentation. Most of these, being statutory instruments (*q.v.*), are liable to annulment within forty days, beginning with the day of presentation. In other cases, the period during which they may be annulled is laid down in the Act under which they are made and presented; it may be defined by reference to days on which the House has sat, by simple reference to the calendar, or by some other method.

When a paper has been presented to the House, a record of the fact, together with a brief description of the paper, appears in an appendix to the Votes and Proceedings on the following day, and this includes the statement that the paper was ordered to lie upon the Table and in some cases, to be printed. A similar entry also appears in due course in the Journal.

* In some cases the powers are exercised by non-governmental statutory bodies, *e.g.* the General Synod of the Church of England or the governing bodies of universities or colleges.

A weekly list is also published of all statutory instruments and other rules, orders, etc., which are liable to annulment during a specified period which has not yet expired.

Although most of the papers are printed, only in some cases is an order made by the House to that effect; these are known as "House of Commons Papers" and are numbered in a series accordingly; this series also includes the reports of joint, select and standing committees. The rest are printed as "Stationery Office Papers" if they are presented in pursuance of a statute, and in the Command Paper series if they are command papers. Many papers are now presented "in dummy"; that is, instead of a copy of the paper itself being delivered to the Votes and Proceedings Office, either the title page is sent, or else a plain sheet of paper, bearing the title of the paper (*see* DUMMY). This practice arose, no doubt, from an anxiety to ensure that the contents of a paper should not by any chance become known before it had been received by the House; since the premature publication might be regarded as a gross discourtesy to the House.

Most of the papers which are presented to the House of Commons are also presented to the House of Lords. Papers are received by the Journal Office of the House of Lords, and are recorded in the Lords Minutes, and subsequently in the Lords Journals. As in the Commons, they are ordered to lie upon the Table and, if necessary, to be printed; they may also be liable to annulment as described above. After presentation they pass into the custody of the Librarian.

PARLIAMENT ACT

The power of the House of Commons to insist on a public bill being passed into law without the assent of the Lords is derived from the Parliament Act 1911, as amended by the Parliament Act 1949. Different conditions are laid down according to whether the bill is a money bill or not.

(1) Any bill which the Speaker certifies as dealing solely with certain matters relating to finance (including the imposition or regulation of taxation, the imposition of charges on the Consolidated Fund or the National Loans Fund or on money provided by Parliament, and the appropriation or issue of public money) may, unless it is passed by the Lords without amendment within one month of being sent to them by the Commons, receive the royal assent and become law, without the Lords having consented thereto.

(2) If a bill is passed (in the same form) by the Commons in two successive sessions, it may receive the royal assent and become law, notwithstanding that the Lords have not consented to it, provided that one year has elapsed between the first time that the bill received a second reading in the Commons and the

PARLIAMENT ACT—*continued*

second time that it receives a third reading in that House. A bill prolonging the duration of Parliament beyond five years is expressly excluded from the operation of the Act.

It should be noted that in the case of bills of both classes the Act says that the bill shall be presented to His Majesty for his royal assent " unless the House of Commons shall direct to the contrary ". This must mean that the Commons are not obliged to insist on a money bill being presented for royal assent within one month or debarred from considering amendments made by the Lords to such a bill. In the case of bills other than money bills, the Act directs the Speaker to certify the bill as the same in the second session as that passed in the first, but allows such changes as are made necessary by the lapse of time—for example, the substitution of a later year for the original year in the title. There is also provision for the incorporation of amendments agreeable to both Houses.

It is provided that the Committee of Selection shall at the beginning of every session nominate two members whom the Speaker shall consult, if practicable, before giving his certificate to a money bill.

Since the passing of the original Act in 1911, only three bills (none of them being money bills) have become law under the procedure which it laid down. These are (1) the Government of Ireland Act 1914, which gave home rule to Ireland, but never came into force, being repealed by the Government of Ireland Act 1920, which in turn was largely superseded by the Irish Free State Agreement Act 1922 and the Irish Free State Constitution Act 1922; (2) the Church of Wales Act 1914, which disestablished the Church in Wales, and came into force in 1920; and (3) the Parliament Act 1949, which reduced from two years to one the period during which the House of Lords could delay the royal assent to a bill passed by the Commons.

PARLIAMENT CHAMBER

The correct title of the debating chamber of the House of Lords, so called because it is used as a meeting place by the constituent parts of the High Court of Parliament, namely, the Queen, the House of Lords and the House of Commons. The two Houses never *deliberate* together; they only come together in order to hear the formal communications which the Queen makes to them, either in person or through a commission of peers appointed to act on her behalf. These communications include the Queen's speeches at the opening and close of each session of Parliament, and the giving of the royal assent which converts a bill into an Act of Parliament or statute (when the royal assent is signified by commission (*see* ROYAL ASSENT)).

PARLIAMENTARY AGENT

A person (usually a solicitor or a barrister) professionally employed in the preparation and promotion of private bills and other legislation of local application and in opposition thereto. Parliamentary agents advise parties who wish to obtain local and personal or private Acts, provisional orders (*q.v.*) or special procedure orders (*q.v.*) whether Parliament or the government department concerned is likely to give them the powers they seek and what steps they should take to obtain such Acts or orders. They also advise parties whose interests would be affected by such legislation as to what steps they should take if they wish to oppose it. They draft bills, amendments, notices, petitions, memorials and all other documents required in the promotion of, or opposition to, private bills, etc. They are allowed to conduct their clients' cases before the Examiners of Petitions for Private Bills, the Standing Orders Committees of both Houses, and committees on unopposed private bills or provisional order bills—before which officers and committees counsel are not allowed to appear—as well as before the Court of Referees, committees on opposed private bills or provisional order bills and joint committees on special procedure petitions. They are personally liable to each House and to the Speaker or the Lord Chairman for the observance of all the rules of that House as well as of all rules laid down by those officers, and for the payment of all fees due from their clients.

There are two classes of parliamentary agents: (1) those who are entitled to practise both in promoting and opposing private bills, provisional orders and special procedure orders, and (2) those who are entitled to practise in opposing such bills, etc., only. But no person may practise as a parliamentary agent of either class unless he has been registered as such agent in the Private Bill Office of the House of Commons and the Committee and Private Bill Office of the House of Lords. It is a breach of privilege for any person who has not been registered as a parliamentary agent to call himself one.

Before a person is registered as a parliamentary agent entitled to practise both in promoting and opposing bills he must satisfy the Speaker and the Lord Chairman that he has a practical knowledge of the private bill standing orders and procedure of their respective Houses. Any person who is actually employed in opposing a private bill, hybrid bill, provisional order or special procedure order is entitled to be registered as a parliamentary agent entitled to practise in opposing bills, etc., only, but if he is neither a solicitor nor a writer to the signet, he must, unless he has been previously registered as a parliamentary agent, produce a certificate of his respectability from a member of parliament, a justice of the peace, a barrister or a solicitor. Registration as a parliamentary agent entitled to practise in opposing bills only

PARLIAMENTARY AGENT—*continued*
ceases to have effect when the session comes to an end, *i.e.* there is no permanent category of parliamentary agents entitled so to practise.

Before any person is registered as a parliamentary agent in either House he must sign a declaration engaging to obey all the rules of that House and any rules prescribed by the Speaker or the Lord Chairman, as the case may be, and to pay all fees due from his clients, and, if required, must enter into a bond in a penalty of £500 with two sureties of £250 each.

Any agent who breaks the rules of either House or is guilty of professional misconduct is liable to be suspended or prohibited from practising by the Speaker or the Lord Chairman. A member of the House of Commons may not practise as, or be in partnership with, a parliamentary agent.

The charges which a parliamentary agent is entitled to make are regulated by the Speaker and the Clerk of the Parliaments under statutory authority and his bill of costs may be taxed (*see* TAXING OFFICER).

PARLIAMENTARY BAR

Those barristers who practise before parliamentary committees.

PARLIAMENTARY COMMISSIONER FOR ADMINISTRATION

An officer appointed under the Parliamentary Commissioner Act 1967 to investigate any action of any government department taken in the exercise of its administrative functions. The Act provides, however, that he may investigate these actions only where a complaint has been made in writing by a member of the public to a member of the House of Commons, and referred by him to the Commissioner with the consent of the complainant. Matters in respect of which the complainant has or has had a remedy by way of legal action or appeal to a legal tribunal may not be examined by the Commissioner except in cases where it would be unreasonable to expect the complainant to resort to his legal rights. The matter of the complaint must normally be referred to the Commissioner within twelve months of the complainant's first notice of the matter, and the matter must relate to a United Kingdom resident.

When the Commissioner receives a complaint he has full discretion, within the limits described above, as to whether and how far to investigate the matter. He must give the department concerned an opportunity to comment on any complaint which he investigates, but apart from that he may conduct his investigation in any way that he thinks fit. He may require the Department concerned and other persons to furnish any information or documents, except where Cabinet proceedings are concerned, and he has power to take evidence on oath.

The Commissioner makes an annual general report to both Houses of Parliament of his proceedings during the year. If he receives a complaint which he decides not to investigate he reports his reasons to the member who referred the complaint to him. In cases which he investigates he sends a report of the results to the member who referred the complaint to him and to the department concerned and he may also make a report of the results to both Houses.

The Commissioner is sometimes referred to as the " ombudsman " as his functions are analagous to those exercised, notably in Scandinavian countries, by an official known there by that name.

PARLIAMENTARY COMMISSIONER FOR ADMINISTRATION, SELECT COMMITTEE ON

A Select Committee, now appointed in every session by the House of Commons, to examine the reports laid before the House by the Parliamentary Commissioner for Administration (*q.v.*), and matters in connection therewith. The function of the Committee is to take up with the department concerned any case on which the Commissioner has made an individual report to both Houses as provided by the Parliamentary Commissioner Act 1967. In this way the departments have an opportunity to comment on the Commissioner's findings ; and the Committee report the views they form in the light both of the Commissioner's report and of the departments' comments.

PARLIAMENTARY COUNSEL

Barristers employed to draft government bills and government amendments to such bills. They are established civil servants. They are required to give the whole of their time to the public service and are not allowed to engage in private practice. After a government bill has been introduced, the draftsman concerned scrutinises amendments of which members have given notice with a view to advising the minister in charge of the bill as to the meaning of the amendments and their effect on the bill. The parliamentary counsel are frequently called upon to advise chairmen of standing committees, the Chairman of Ways and Means and the Speaker as to the meaning and effect of proposed amendments. The Parliamentary Counsel's Office is subordinate to the Treasury. The permanent staff at present consists of twenty barristers and solicitors.

PEER

There are five classes of peers, viz. (1) peers of England, *i.e.* holders of peerages created before the Union of England and

PEER—*continued*

Scotland, (2) peers of Scotland, *i.e.* descendants and representatives of persons who held peerages in Scotland before the union of Scotland with England, (3) peers of Great Britain, *i.e.* holders of peerages created after the Union of England and Scotland and before the Union of Great Britain and Ireland, (4) peers of Ireland and (5) peers of the United Kingdom, *i.e.* holders of peerages created since the union with Ireland other than Irish peerages. The right to create peers is one of the royal prerogatives. The Queen can create any number of new peers of the United Kingdom, but she cannot create a new peer of England, Scotland or Great Britain, and she can create only a limited number of new Irish peerages. (The last Irish peerage created was that bestowed on the Hon. George Nathaniel Curzon, who on November 11, 1898, was created a baron of the Kingdom of Ireland, on being appointed Viceroy of India.) Peers may be created by the sending of a writ of summons or by letters patent under the great seal. The latter mode is now always employed, except where the eldest son of a peer is called up to the House of Lords in his father's lifetime.

Peers of England, Scotland, Great Britain or the United Kingdom are entitled to sit and vote in the House of Lords, but peers of Ireland are not so entitled. The peers of Ireland were formerly represented by twenty-eight of their number elected for life by their fellow Irish peers, but the abolition of the office of Clerk of the Crown and Hanaper* when the Irish Free State was established in 1922 destroyed the machinery for filling vacancies among the Irish representative peers and none now survive.

A peer is not summoned and is disqualified for sitting or voting in the House if he is under twenty-one, or is an alien and has not been naturalised, or if he is a bankrupt, or has been convicted of treason and has neither received a pardon nor served his sentence. Save in the cases mentioned, every peer of England, Scotland, Great Britain or the United Kingdom is entitled to a writ of summons. A peeress in her own right is entitled to sit and vote in the House of Lords.

Peers other than Irish peers are ineligible for election as members of the House of Commons. An Irish peer is eligible for election for any constituency in the United Kingdom.

Peers other than Irish peers may not vote at parliamentary elections.

By the Appellate Jurisdiction Act 1876, as amended by subsequent legislation, the Queen appoints Lords of Appeal in Ordinary (*q.v.*) who rank as barons and are members of the House of Lords for life, but whose dignity does not descend to their heirs. To qualify for appointment as a Lord of Appeal in Ordinary a

* Or, according to some authorities, that of Lord Chancellor of Ireland.

person must either have held high judicial office for at least two years or have been in practice at the bar for not less than fifteen years. Life peerages enabling the holder to sit and vote in the House of Lords may also be created by the Queen under the Life Peerages Act 1958. Such peerages may be conferred on women as well as men.

A peer, as one of the hereditary counsellors of the Crown, has a right of audience of the Queen. He cannot be arrested except on a criminal charge or for refusing to give security for the peace. Peers are exempt from serving on juries. The right of peers accused of treason or felony to be tried by their peers was abolished by the Criminal Justice Act 1948.

Peers who are lords of parliament have the same privileges as members of Parliament.

Peeresses in their own right other than Irish peeresses have all the privileges of a peer including, since the enactment of the Peerage Act 1963, the right to receive a summons to attend the House of Lords and to sit and vote in that House. Equally with peers they are ineligible for election as members of the House of Commons and may not vote at parliamentary elections. Irish peeresses in their own right and peeresses by marriage have all the privileges of a peer except the right of sitting and voting in the House of Lords. They are eligible for election as members of the House of Commons and may vote at parliamentary elections.

When a peer dies his heir is not summoned to parliament automatically ; he must apply to the Lord Chancellor for a writ of summons. If there is any doubt as to whether the applicant is the rightful heir, the Lord Chancellor will decline to issue a writ, leaving it to him to petition the Queen for one. Such a petition is referred to the Attorney General for examination and report. If he thinks that there is a *prima facie* case, he reports that in his opinion the petition should be referred to the House of Lords. The petition, together with the Attorney General's report, is then referred to the House of Lords, which refers it to the Committee for Privileges (*q.v.*). The procedure is the same in cases (*a*) where a person claims to be heir to a dormant peerage, *i.e.* a peerage in respect of which no writ of summons has been issued for some time because the line of male heirs has been lost sight of, or (*b*) where a person who claims to be one of the co-heirs to a peerage which has fallen into abeyance asks that the abeyance may be terminated in his favour. Only peerages created by writ of summons can fall into abeyance because they descend to the heirs-general of the holder. Such a peerage falls into abeyance when the holder dies leaving no son and several daughters, or, to be exact, female descendants but no male issue. It remains in suspense until all the lines but one become extinct or the

PEER—*continued*

Sovereign terminates the abeyance in favour of one of the co-heirs.

Under the Peerage Act 1963, a person who succeeds to a peerage may disclaim his peerage for his life by delivering an "instrument of disclaimer" to the Lord Chancellor. (Delivery of the instrument is effected by presenting it to the Clerk of the Crown in Chancery.) The right to disclaim must normally be exercised within twelve months from the date of succession. In the case of minors or persons incapacitated by bodily or mental infirmity time does not begin to run against them until they come of age or cease to be incapacitated. A peer who succeeds after the Act comes into force forfeits this right to disclaim by applying for a writ of summons to the House of Lords. A member of the House of Commons who succeeds to a peerage is allowed a month from his succession, and a person who succeeds to a peerage after having been nominated as a candidate at a parliamentary election or who, after succeeding to a peerage, is nominated as a candidate at a parliamentary election for which the writ was issued before his succession, is allowed a month from his election in which to disclaim his peerage. During this period he is exempt from disqualification for membership of the House of Commons, but may not sit or vote in that House. The effect of the disclaimer of a peerage is to divest the holder (and his wife) of all right and interest to or in the peerage and all incidents, etc., attaching thereto and to render him eligible for election to the House of Commons. A peer who has disclaimed his peerage cannot subsequently be created a hereditary peer. A person upon whom a peerage, whether hereditary or for life, has been conferred cannot disclaim it.

PERSONAL BILL

A private bill which relates solely to the estate, property, status or style of an individual or in any other way to his personal affairs. The most common type of personal bill is the estate bill (*q.v.*). In 1947, however, a petition was presented to the House of Lords for leave to bring in a bill to enable the petitioner to marry the former wife of his brother who had been divorced by her and was still living, but the Personal Bills Committee reported adversely on the application and the bill was not proceeded with. A bill to alter the Christian name of an individual (which is said to be unalterable save by Act of Parliament) would be a personal bill.

Personal bills are in practice invariably introduced in the House of Lords. The promoters are required to deposit a petition for leave to bring in the bill, with a printed copy of the proposed bill annexed, in the Committee and Private Bill Office of the House of Lords. This petition stands referred to the Personal Bills

Committee (*q.v.*), which reports whether the objects of the bill are proper to be enacted by a personal bill and whether the provisions of the bill are proper for carrying its purposes into effect and what amendments, if any, are required. (If the proposed bill affects private interests in Scotland, the Personal Bills Committee must refer the petition to two judges of the Court of Session, who hear the parties and receive proof of the allegations made in the preamble of the bill and such consents of the parties interested and acceptances of trusts as are tendered. They then report to the Personal Bills Committee the state of the case and their opinion thereon and what amendments, if any, are required in the bill. The Personal Bills Committee must not report on the petition for the bill until they have received and considered the judges' report.)

If the report of the Personal Bills Committee is favourable, the bill may then be presented and read the first time ; if the report is adverse, the bill is not presented at all. The proceedings on a personal bill after first reading are not materially different from the proceedings on a private bill of the ordinary kind. Personal bills are rarely opposed. If such a bill is opposed the Lord Chairman fixes the time by which petitions against the bill must be presented.

When a personal bill is received by the Commons from the Lords it is referred to the Examiners of Petitions for Private Bills like any other private bill, but if the Chairman of Ways and Means reports that the bill relates to the estate, property, status, style, or personal affairs of an individual, the reference to the Examiners is discharged. The subsequent procedure is the same as that on any other private bill.

PERSONAL BILLS COMMITTEE

A committee appointed by the House of Lords at the commencement of every session to which all petitions for personal bills (*q.v.*) stand referred. It consists of the Lord Chairman and six other lords. Three form a quorum.

PERSONAL EXPLANATION

A member who wishes to explain, excuse, justify or apologise for, his conduct is allowed to make a statement, known as a personal explanation, immediately after question time. Examples of such statements are those made by ex-ministers explaining their reasons for resigning office, and those made by members whose conduct has been subject to criticism. These statements are made by the indulgence of the House, and not of right, since there is no question before the House at the time, and no debate can take place.

PERSONS, PAPERS AND RECORDS, POWER TO SEND FOR

A power which is given by the House of Commons to nearly all select committees except committees on hybrid bills or private bills. It gives the committee power to summon any person other than a member of either House or an officer of the House of Lords to appear before the committee and to bring with him specified documents in his possession. If a committee has not been given this power, it cannot request witnesses to attend or even examine witnesses who appear voluntarily before it without receiving power for the purpose from the House. Members of a select committee on a private, provisional order, or hybrid bill may, however, ask questions of any witnesses who are called by either the promoters or the opponents of the bill.

PETITION, PUBLIC

Public petition is a somewhat misleading term, all petitions except those which relate to private bills (*see* PETITIONS RELATING TO PRIVATE BILLS), provisional order bills (*see* BILL, PROVISIONAL ORDER) and special procedure orders (*q.v.*) being classed as public petitions regardless of whether they relate to public measures and matters of general policy or pray for redress of local or personal grievances.

A petition to either House of Parliament may be on parchment or paper. If a petition is in any language other than English it must be accompanied by a translation certified as correct by the member who presents the petition. A petition to the House of Commons must be written by hand ; a petition to the House of Lords need not. There must be no erasures or interlineations in a petition.

A petition should begin : " To the Right Honourable the Lords Spiritual and Temporal in Parliament assembled ", or " To the Honourable the Commons of the United Kingdom of Great Britain and Northern Ireland in Parliament assembled ", according as it is intended for the House of Lords or the House of Commons, and should continue : " The humble petition of A.B., gentleman (*or other occupation*), sheweth that (*or* as follows) ". A peer petitioning either House omits the word " humble ". If there are a great number of petitioners they should describe themselves in general terms, *e.g.* " the inhabitants of (such-and-such a place) ". The facts which the petitioners wish to bring to the notice of the House should then be set out, and the petition should conclude with a prayer, *i.e.* a request to the House to do or refrain from doing something. The words "and your petitioners, as in duty bound, will ever pray ", are often added after the prayer but they are not necessary.

Petitions must be signed by the petitioners themselves. One person cannot sign for another unless the latter is unable to sign owing to sickness. If the petitioners are a corporate body with a common seal, the seal must be affixed to the petition. One person cannot sign as the agent or on behalf of another unless he holds a power of attorney, but where a person signs a petition on his own behalf as well as for others, *e.g.* where the chairman of a public meeting signs on behalf of the persons there present, the petition may be received as a petition from him alone. A petitioner must write his address after his signature ; otherwise it will not be counted. (This rule does not apply to petitions to the House of Lords).

A petition must be signed on the sheet on which the prayer is written or have at least one signature on that sheet. Sheets containing additional signatures should be headed with at least the prayer, otherwise the signatures will not be counted. (This rule does not apply to petitions to the House of Lords). The heading on such sheets may be printed, typewritten, etc.

Affidavits, letters and other documents must not be attached to petitions.

A petition must not contain any indecorous or intemperate expressions or any language disrespectful to the House to which it is addressed or to any member of that House, or any offensive imputations on the character or conduct of the Sovereign, Parliament, the other House, the Courts of Justice or any other constituted authority. It must not refer to anything said by a member in either House or to any motion of which notice has been given unless the notice has been printed in the order book. It must not relate to a matter in which the House cannot interfere and must not ask for something which the House has not power to do, *e.g.* some exercise of the royal prerogative.

A foreigner may not petition either House unless he lives in the United Kingdom. British subjects, however, living abroad may petition the House. A member may himself petition the House, but his petition must be presented by another member. A paper setting out the rules regarding the form and character of public petitions, to which a form of petition is subjoined, is available to members at the beginning of the session and copies may be obtained at any time from the Vote Office.

Public petitions must be presented by members, except petitions to the House of Commons from the Corporation of London, which may be presented at the bar by the sheriffs. The last instance of a petition being presented by the sheriffs of the City of London was on February 16, 1948, when a petition by the Corporation of London praying that the Representation of the People Bill might not be allowed to pass into law in its present form and that it might be amended so as to leave undisturbed the separate representation of the City of London was so presented.

A member cannot present a petition from himself. He may, however, present a petition which he has signed in a representa-

PETITION, PUBLIC—*continued*

tive capacity, *e.g.* as chairman of a County Council. The Speaker cannot present a petition to the House. A member is not obliged to present a petition, even from a constituent. It is the duty of the member before presenting a petition to read it through and make sure that it is in order. If he is not satisfied of this, he should decline to present the petition. A member of the House of Commons who is in doubt whether a petition is in order should consult the Clerk of Petitions in the Journal Office or the clerks in the Table Office.

Petitions may be presented to the House of Commons either formally at the end of private business and before the beginning of question time or informally by dropping them into the bag kept at the back of the Speaker's chair at any time while the House is sitting. A member must write his name at the head of the the petition before he presents it.

If a member wishes to present a petition formally, he must enter his name on the public petitions list which is kept in the Table Office; before doing so he should have the petition examined by one of the clerks in the Journal Office to make sure that it is in order, otherwise he will not be allowed to enter his name on the list. The Speaker will then call him when the time arrives for presenting petitions. In presenting the petition the member must confine himself to stating from whom the petition comes, how many signatures it bears, and what its material allegations are, and to reading the prayer. He may not read the whole petition or any part of it except the prayer. If the petition does not appear to contain anything in breach of the privileges of the House and seems fit to be received, the Speaker at once requests the member to bring the petition to the Table.

When the petition has been brought to the Table, the member who presented it, or any other member, may move that it be read. If such a motion is made, the Speaker, without putting any question, directs the Clerk to read the petition. But the petition cannot be debated unless it complains of a present personal grievance urgently requiring instant remedy, or of a matter affecting the privileges of the House, or contains charges against a member. No petition has been held to come within the first category since 1844.

All petitions, unless they are taken into consideration forthwith or appointed for consideration on a future day, stand referred to the Committee on Public Petitions (*q.v.*). This committee has power to direct the printing of any petitions or parts of petitions which appear to require it. But if the petition relates to a subject with respect to which the member who presented it has given notice of a motion, the petition, if not printed by the committee, may be printed and circulated with the Votes and

Proceedings on the motion of the member who presented it. Such a motion requires notice and is not entitled to precedence.

All petitions whether presented formally or informally are examined, after presentation, by the officers of the House and if they are found to contravene any rule of the House or to be duplicates of petitions already presented in the current session, are not recorded in the Votes and Proceedings as having been presented and are returned to the members who presented them.

Before presenting a petition which contains a charge against another member, a member should give the member in question notice privately of the day on which he intends to present it in order that the latter may have an opportunity of replying to the charge at once.

A petition which asks for a grant of public money or the release of a debt to the Crown or for the remission of duties payable by any person or for compensation for losses out of the public revenues will not be received by the House of Commons unless the recommendation of the Crown is signified by a minister. Petitions for legislation involving expenditure, however, do not require the royal recommendation.

A petition to the House of Lords is usually presented at the beginning of public business unless it relates to a public bill, in which event it may be presented immediately before the motion that the bill be now read a second (or third) time or that the House do now resolve itself into a committee on the bill is moved.

A lord who presents a petition may speak on its subject matter when presenting the petition, but the petition is not read unless the lord who presents it himself reads it in the course of his speech. Although comments may be made at the time by other lords, no *debate* can take place on the subject matter of the petition unless the lord presenting the petition has given previous notice of his intention either to call attention to such and such a subject and to present a petition or simply to present a petition relating to such and such a subject.

Petitions for presentation to either House may be sent post free to members of that House provided they are sent without covers or in covers open at the sides, marked on the outside " parliamentary petitions ", and that they do not weigh over 2 lb.

PETITIONS FOR OR RELATING TO PRIVATE BILLS

Petitions for or relating to private bills are presented by being deposited in the Private Bill Office of the House of Commons or the Committee and Private Bill Office of the House of Lords. They may be deposited by the petitioners themselves or by their agents. The rules applicable to petitions generally (*see* PETITION, PUBLIC) apply to these petitions also except that petitions against private bills need not be written by hand.

PETITIONS FOR OR RELATING TO PRIVATE BILLS—*continued*

Petitions for private bills, that is, petitions for leave to introduce private bills other than personal bills (*see* PERSONAL BILL) or late bills which it has been decided shall begin in the House of Lords, must be presented to the House of Commons on or before November 27. A petition for a private bill must be signed by the party promoting the bill or some of them and a printed copy of the proposed bill must be annexed to the petition. (If the bill is promoted by a limited company, corporation or local authority, the common seal of that body must be affixed to the petition and is in itself sufficient without any signatures.)

Petitions against private bills are presented by parties other than members of Parliament who wish to oppose a private bill. If the bill is to begin in the House of Commons they must be deposited on or before January 30 or in certain cases within ten days from the second reading of the bill. In order to secure a hearing the petitioners must pray to be heard either in person or by their counsel or agents and the grounds on which they object to the bill must be distinctly specified.

Petitions in favour of a private bill may be deposited at any time after the introduction of the bill. Petitioners in favour of a bill have not the right of appearing before the committee on the bill. Counsel may allude to the fact of such petitions having been presented, but may not examine or cross-examine with reference to their contents, signatures, etc.

Petitions against alterations, that is, petitions by parties who object to amendments proposed to be made in a private bill (whether they are proposed by the promoters of the bill and contained in the " filled-up bill "* or are sought by petitioners against the bill), may be presented at any time before the bill has been reported to the House by a committee. (Petitions against alterations are sometimes presented by parties who are apprehensive of opposition by other parties to amendments which have been made to the bill in the House in which it was introduced for the protection of the petitioners.) Petitioners against alterations sought by opponents of a private bill are not heard by the committee unless the promoters are ready to concede the amendments or do not care whether they are made or not.

* The " filled-up bill " is a printed copy of the bill showing the amendments which the promoters propose to ask the committee to make in the bill. It must be signed by the agent for the bill and deposited in the Private Bill Office of the House of Commons, or if the bill was introduced in the House of Lords in the Committee and Private Bill Office of that House, two clear days before the committee on the bill is due to meet (the day before if the bill was unopposed). Copies of the filled-up bill are laid before the members when the committee meets.

Petitions for additional provision are presented by promoters of private bills who wish to insert additional provisions in such bills. A printed copy of the provision proposed to be added must be annexed to such a petition. Petitions for additional provision must be endorsed by the Chairman of Ways and Means or the Lord Chairman according as the bill is pending in the House of Commons or the House of Lords. In practice they require the approval of both these officers. Petitions cannot be presented for the insertion of additional provision in bills brought from the other House. Petitions against additional provision may be presented at any time before the bill is reported by the committee.

Petitions for late bills, that is, petitions for leave to introduce a private bill (other than a personal bill), a petition for which has not been presented on or before November 27, can only be presented with leave of the Lord Chairman and the Chairman of Ways and Means who decide in which House the bill shall be introduced. Petitions against a late bill must be deposited within ten days from the first reading of the bill.

Petitions relating to Standing Orders are either petitions praying that particular standing orders should be dispensed with or petitions opposing such applications. The former category includes, amongst others, petitions from opponents of private bills whose petitions have not been deposited within the time limited praying that they may be heard before the committee on the bill.

Petitions against provisional order bills, hybrid bills and special procedure orders, and counter petitions to petitions against special procedure orders are presented to the House of Commons and the House of Lords by being deposited in the Private Bill Office of the former House and the Committee and Private Bill Office of the latter respectively.

PETITIONS, PUBLIC, COMMITTEE ON

A select committee appointed by the House of Commons at the beginning of each session. To this Committee are referred all petitions presented to the House with certain exceptions, of which petitions deposited in the Private Bill Office form the chief. The function of the Committee is to classify and prepare abstracts of the petitions referred to it in whatever manner the Committee considers best suited to convey to the House all requisite information respecting their contents, and to report such information to the House from time to time. The Committee is given power to direct the printing in full of any petitions or parts of petitions which appear to require it. If the Committee orders a petition to be printed, it is printed as an appendix to the Committee's report. The Committee has no power to inquire into

PETITIONS, PUBLIC, COMMITTEE ON—*continued*
the truth of the allegations of any petition. The Committee usually consists of fifteen members. The quorum is three.

PRAYERS

In both Houses the sitting begins with prayers, which are read in the House of Commons by the Speaker's Chaplain and in the House of Lords by a bishop, or, if no bishop is present, by the Lord Chancellor or Lord Speaker. The Speaker does not take the chair of the House of Commons until prayers are finished; instead he occupies the Clerk's place at the Table. Members stand at their places among the benches on the floor of the House. The Clerks do not enter the Chamber, nor are strangers admitted to the public galleries, until after prayers. If a member wishes to secure for himself a particular seat in the chamber at any sitting he may place on it a card (obtained from an attendant) before the meeting of the House, and must then be present during prayers to establish his right. If he must attend a committee during prayers, he may use a pink card, which secures his right in his absence.

The expression "prayer" is also commonly applied to any motion, in pursuance of a statute, for an address requesting the annulment of a statutory instrument. It is so called because the address "prays" that the Queen "will be graciously pleased" to use her statutory powers in the desired manner. Any motion to oppose or annul a statutory instrument, or other rule, order or regulation is now, by extension, commonly referred to as a prayer.

PREAMBLE

An introductory paragraph in which the reasons for introducing the bill are set forth. Public bills now rarely contain a preamble, but a preamble is always inserted in private bills. The preamble of a private bill sets forth the facts upon which the application for the intended Act is founded, and as these are the whole inducement for the enactment, their truth must be established by evidence. The procedure in committee in regard to the preamble differs in the case of public and private bills. In the case of a public bill, the preamble stands* postponed until after the clauses of the bill and the schedules, if any, have been considered, when it is amended, if necessary, so as to make it consistent with the provisions of the bill as passed by the committee. In the case of a private bill, however, if the bill is opposed, the preamble is considered before the clauses, counsel for the bill calling witnesses to prove the allegations contained in the preamble. Petitioners against the bill are then heard, and, after counsel for the bill has

* In the House of Lords a question "that the preamble of the bill be postponed" is formally put at the beginning of the proceedings in committee.

replied, the committee decides whether the preamble has or has not been proved. Unless the committee finds that the preamble has been proved the bill can make no further progress.

PRESS GALLERY

A gallery for the accommodation of reporters. There is one in each House. In the House of Commons the Press Gallery is above and behind the Speaker's Chair.

PREVIOUS QUESTION

A motion the object of which is to avoid coming to a decision on the subject under discussion. It differs from other motions in that it is not moved in the terms in which it is proposed to the House. The mover merely says, " I move the previous question"; the question proposed and put to the House is " That that question be *not* now put " in the House of Commons.

The previous question cannot be moved by a member who has spoken on the question under discussion.

If the previous question is carried, the question during the discussion of which it was moved drops and the House proceeds to the next business. If, however, the previous question is defeated, the question during the discussion of which it was moved must be put immediately, without further debate. The reason for this is that the previous question used to be put in the form " That that question be now put ". The form of the question was changed in order to avoid confusion with the closure.

The previous question cannot be moved on an amendment or on a motion relating to the transaction of public business or to the meeting of the House. Nor can it be moved in committee.

When the previous question has been proposed from the chair, it is not in order then to move to amend the original question. The adjournment either of the House or of the debate on the previous question may, however, be moved.

Debate on the previous question is not confined to the expediency of taking a vote on the subject under discussion. The merits of the original question can continue to be discussed.

The carrying of the previous question does not prevent the motion on which it was carried from being made again on a subsequent day.

In the House of Lords the previous question is proposed from the chair in the form " Whether the said original question be now put ". The mover and those who agree with him vote *against* the motion. If the question is decided in the negative the original motion drops, but if the question is resolved in the affirmative, the original question is put immediately.

The previous question derives its name from the fact that the question whether the original question shall be put at all is previous in its nature, *i.e.* logically prior to that question.

PREVIOUS QUESTION—*continued*

The previous question is not often moved nowadays in either House. It was last moved in the Commons on January 20, 1943—on a motion " that Colonel Clifton Brown be the Chairman of Ways and Means and that Major Milner be the Deputy Chairman "—but was withdrawn. On May 2, 1950, the previous question was moved and carried in the Lords on a motion, moved by Lord Stansgate, " That this House, ever jealously regarding the privilege of parliament, is no less jealous to provide against its abuse, and regrets that the Lord Vansittart, in the speech which he made in this House on March 29 last, did not use due care in the exercise of the privilege of parliament."

PRINTED PAPER OFFICE

An office in the House of Lords where printed copies of documents which have been laid on the table of that House, other parliamentary papers, Hansard, etc., may be obtained by members of the House of Lords.

PRIVATE BILL OFFICE

A public office where much of the business relating to private bills in the House of Commons is transacted. The office is open from 11 a.m. to 5 p.m. on days on which the House sits, and from 11 a.m. to 1 p.m. on days (other than Sundays) on which the House does not sit. Private bills, petitions and other documents connected with private legislation are required by the standing orders to be deposited, and are kept, in the office; and those notices which must be given by the parties in connexion with proceedings on private bills are handed in here, and printed with the Votes and Proceedings. The clerks in the office are responsible for staffing committees on opposed private bills and other opposed private legislation and for the publication of the Private Business List issued with the Votes and Proceedings and other information connected with proceedings on private bills. Among their other duties is the examination of each private bill between the first and second reading to see whether it is in conformity with the rules and standing orders of the House.

PRIVATE BUSINESS

Includes proceedings on private bills (*see* BILL, PRIVATE) or provisional order bills (*see* BILL, PROVISIONAL ORDER), including bills for the confirmation of provisional orders issued under the Private Legislation Procedure (Scotland) Act 1936 (*see* SCOTTISH PRIVATE LEGISLATION), and motions for the making, amendment, repeal or suspension of standing orders relating to such bills or to special procedure orders (*q.v.*).

Private business is usually considered immediately after the meeting of the House, but, if opposed, may, at the discretion of the Chairman of Ways and Means, be considered on Mondays, Tuesdays, Wednesdays and Thursdays at 7 p.m.

No private business may be considered after 2.45 p.m. on Mondays, Tuesdays, Wednesdays and Thursdays. On the arrival of that hour any business which is in hand is interrupted, and its further consideration is deferred to a future day named by the Chairman of Ways and Means. Any business on the printed private business list which is not reached before 2.45 p.m. goes over to the next sitting, or in the case of opposed business until the next sitting day other than a Friday.

If a proceeding on a private bill or a provisional order bill is opposed, it is deferred to a future day (other than a Friday) named by the Chairman of Ways and Means. A proceeding so deferred is deemed to be opposed business as long as a notice of an amendment to the question that the bill be now read a second or third time or that the bill as amended be now considered, as the case may be, stands on the order paper. Notice of such an amendment remains effective for one week only after which it lapses unless renewed. If the proceeding continues to be opposed, the Chairman of Ways and Means ultimately appoints it for some evening at 7 p.m. If a motion which does not relate to a bill which stands on the notice paper for that particular day is opposed, it lapses unless the mover renews the notice for a future day. This he may do either by naming a day directly the motion is opposed or by handing in a notice at the table or the Table Office in the ordinary way. The Chairman may assign some evening for the consideration of a motion which is opposed.

If, on a day on which opposed private business is to be considered at 7 p.m., some member obtains leave to move the adjournment of the House at that hour (*see* ADJOURNMENT OF THE HOUSE, MOTION FOR), the opposed private business is considered as soon as the motion for the adjournment of the House has been disposed of.

Opposed private business is set down for 7 p.m. by direction of the Chairman of Ways and Means and is distributed by him in such a way that a proportion of the total time given by the House to opposed private business is taken on allotted days (*q.v.*) on which, by convention, the choice of subject for debate lies with the Opposition.

PRIVATE MEMBER

Strictly speaking, all members of the House of Commons who are not members of the Government are private members. But neither the Leader of the Opposition nor the other occupants of the opposition front bench are usually regarded as private

PRIVATE MEMBER—*continued*

members, though some of the latter have been known to take part in the ballot for private members' motions.

PRIVILEGE

A privilege in the legal sense of the term is an exemption from some duty, burden, attendance or liability to which others are subject. In parliamentary language, however, the term is also applied to the powers other than legislative possessed by either or both Houses and to the exclusive right of the Commons to grant supplies and to originate measures of taxation (*see* BILL, PUBLIC). (The right of access to Her Majesty's royal person whenever occasion may require and the right to have a favourable construction placed upon their proceedings which the Speaker claims at the beginning of each Parliament, are, as Sir T. Erskine May says, "matters of courtesy rather than privilege".)

The privileges which attach to members of Parliament individually are freedom of speech, freedom from arrest, and exemption from serving on juries, attending as witnesses or serving as sheriffs.

The most important of these is freedom of speech. No action for defamation will lie against a member, nor can he be prosecuted, for anything which he says in the House or any committee of the House or for anything contained in any written notice given by him, *e.g.* of a motion or of a question to a minister. (The right of freedom of speech does not mean that a member can say anything he likes in the House whenever he likes (*see* DEBATE).) A similar privilege attaches to statements made by petitioners in petitions, by parties promoting or opposing private bills or their advocates before committees of either House, or witnesses giving evidence before either House or its committees.

The privilege of freedom from arrest was of particular worth in the days when a debtor could be imprisoned for non-payment of his debt, but is now of little importance. It does not extent to arrest or imprisonment for indictable offences, criminal contempt of court, or refusal to give surety of the peace or for good behaviour. During the Second World War it was held not to extend to preventive detention under Regulation 18B of the Defence Regulations.

The exemption from obeying subpoenas is usually waived.

Peers who are members of the House of Lords have practically the same privileges as members of the House of Commons. In addition they enjoy the privilege, or rather the right, of personal access to the Sovereign (the right of access to Her Majesty's royal person is not enjoyed by members of the House of Commons individually but only by the House as a body) and the right of entering a protest on the Journals of the House (but the House may order a protest to be deleted).

The powers other than legislative possessed by the House of Commons as a body and usually termed privileges are as follows :

(1) The right to provide for its due composition. This includes (*a*) the right to secure the issue of writs out of chancery to fill vacancies caused by the death of members or otherwise ; and (*b*) the right to determine whether members are duly qualified to sit, but not whether they have been duly elected.

(2) The right to regulate its own internal affairs and procedure. This includes (*a*) the right to punish members who are guilty of disorderly conduct by suspending them from the service of the House, committing them or even expelling them ; (*b*) the right to debate behind closed doors ; and (*c*) the exclusive power of interpreting a statute so far as the regulation of its own proceedings within its own walls is concerned. Even if that interpretation should be erroneous, the courts have no power to interfere with it directly or indirectly (*Bradlaugh* v. *Gossett*). This privilege is not confined to the chamber in which the House sits. For instance, it extends to the sale, within the precincts of the House, of intoxicating liquor without a licence through its employees in the Refreshment Department of the House (*R.* v. *Graham Campbell* ; *Herbert, Ex parte,* (1935) 1 K.B. 594). (A crime committed in the House or within its precincts would probably be tried and punished by the ordinary courts.)

(3) The right to publish papers containing matter defamatory of individuals. (This right is secured by the Parliamentary Papers Act 1840.)

(4) The right to direct the Attorney General to prosecute persons guilty of contempts of the House which are also offences at law and persons accused of offences against a law in connection with elections.

(5) The power to compel the attendance of witnesses and the production of papers.

(6) The power to compel the attendance of persons charged with contempt or breach of privilege.

(7) The power to commit persons, whether members or not, for breach of privilege or contempt. (The House of Commons has not exercised the power of imposing fines since 1666.)

(8) The right to expel members whom the House considers unfit to be members, *e.g.* members convicted of grave misdemeanours.

The House of Lords has powers of a similar character to those possessed by the House of Commons, but differing in extent. The House of Lords can impose fines on persons guilty of breach of privilege or contempt instead of, or in addition to, sentencing them to imprisonment, and can sentence them to be imprisoned for a definite period, in which event they are not released, as persons committed by the House of Commons are, when Parliament is prorogued or dissolved. On the other hand, it cannot

PRIVILEGE—*continued*
expel one of its members. The House of Lords has the right to require the judges to attend, not only when it is acting in a judicial capacity, but whenever it needs their advice.

At the commencement of every Parliament the Speaker " on behalf of the Commons lays claim by humble petition to their ancient and undoubted rights and privileges ", and the Queen, by the mouth of the Lord Chancellor, confirms them. But though the privileges may originally have been dependent on royal grant, they are now part of the law of the land and the Commons would continue to enjoy them even though the Speaker did not ask for them and the Queen did not confirm them. The Speaker's petition is a mere formality. The Lords make no corresponding claim for their privileges.

The Relation of Privilege to the Law. From the fact that the privileges of the two Houses are part of the law of the land, it follows (1) that neither House can add to, or alter, its privileges by its own resolution; (2) that if the question of the existence or extent of a privilege claimed by either House arises in a case before a court of law, the court will decide it in accordance with its own views of the law, not in accordance with the decisions of the House concerned. On the other hand, the courts admit that each House has exclusive jurisdiction over its own internal proceedings, including the interpretation of relevant portions of the statute law. And though the courts do not consider that the decisions of the Houses are binding on them, they admit that no appeal lies to them from the decision of either House that a given act constitutes a breach of its privileges. The determination of this question necessarily involves deciding whether the House has got the privilege and what it covers. To this extent, therefore, each House *is* the sole judge of its privileges; and though neither House can stay an action, or, by passing a resolution that an act which forms the subject matter of an action before a court is within the privileges of the House, prevent the court from coming to a contrary decision, the House can *indirectly* enforce its interpretation of the law by committing the plaintiff for contempt.

PRIVILEGES, COMMITTEE FOR

A committee appointed by the House of Lords at the beginning of each session, " to consider of the orders and customs of the House and privileges of parliament and of the peers of Great Britain and Ireland and lords of Parliament ". It consists of " all the lords who have been or shall be present this session ", *i.e.* any lord who attends a sitting of the Committee is *ipso facto* a member, but the Committee cannot function unless at least three Lords of Appeal (*q.v.*) are present. The Committee may sit in the

House of Lords before prayers or while the House is temporarily adjourned. To this Committee are referred for hearing:

(1) petitions from

(*a*) persons claiming to be entitled to existing peerages—usually dormant ones—praying for the issue of a writ of summons to Parliament, or

(*b*) persons claiming to be co-heirs to peerages which have fallen into abeyance and praying that the abeyance may be terminated in their favour,

which have been presented to the Queen and referred by her to the House of Lords;

(2) petitions to the House of Lords from persons claiming to have succeeded to Irish peerages in cases where the Lord Chancellor has reported that the claim is of such a nature that it ought to be referred to the Committee for Privileges.

The Committee may examine witnesses on oath, order the production of documents and hear counsel. Its findings are usually adopted by the House.

Other matters are sometimes referred to the Committee by the House. In 1905, for instance, the question of the right of a peer to be heard as counsel at the bar of the House was so referred.

PRIVILEGES, COMMITTEE OF

A select committee appointed by the House of Commons at the beginning of each session. It consists, as a rule, of fifteen members, including the Leader of the House (who is usually chosen chairman), the Leader of the Opposition and one of the Law Officers. The quorum of the Committee is six. Complaints of breach of privilege (*q.v.*), unless disposed of by the House itself, are referred to this Committee. The Committee is given power "to send for persons, papers and records". It has no power to hear counsel or solicitors.

PROCEDURE, SELECT COMMITTEE ON

A Committee which has been appointed by the House of Commons in every session since that of 1961–62, to consider the procedure in the public business of the House and to report what alterations, if any, are desirable for the more efficient dispatch of such business.

Formerly the matters to be examined by the Committee were set out either in the Committee's order of reference when it was appointed for the session or in instructions agreed to in the House from time to time. But now the Committee is left to decide which part of the procedure of the House is to be examined.

A series of reports from the Committee has led to a number of changes in the procedure of the House, but not all the changes recommended by the Committee have been agreed to, even with

PROCEDURE, SELECT COMMITTEE ON—*continued*

modifications by the House; nor has the existence of the Committee precluded the House from altering its procedure from time to time without reference to the Committee.

PROCEDURE OF THE HOUSE, SELECT COMMITTEE ON

A select committee appointed by the House of Lords at the beginning of every session. Its function is to consider any proposals for alterations in the procedure of that House which may arise from time to time and whether the standing orders should be altered to effect such alterations. It consists of the Lord Chancellor, the Chairman of Committees and a number of other lords.

PROGRESS, MOTION TO REPORT

The colloquial name for a motion "that the chairman do report progress and ask leave to sit again", moved when the House is in committee for the purpose of suspending the business until some other day. It is the analogue of a motion for the adjournment of the debate (*q.v.*) which cannot be moved when the House is in committee because a committee of the whole House has no power to adjourn its sittings or a debate to a future day. Members speaking on a motion to report progress must confine themselves to giving reasons why the committee should or should not proceed any further with the business at that time. A member who has moved a motion to report progress during a debate on a question is not entitled to move a similar motion during the same debate. If the chairman thinks that a motion to report progress is "an abuse of the rules of the House" (*q.v.*), he may either refuse to accept it, or accept it but put the question on it at once without allowing the motion to be debated. The fact that no progress has been made with a bill will not, of itself, render a motion to report progress an abuse of the rules of the House. If a motion to report progress is moved during the debate on a question, but is defeated, a motion to report progress cannot be moved again during that debate unless the question on some other motion, *e.g.* a motion "that the chairman do leave the chair", has in the meantime been proposed from the chair. If a motion to report progress is carried, the chairman leaves the chair of the committee and, when the Speaker has resumed the chair of the House, the chairman, addressing him, informs the House that the committee have made progress in the bill and have directed him to move that the committee may have leave to sit again.

PROMOTERS

Persons or bodies applying to Parliament for a local and personal or a private act, or to a minister of the crown for a provisional order.

PROROGATION

The act by which the Queen brings a session of Parliament to an end. Parliament is then said to be " prorogued " until the day named for its next meeting. Prorogation automatically closes all proceedings and business in progress at the time, unless provision is expressly made to the contrary, *e.g.* by " suspending " a bill till the next session. The time, however, during which certain statutory instruments are liable to be annulled by resolution of either House ceases to run when the House is prorogued ; it begins to run again on the day when Parliament meets again (*see* STATUTORY INSTRUMENTS).

The House of Lords may sit and act for the purpose of hearing and determining appeals during the prorogation of Parliament (Appellate Jurisdiction Act 1876, s. 8).

PROTEST

A statement of the dissent of a lord from a vote of the House of Lords, with or without reasons, entered on the Journal of the House. Where several lords dissent from a vote for the same reasons, it is customary for all of them to sign the same protest. A lord may add his signature to a protest drawn up by another lord or he may sign the protest for some of the reasons given, specifying which, or for certain of the reasons given, and for other reasons which he sets out.

A protest must be entered in the Clerk's book in the Printed Paper Office before 2 p.m. on the next sitting day, and must be signed before the sitting of the House on the same day. The House sometimes grants an extension of time.

A lord cannot, without leave from the House, enter a protest against a vote unless he was present and (in the case of a division) voted when the question was put.

The right of protest is dependent on the good will of the majority. If a majority of the House choose, they can order a protest, or part of it, or some of the reasons given to be expunged.

The right of entering protests against decisions of the House of Lords has not often been exercised in recent years. Only five protests have been entered in the last forty-four years. The most recent instance of the exercise of the right occurred on November 18, 1954, when Lord Saltoun entered a protest against the House agreeing to an Amendment on the report stage of the Town and Country Planning (Scotland) Bill.

PUBLIC ACCOUNTS, COMMITTEE OF

A select committee of the House of Commons, appointed by standing order, " for the examination of the accounts showing the appropriation of the sums granted by Parliament to meet the public expenditure and of such other accounts laid before Parliament as the committee may think fit ". It consists of

PUBLIC ACCOUNTS, COMMITTEE OF—*continued*

fifteen members, of whom five are a quorum. The Committee has power to send for persons, papers and records and to report from time to time. The chairman is usually a member of the Opposition. The Financial Secretary to the Treasury is a member of the Committee but hardly ever attends.

In practice the Committee considers chiefly those matters to which its attention is directed by the Comptroller and Auditor General. Where it appears that a department has spent more than the amount granted by Parliament, the Committee inquires into the causes which led to this expenditure being incurred and reports whether it sees any objection to providing the sums necessary to meet the deficiency by an Excess Vote (*q.v.*). Although the primary function of the Committee is to ascertain whether any department has spent more money than Parliament has granted or has spent money on objects other than those for which Parliament granted it, the Public Accounts Committee does not restrict its inquiries to these matters. Where the Comptroller and Auditor General brings to its notice what appears to him to have been waste of public money, the Committee investigates the matter.

The Comptroller and Auditor General and one of the Treasury Officers of Accounts attend the Committee whenever evidence is taken, but members of the public are not admitted.

Reports of the Committee may be considered on an allotted day (*q.v.*) if the Opposition wishes.

PUBLIC BILL OFFICE

The Public Bill Office of the House of Commons forms part of the Department of the Clerk of the House of Commons. Its chief duty is to supervise the passage of all public bills through the House from their introduction onwards, and to make the necessary arrangements for their printing.

The clerks in the office examine all public bills before they are printed to see that the rules of the House are complied with. In particular they have to be satisfied that each bill conforms to its title and that the rules with regard to public money are observed; and they are responsible for ensuring that public bills which may affect private rights are referred to the Examiners of Petitions for Private Bills. All notices of amendments to bills and of motions for money resolutions in connexion with bills are examined to see that they are in order, and also Lords amendments to Commons bills, so that the House may be informed of any which may appear to infringe its privileges.

The office is responsible for the printing of all public bills and amendments proposed thereto, for the insertion of amendments in the " House copy " of bills, for supplying clerks to standing committees and to the Chairmen's Panel, for making arrangements with regard to ballots and the taking and recording of divisions, and for issuing to every member returned at a by-election the certificate which he must present at the Table of the House on taking his seat. Consolidated Fund Bills (including the Appropriation Bill) are drafted in the office.

The Clerk of Public Bills, as Clerk of the Fees, has certain responsibilities with regard to the fees payable in connexion with private bills.

PUBLICATIONS AND DEBATES REPORTS, SELECT COMMITTEE ON

A select committee formerly appointed by the House of Commons at the beginning of each session to assist the Speaker in the arrangements for the official report of debates and to inquire into the expenditure on stationery and printing for the House and the public service generally. Arrangements for the official report of debates, for the provision of stationery, and for printing for the House are now among the matters controlled by the Speaker on the advice of the Select Committee on House of Commons (Services) (*see* HOUSE OF COMMONS (SERVICES), SELECT COMMITTEE ON).

QUEEN'S CONSENT

In certain cases the Queen's consent must be given to the consideration of a bill by either House. This must not be confused with the royal assent, the act by which the Crown concurs with the two Houses in passing a bill and thereby converts it into a statute, or with the Queen's recommendation to the expenditure of public funds. The Queen's consent is needed in the case of a bill which touches the property, rights, interests, privileges or prerogatives of the Crown; it is an intimation that the Queen is willing to allow the bill to be considered by the House, and it in no way prejudices her constitutional rights in the eventual giving or withholding of her royal assent when the bill has been passed by both Houses.

The Queen's consent is most often needed in the case of bills which affect the property of the Crown, and more often for private than for public bills. The procedure in the House of Commons is as follows. (The procedure in the House of Lords is substantially the same.) Soon after the introduction of the bill, the government department concerned informs the Public Bill Office, or the Private Bill Office, as the case may be, that the Queen's consent will require to be signified. If the interests of the Crown are only involved to a small extent or incidentally, her consent is deferred till the third reading, but if the whole principle of the bill depends on it, the consent will be required at the point at which the bill is first submitted to the judgment of the House, that is, at the second reading. In one instance the Speaker gave instructions

QUEEN'S CONSENT—*continued*
that a bill should not be printed until it was known that such consent would be forthcoming. When the appropriate stage is reached, the words " Queen's Consent, on behalf of the Crown, to be signified " appear on the order paper after the name of the bill. The Speaker must then require the consent to be signified before he proposes the question for the second (or third) reading. The consent is actually signified by a minister, who must be a privy counsellor (in the case of a private bill, it is done by the Chairman or Deputy Chairman of Ways and Means, if a privy counsellor). The minister usually indicates by a bow that the Queen's consent has been granted ; if the minister were to recite the formula in words, he would no doubt say (as the Journal records) that " Her Majesty, having been informed of the purport of the bill, gives her consent, as far as Her Majesty's interest is concerned, that the House may do therein as they shall think fit ".

A similar procedure is followed with regard to bills affecting the property of the Duchies of Lancaster and Cornwall. In the former case, the Queen's consent is signified " in right of her Duchy of Lancaster ", in the latter the consent is that of the Prince of Wales as Duke of Cornwall. When the Prince is a minor, the Sovereign's consent is given " on behalf of the Prince of Wales ".

The procedure is substantially the same in the case of a bill affecting the privileges or prerogative of the Crown. This may occur where a bill proposes to make legislative provision in a matter within the Crown's constitutional prerogative. If the Government is prepared to advise the Crown that such a bill should be allowed to proceed, the House is informed that " Her Majesty places her prerogative and interests at the disposal of Parliament, that the House may do therein as they shall think fit " (the formula may vary slightly according to circumstances). Such an intimation is conveyed by a minister of the Crown.

An example of the above is furnished by the Peace Bill, which was introduced several times by a private member during the 1930s. This bill, which sought to make the obligations imposed by the Covenant of the League of Nations a part of the statute law of the United Kingdom, came up for a second reading in December 1937, when the King's consent, " so far as His Majesty's prerogative is concerned ", was given to the bill. This was no doubt necessary since the declaring of war is a part of the royal prerogative. In this case the consent was signified when the bill came up for a second reading, but it did not receive a second reading as the House was counted out before the question could be put. More recent examples of bills requiring the Sovereign's consent in this form are the Crown Proceedings Bill of 1947, which (among other things) made it legal to bring a civil action against the Crown (on second reading), the Indian Independence Bill of

1947 (on second reading), the Palestine Bill of 1948, which brought to an end the British mandate in Palestine (on third reading), the Ireland Bill of 1949, which recognised the new Republic of Ireland (on second reading) and the Swaziland Independence Bill of 1968 (on second reading).

The Sovereign's consent is occasionally required to a motion affecting the royal prerogative. Of the following examples the first three concern the execution by deputy of the duties of the Speaker, whose appointment always needs the royal approval. (1) In 1855 a select committee was appointed to consider what improvement might be made in the provision for the execution of the office of Speaker in the event of his unavoidable absence. The Queen's consent was signified to the motion for taking the committee's report into consideration; and, on consideration of the report, the standing order directing the Chairman of Ways and Means to act as Deputy Speaker was passed. (2) In 1902 the King's consent was signified to an amendment which had recently been made to that standing order, extending the chairman's powers to a deputy chairman. (3) In 1964 the Queen's consent was signified to a motion appointing a member an additional deputy chairman and authorising him to exercise all the powers vested in that office, during the illness of the Speaker. (4) in 1856 the Queen's consent was signified to a motion for the appointment of a select committee to "consider the best means of communication between those parts of the Metropolis which lie to the north of Saint James's Park and those which lie to the south and west thereof".

QUEEN'S RECOMMENDATION

This is required to be signified to the House of Commons before the consideration of any motion* authorising the expenditure of public funds is entered upon. This rule, which is the subject of one of the oldest standing orders (dating from 1713) effectively reserves to the Government the right of initiating all expenditure. The Queen's recommendation is most often required in the case of the proposals for expenditure contained in bills; in such cases the Public Bill Office is informed by the Parliamentary Counsel in charge of the bill that the recommendation has been signified, and a note to that effect appears on the order paper containing a notice of motion approving the expenditure (*see* BILL, PUBLIC; FINANCE). The Queen's speech at the opening of the session invariably informs the Commons that the estimates for the public services will be laid before them, and this intimation is held to convey the necessary recommendation in the case of the regular yearly expenditure on the public services.

* The Queen's recommendation would also be required in the case of a petition asking for a grant of public money, unless the petitioner prayed for legislation to achieve the desired object.

QUEEN'S SPEECH

When the Queen opens Parliament at the beginning of the session, she reads a speech which is prepared for her by her ministers, and which sets forth the policy which they intend to pursue and the legislation which they propose to introduce during the session. In making the speech the Queen acts as the mouthpiece of her ministers and they are entirely responsible for its contents. When the Commons have returned to their own chamber, a backbench supporter of the Government moves an address of thanks to the Queen "for the gracious speech which Your Majesty has addressed to both Houses of Parliament".

The debate which follows, and lasts for several days, may range over the whole policy of the Government and a number of amendments are moved criticising the policy set forth in the speech. Any divisions arise on questions for making these amendments to the address, and the question for the address itself is agreed to without a division, out of courtesy to the Queen. The debate is known as "the debate on the Queen's speech", or (more accurately) as "the debate on the address". A similar debate takes place in the House of Lords. A Queen's speech is read by the Lord Chancellor on proroguing Parliament, but this is never debated, nor is an address of thanks moved, since it is immediately followed by the reading of the commission for prorogation, after which there can be no further proceedings in Parliament before the day to which it stands prorogued. This speech reviews the session which it concludes.

QUESTION

A matter which is to be, or is being, determined by the House or a committee. A question may not be debated until it has been "proposed from the chair", *i.e.* until it has been read or stated to the House or committee by the Speaker or the chairman. Generally speaking, a question is founded on a motion moved by a member. In certain cases, however, the Speaker or the chairman proposes a question without a motion being moved. Thus, in a committee on a bill, if no amendment is proposed to a clause, or when all the amendments to it have been disposed of, the chairman at once proposes the question "that the clause (or the clause as amended) stand part of the bill". And whenever a resolution is reported from a committee of the whole House the Speaker (unless an amendment is proposed to the resolution or a motion is moved for its recommittal or postponement) at once proposes the question "that this House doth agree with the committee in the said resolution".

In the House of Commons a motion, when moved, is itself proposed as the question, but in the Lords the question proposed is "that the motion be agreed to".

Once a question has been proposed from the chair, it must

be disposed of before the House or committee can proceed with any other business unless the motion or amendment on which it is founded is withdrawn. A question may be disposed of—

(*a*) by being agreed to, with or without amendment, or
(*b*) by being decided in the negative, or
(*c*) by the adjournment of the debate, or
(*d*) by the previous question being carried, or
(*e*) by the adjournment of the House.

(*For* Questions to Ministers, *see that title*).

QUESTION, PUTTING THE

Ascertaining the sense of the House or of a committee with regard to a motion, an amendment or any other matter which requires to be determined by the House or committee. In the House of Commons the question on a motion is " put " in the following manner. When the debate, if any, is finished, the Speaker reads the motion to the House, prefacing it with the words " the question is " and concluding with the words " as many as are of that opinion say ' aye ' ".* After pausing long enough to allow the supporters of the motion to answer, he continues " as many as are of the contrary opinion say ' no ' ". (This is termed " collecting the voices ", and when the voices of both the ayes and the noes have been given, the question is said to be " fully put " and no member may speak to it.) After giving the opponents of the motion time to call out " no ", the Speaker says, " I think the ayes (or the noes) have it ", *i.e.* are in the majority. In theory he judges by the loudness of the respective cries whether the ayes or the noes are the more in number. In practice his decision is based on his knowledge of the balance of opinion in the House. Unless some member challenges the Speaker's decision by calling out " no " when he says that he thinks the ayes have it or *vice versa*, the Speaker *declares* that the ayes or the noes, as the case may be, " have it ". If, however, the minority or any individual member challenges his decision, the Speaker directs the lobby to be cleared† and, after an interval of two minutes, puts the question a second time. If the minority persists in demanding a division, the Speaker (unless he thinks that the division is unnecessarily claimed, in which event he can take the vote by calling first on one side and then on the other to stand up) directs the ayes to go to the right and the noes to the left, and names four members, two from each

* When he puts the question on an amendment to a motion, the Speaker says : " The original question was (reading it). Since which an amendment has been proposed to (reading the terms of the amendment). The question I have to put is ' that the amendment be made '. "

† When the Speaker thinks that the members who challenge his decision do not intend to divide the House, he sometimes tries to wear them down by repeating " I think the ayes (or the noes) have it ".

QUESTION, PUTTING THE—*continued*

side, to act as tellers. In a committee of the whole House questions are put by the chairman in the same manner as in the House. In the House of Lords questions are put in much the same manner as in the House of Commons. The chief differences are—

(i) that (except in the case of motions for advancing bills a stage and similar motions) the Lord Chancellor does not read out the motion, but simply says: "The question is that this motion be agreed to";*

(ii) that the words "content" and "not content" are used instead of "aye" and "no";

(iii) that if, when the Lord Chancellor says that he thinks the contents (or the not contents) have it, his decision is challenged, he directs not the lobby, but the bar, to be cleared; and

(iv) that if, when he puts the question a second time, his decision is again challenged, he says: "The 'contents' will go to the right by the throne; the 'not contents' to the left by the bar".

Neither the Lord Chancellor nor the Lord Chairman has power, where a division is, in his opinion, unnecessarily claimed, to take the vote by calling first on one side and then on the other to stand up.

QUESTION TIME

The time set apart in the House of Commons for the oral answer by ministers of questions from members; it begins when the various matters (including private business) which are dealt with immediately after the beginning of the sitting have been disposed of, and not later than a quarter to three, and ends not later than half-past three. As a rule nearly an hour is available, which is rarely enough for all the questions on the paper. Private notice questions are taken immediately afterwards and are not bound to be finished by half-past three (*see also* QUESTIONS TO MINISTERS).

QUESTIONS TO MINISTERS

In both Houses members may put questions to ministers about the matters for which they are responsible to Parliament. In the House of Commons a member who wishes to ask a question must give written notice beforehand, either at the Table or in the Table Office, of the terms of his question. If he wants an oral answer, he puts an asterisk or "star" on the piece of paper on

* When he puts the question on an amendment, the Lord Chancellor begins with the words "the original motion was", and concludes by saying "the question is that this amendment be agreed to".

which his question is written, and he must give two clear days' notice. He must give notice before 10 p.m. on a Thursday, for questions to be asked on the following Monday, before the rising of the House on a Friday for questions to be asked on the following Tuesday and before 2.30 p.m. on a Monday and Tuesday for questions to be asked on the following Wednesday and Thursday respectively. No notice may be given for a day more than twenty-one days ahead, but in reckoning the twenty-one days periods in which the House will not sit for more than two consecutive days are disregarded. The notice is printed on the following day among the " notices given " (*see* ORDER PAPER). No member is allowed more than two oral question on one day.

On specially urgent matters, "private notice questions" may be asked after the end of the time allotted by the standing orders to questions for oral answer. A member who wishes to avail himself of this privilege must give notice of the terms of his question to the minister and to the Speaker not later than twelve o'clock on the day on which he is to ask it. Provided that it complies with the ordinary rules of order applicable to questions, and is of some public importance, the Speaker will allow it, if he is satisfied that the matter is really urgent, that no previous opportunity has occurred of raising it, and that it does not anticipate a question already on the notice paper.

While ministers make every effort to supply answers to oral questions on the desired day, there is not the same urgency to provide non-oral answers. In the case of such " written questions ", as they are called, the minister is not obliged to provide the answer, which is printed in Hansard as well as being sent direct to the member, on the day on which the question appears on the paper ; if, however, the answer is not furnished within a reasonable time, the member is entitled to put the question down again. Non-oral answers are often preferred for questions which deal with personal cases, or involve lists of figures.

Oral questions are dealt with at the beginning of the sitting on Mondays, Tuesdays, Wednesdays and Thursdays after private business and one or two other items of business have been disposed of. Questions last till half past three, the time available being, as a rule, a little less than one hour. As there is often not time to answer all the questions of which notice has been given, their position on the paper is of some importance, and they are therefore arranged in an order which varies from week to week according to a regular schedule, each minister appearing on a particular day or days each week ; within the group of questions for each minister, questions are arranged giving priority according to the days on which notice of the questions was originally given. The Speaker calls in turn each member whose question appears on the paper ; on being called, the member rises, says " Question number so-and-so ", and sits down ; whereupon the minister

QUESTIONS TO MINISTERS—*continued*
rises and reads out from the despatch box the answer prepared for him by his department. A supplementary question from the member usually follows, and a further answer from the minister, the process perhaps continuing, with other members joining in, for several minutes before the Speaker calls the next question. The forms of question and answer must be strictly adhered to, and anything in the nature of speeches or debate at question time is out of order. The answers to questions which have not been reached for lack of time, or have been otherwise omitted, are printed in "Hansard" with the non-oral questions except in cases where the member has asked for his question to be postponed or withdrawn.

Notices of questions must, as has been said above, be handed to the Clerks Assistant at the Table, or to the clerks in the Table Office. They may also be sent by post (in which case they must bear the member's signature), but not by telephone or telegram. One member may give notice on behalf of another. It is the duty of the clerks to scrutinise each question on behalf of the Speaker, to see that it complies with the rules of order. If it is out of order, it is not printed, and the member is informed accordingly by card. The question can then often be put in order by a minor alteration. A member who is not prepared to accept the clerk's opinion may have the matter referred to the Speaker for decision.

The rules of order governing the content of speeches (*see* DEBATE) apply generally to questions, but there are additional rules defining their form and scope. In the first place, a question must be interrogative in form, and it must either seek information or press for action. It may not suggest its own answer, and, though it may include a statement (for the accuracy of which the member is expected to assume responsibility) of the facts on which it is based, it may not be argumentative or hypothetical. Secondly, the subject of the question must be one for which the minister is responsible. In these days when the functions of government are continually widening in scope, and the system of grants and subsidies has greatly extended its influence, it is not always easy to decide just how far a minister's responsibilities do extend. It is certainly far easier to name a number of matters about which members sometimes seek unsuccessfully to ask questions. These include the internal affairs of foreign and Commonwealth countries, the activities of local authorities (except in such matters as roads and education, where the central government makes grants and contributions to local funds on condition of satisfactory standards being maintained), the Church of England and other religious bodies, banks, trade unions, and unofficial bodies generally. The "public corporations" and nationalised undertakings give rise to many problems.

Under the Acts constituting these authorities, a minister may have the right to secure such information as he wishes or to give directions in matters affecting the national interest, but ministers have usually declined expressly to intervene in matters of day-to-day working, and have referred members to the managements themselves, thus in effect delegating the responsibility to those bodies, and, by implication, removing those matters from the scope of parliamentary question. It may be observed that the Foreign and Commonwealth Secretary accepts complete responsibility for answering questions about the British colonies ; on the other hand, the Minister of Posts and Telecommunications declines to intervene in any way on the contents of the B.B.C.'s programmes.

Questions may not be asked about the Sovereign and the Royal Family, officials of the Court (for whom no minister is responsible), foreign ambassadors, and judges.

Further rules exclude questions which seek the interpretation of a statute or a legal opinion, or ask for information already published, or recently supplied in answer to a parliamentary question, or for the confirmation of rumours or press reports. Questions which are tendentious, controversial, ironical, frivolous, vague or repetitive are also out of order. Finally it may be noted that questions may not be asked about matters which are of their nature secret (such as the proceedings of the Cabinet and the advice given to ministers by the Law Officers) ; and that a minister may decline to answer a question if he thinks it desirable in the public interest.

It is for ministers to choose which of them shall answer any particular question ; and if a member addresses a question to the wrong minister, it is transferred to the right one, on the advice of the former's department, by the Clerks at the Table without reference to the member, who cannot then insist on putting his question to the original minister. The member is informed of the transfer by the department transferring the question.

Questions may be put by peers to ministers in the House of Lords. Notice thereof may either be handed to the Clerks at the Table or sent by post to the Clerk of the Parliaments. A question which is intended only to elicit information, and not to provide the occasion for a debate, may be put down for any day on which the House sits and must be starred. An unstarred question may be followed by a debate, though if the peer asking it wishes to secure for himself the right of reply at the end of the debate he must add the words " and to move for papers " at the end of the notice which he hands in. No notice may be given for a day more than four weeks ahead (excluding periods of recess). Questions may be put down " not for oral answer ", as in the House of Commons ; the answers are printed in the official report of debates (Hansard).

QUORUM

The quorum of the House of Commons is forty, including the Speaker. Formerly the Speaker did not take the chair at the beginning of the sitting unless and until the required number were present, but under the present practice he always takes the chair at the appointed time, and does not count the House unless his attention is called to the fact that less than forty members are present.

If this happens, the proceedings are suspended, strangers are directed to withdraw and the division bells are rung intermittently for a period of one minute (instead of for two continuous periods with a short interval, as for a division). If within four minutes enough members enter the chamber, the Speaker, as soon as a quorum is present, calls upon the member who was interrupted by the count to continue his speech. If not enough members are present after four minutes, and the time is past 4 p.m. (1 p.m. on Friday), the Speaker adjourns the House. Up till 4 (or 1) p.m., however, the House may not be adjourned on this account; instead the Speaker suspends the sitting, which is resumed when the required number of members are present. If this has not occurred by 4 (1) p.m., the Speaker then counts the House again, and, if a quorum is still not present when he has finished counting, he adjourns the House.

The same procedure is followed in a committee of the whole House, except that, if less than forty members are present after the four minutes have expired, the chairman leaves the chair of the committee and reports the fact to the House when the Speaker has resumed the chair of the House. The Speaker then counts the House again, and leaves the chair again (if enough members are present), when the House again resolves itself into the committee, or adjourns the House, or, if it is not yet 4 p.m., suspends the sitting till that hour. The House may not be counted between 7.30 and 8.30 p.m. (on Fridays between 1.15 and 2.15 p.m.) or after 10 p.m., but if a division at those times shows less than forty members present the House proceeds to the next business. The House may not be counted during proceedings on any Consolidated Fund Bill or Appropriation Bill, or during any proceedings (such as a bill on which a guillotine order is in force) in the course of which the Speaker is directed forthwith to put any question. The Speaker will not count the House, though his attention has been called to the lack of a quorum, if he has recently satisfied himself, on counting the House, that enough members are present, or if the numbers in a recent division have conveyed the same information.

Since a member is not obliged to vote in a division, it is clearly not proper to regard the numbers shown in a division as necessarily representing the number of members present in the House. If the figures in a division amount, with the tellers and the Speaker or chairman, to less than forty, the question is not decided and if the division has taken place at a time when the House can be counted, the Speaker or chairman announces that the business in progress is " dropped " (*see* DROPPED ORDER) and then proceeds to count the House. If this occurs while the House may not be counted, the business stands over until the next sitting and the House proceeds to the next business on the order paper.

The quorum of a standing committee is seventeen or one-third of the membership of the committee, excluding the chairman, whichever is the less. Here, as in a select committee, the chairman does not take the chair until a quorum is present, and once the committee has proceeded to business, it is the duty of the committee clerk to draw his attention to the lack of a quorum. A reasonable time is allowed for members to reach the committee room to make up the quorum (the count being announced by the policeman on duty at the door), and, if the required number is not attained, the chairman adjourns the committee to the next day on which it normally sits. The quorum of a select committee is fixed by an order of the House, and varies generally with the size of the committee. For a committee of eleven members three is the usual figure, although the Committee of Privileges (fifteen members) has a quorum of six, and the Committee on Public Petitions (fifteen members) has a quorum of three, and the Estimates Committee (forty-three members) a quorum of seven. The quorum of a committee on an opposed private bill (four members) is three, unless the House gives special leave to the committee to proceed with less, and of a committee on an unopposed private bill (five members), three.

The quorum of the House of Lords is thirty, or (when it is sitting judicially) three. The House may, however, proceed with ordinary business with only three peers present ; but if a division should disclose that less than thirty are in the chamber, the question is not decided and the debate is adjourned.

READINGS, FIRST, SECOND AND THIRD

Stages through which a bill must pass in its progress in each House. Before the invention of printing the only practicable means of informing members of the contents of a bill was by the Clerk's reading it aloud. By the end of the sixteenth century it had become the practice in both Houses to have a bill thus read on three separate occasions before passing it. After the Clerk had read the bill, the Speaker " opened the bill ", *i.e.* explained its substance and effect or read a summary of the bill, known as a breviate. It was not usual to debate a bill on the first reading, but after the second reading a debate might take place. On the conclusion of the debate or, if no debate took place, after he had " opened the bill ", the Speaker put the question either that the bill be committed or that it be ingrossed. The bill might again

READINGS, FIRST, SECOND AND THIRD—*continued*

be debated on the third reading when the question put was "that the bill do pass".

Originally the Speaker determined what bills should be read and when, though the House sometimes interfered and insisted upon having a particular bill read, but in the course of the seventeenth century the House took the determination of this matter into its own hands.

During the eighteenth century it became the practice, on the day appointed for the second or third reading of a bill, to move that the bill "be now read a second (or the third) time" before the bill was read. Members took to debating the merits of the bill and, if they objected to it, dividing, on the question that the bill be now read a second or (the third) time, and the questions for committing and passing the bill became merely formal questions and eventually ceased to be put.

The circulation of printed copies of bills made it unnecessary to read bills at length and by the end of the eighteenth century it had become the practice for the Clerk to read only the title and the first words. Later even this formality was dispensed with.

RECESS

When Parliament has been prorogued, it is said to be "in recess"; and the period between the prorogation and the next meeting of Parliament, that is, between two sessions of a Parliament, is known as a recess. The word is, however, often loosely used in speaking of any period during which the two Houses are adjourned for more than a week-end.

RE-COMMITTAL OF BILLS

In certain circumstances a bill may be re-committed after it has been reported to the House by the committee which has considered it. This is rarely necessary nowadays, since any amendment which could have been proposed in committee without an instruction (which would have been necessary if the amendment was outside the scope of the bill) is now also admissible, on consideration of the bill, provided that, if it imposes a charge, it is covered by a money resolution. If it is desired to widen the scope of a bill, the bill may be re-committed to a committee of the whole House, and an instruction to the committee may then be moved. Re-committal is occasionally resorted to "on third reading"—*i.e.* immediately before the third reading—when it appears necessary to make an amendment to a bill at the last moment before it leaves the House. Re-committal may, however, be necessary for other reasons. For instance, if a committee has made some mistake in procedure (such as by exceeding its powers), it is usual for the House to re-commit the bill to that same committee which formerly considered it, and which is thus given the opportunity of rectifying its error. When a bill has been committed to a select committee or a joint committee and reported to the House it is afterwards re-committed to a committee of the whole House. When a re-committed bill has been reported to the House, a consideration stage always follows if the bill has been amended on re-committal, or if it has been reported from a standing or select committee. The Speaker has the power to decide whether any proposed motion to re-commit a bill, and, if there are more than one, which such motion, shall be moved.

RECORD OFFICE OF THE HOUSE OF LORDS

This office, which was established in 1946 at the southern end of the Houses of Parliament, also occupies almost the whole of the twelve floors of the Victoria Tower. In it are kept bills, papers, plans, petitions and other documents presented to the Houses of Parliament, or produced in the course of their work, since the year 1497, and numbering several million in all. Two of the most important series are the original manuscript Journals of the House of Lords, dating from 1510, and the original manuscript Journals of the House of Commons, dating from 1547 to 1800 (with the exception of a period from 1584 to 1601 which is covered by D'Ewes' *Journals*). In addition there is an increasing quantity of material deposited by private individuals, including, for instance, the papers of the first Viscount Samuel. The office is open to all members of the public throughout the year between ten and five o'clock except on Saturdays, Sundays and public holidays. No passes or introductions are needed, but before a first visit a preliminary letter should be sent to the Clerk of the Records at the House of Lords. Guides to certain classes of parliamentary documents are available on application, and a complete *Guide to the Records of Parliament* is published by H.M. Stationery Office.

REFEREES, COURT OF

A tribunal, consisting of the Chairman and Deputy Chairman of Ways and Means, seven other members of the House of Commons appointed by the Speaker, and the Speaker's Counsel, whose function it is to determine whether a petitioner against a private bill whose right to be heard is contested by the promoters has a *locus standi*. Three referees are sufficient to constitute the Court. The practice and procedure of the Court, its times of sitting, order of business and the forms and notices required in its proceedings are regulated by rules framed by the Chairman of Ways and Means. Only one counsel may be heard on either part unless specially authorised by the Court. The promoters are required to state in writing beforehand the grounds on which they object to the right of the petitioner to be heard. When the Court meets, counsel for the petitioner is heard in support of his

REFEREES, COURT OF—*continued*

client's right to be heard, and counsel for the promoters is heard in reply. The Court is bound by former decisions except in cases where it is given, by standing order, a discretion to grant petitioners a right to be heard if it thinks fit.

REPLY, RIGHT OF

The mover of a substantive motion, but not the mover of an amendment or a subsidiary motion, has a right of reply. If, however, the mover of a motion to proceed with an order of the day moves it without rising to address the chair, *e.g.* by raising his hat or bowing, he may speak later in the debate. Now that it has ceased to be the custom for members to wear hats in the chamber, it is even possible that he might be allowed to speak again if he had confined himself, when moving the motion, to saying " Now, sir " or " I move ". On the report stage of a bill which has been considered by a standing committee, the member in charge of the bill and the mover of an amendment or a new clause are allowed to speak more than once.

REPRIMAND

A formal reproof addressed to a person who has been adjudged guilty of a breach of privilege or of a contempt of the House by the Speaker in pursuance of an order of the House of Commons or by the Lord Chancellor in pursuance of an order of the House of Lords. This punishment is inflicted in cases where the House considers that the offence cannot be passed over, but is not serious enough to be punished by imprisonment. The last occasion when it was inflicted occurred in 1968, when a member of the House was ordered to be reprimanded by the Speaker for having disclosed to a newspaper minutes of evidence which had been taken before a select committee and not reported to the House.

When the House orders a person (other than a member) to be reprimanded, the Speaker, if the person is in attendance in the lobby, directs the Serjeant at Arms to bring him to the bar, and when this has been done, reprimands him " in the name of the House ", after which he directs him to withdraw. The Serjeant (with his mace on his shoulder) stands by the offender when he is at the bar. If the person who is to be reprimanded is not in attendance, the House either orders the Serjeant at Arms to take him into custody and bring him to the bar on a certain day or makes an order that the person is to attend the House on a certain day to be reprimanded. When a member is reprimanded, he receives the reprimand standing bare-headed, in his place, unless he is in the custody of the Serjeant at Arms, in which case he is brought to the bar to receive the reprimand.

RESCINDING OF RESOLUTIONS

No question which is substantially the same as one upon which the House has pronounced judgment can be offered, *i.e.* no motion or amendment may be moved which is substantially the same as a motion or amendment which has been either carried of defeated during the current session. This rule does not, however, preclude an amendment to a bill which has been rejected in committee from being again proposed on the report stage. The inconvenience which the rule sometimes causes can, moreover, be obviated in the case of a resolution or order, by rescinding the one or discharging the other. The rule is not thereby infringed because the question, that the resolution be rescinded, or that the order be discharged, is technically a new question. A negative decision, however, cannot be rescinded because this would involve offering the same question again.

RESERVED SPEECH

A member who moves an order of the day may, instead of speaking at the time when he moves, reserve his speech in order to make it at a later point in the debate. In this case he " moves formally " without a speech, and retains the right to speak, when called upon to do so, later on. This only applies to proceedings in the House, since in a committee a member may speak more than once to a question.

RESIGNATION OF MEMBERSHIP

A member of the House of Commons may not resign his seat. Except at a dissolution, he only ceases to be a member if he becomes ineligible for membership, for instance by receiving a peerage or by accepting an office which disqualifies him. A member who wishes to retire applies for one of the ancient (and sinecure) offices which have been preserved for this purpose. The office most used is that known as " the Chiltern Hundreds " (*q.v.*).

RESOLUTION

An expression of the opinion of the House with reference to some subject or a declaration of its intention to do something. A resolution is sometimes ordered to be communicated to the other House with a request for its concurrence, *e.g.* a resolution that it is expedient that a joint committee be appointed to consider a certain subject. A resolution may be rescinded.

Resolutions must be distinguished from orders, *i.e.* directions or commands addressed by one or other House to members or officers of that House or to other persons. Thus the House of Commons *resolves* that an address be presented to the Queen, but *orders* it to be presented to her by those members who are privy counsellors or members of the royal household.

RESOLUTION—*continued*

The recommendations of certain select committees (*e.g.*, the Standing Orders Committee and the Business Committee) are expressed in the form of resolutions, which, when the House has agreed to them, have the same effect as if they were resolutions or orders of the House.

RESTITUTION BILL

Restitution Bills, that is, bills for the reversal of attainders, the restoration of forfeited honours and lands, or for restitution in blood, originate in the House of Lords. They are first signed by the Queen and are then presented by a peer to the House by her command. They are treated as public bills and are sent in due course to the House of Commons where the Queen's consent must be signified before the bill is given a first reading.

RETURN

A paper or document presented to either House in pursuance either of its order or of an address from the House to the Queen praying her to be graciously pleased to give directions that the document desired may be laid before the House. If a motion for a return is unopposed, *i.e.* if the minister in charge of the department which would have to supply the information sought for consents, it may be made after private business (*q.v.*) is finished and before questions, or when questions are over and before public business is entered on, as well as at the usual time for moving substantive motions. If, however, it is opposed, the motion must appear after the government orders of the day; and, unless the mover succeeds in obtaining a favourable place for it during private members' time, he will be unlikely to be able to bring it before the House.

ROYAL ASSENT

The final stage in the making of a law; it is the act whereby the Queen concurs with the two Houses in passing a bill and thereby converts it into an Act of Parliament or statute. Although the royal assent is a part of the Queen's prerogative, it has not been refused to a bill since Queen Anne withheld her assent from the Scottish Militia Bill in 1707; and it is difficult to conceive of circumstances in which it could be refused today.

The royal assent may be given to a number of bills at one time. Until 1967 it had for many years been signified by a commission of peers on behalf of the Queen; the Sovereign has not attended in person for this purpose since 1854. The royal commission has in its turn been largely superseded; the Royal Assent Act 1967 allows the Queen's assent to be signified by Letters Patent, under the Great Seal, signed with her own hand and notified to each House by its presiding officer. The older method has not been abolished and is, in fact, used at least once in every session. In this case the commission usually consists of three peers, of whom the Lord Chancellor is one. At the time appointed, the Gentleman (or in his absence, the Yeoman) Usher of the Black Rod is sent by the Lords Commissioners to summon the Commons to the House of Lords or Parliament Chamber. This officer, attired in court dress and wearing a sword, makes a ceremonial entry to the House of Commons; as he approaches, the outer door of the chamber is shut, in accordance with the practice traditionally observed on the approach of a messenger from the Sovereign. He knocks three times on the door with his staff; he is admitted, and the business in progress is immediately suspended. If the House is in committee, the chairman leaves the chair of the committee and the Speaker resumes the chair of the House. Black Rod then walks up the floor of the House, bowing three times as he goes, and addresses the Speaker in these words: "Mr. Speaker, the Lords, who are authorised by virtue of Her Majesty's commission, to declare Her royal assent to acts passed by both Houses, desire the presence of this honourable House"—(he bows to left and right) —"in the House of Peers, to hear the commission read". He bows once more, and retires. The Speaker leaves the chair, and, preceded by the Serjeant at Arms carrying the mace, and followed by the Clerk of the House and by members walking two by two, he walks to the bar of the House of Lords, where the Commons stand during the ceremony which follows. After the arrival of the Commons, the commission is read by the Reading Clerk; the Clerk of the Crown then reads out the name of each bill in turn, and to each the royal assent is signified by the Clerk of the Parliaments, in Norman French, with the words "la Reyne le veult". At these words, the bill becomes an Act of Parliament. A bill for granting money to the Crown, such as a Consolidated Fund Bill, having been returned to the House of Commons to await the Royal assent is brought to the House of Lords by the Clerk of the House of Commons, who gives it to the Speaker when they reach the bar of the House of Lords. The Speaker hands the bill to the Clerk of the Parliaments, who goes to the bar to receive it. The royal assent is given to such a bill in the words, "La Reyne remercie ses bons sujets, accepte leur benevolence et ainsi le veult". Personal bills receive the royal assent with the words "Soit fait comme il est desire".

When the royal assent is given by notification, a bill becomes law when the notification is given to the second House. Church measures receive the royal assent in the same way as bills. Church measures are the legislative enactments of the General Synod of the Church of England, which, after being approved by resolution of both Houses of Parliament, are presented to the Queen for her royal assent in the same way as bills (*see* MEASURES).

SCHEDULE

An appendix to a bill containing matter which cannot readily be reduced into the proper form for a clause or which would be inconvenient for the reader if inserted in the body of the bill, *e.g.* blank forms, tables, lists, etc. A schedule forms part of the bill to which it is attached.

In committee the schedules to a bill are considered after the committee has gone through the clauses of the bill and has dealt with any proposed new clauses. The procedure on a schedule is similar to the procedure on a clause, the final question put, however, being : " That this schedule (as amended) be the (first) schedule to the bill ", or, in the case of a new schedule : " That this schedule (as amended) be added to the bill ".

SCOTTISH BILLS

If the Speaker is of opinion that a public bill relates exclusively to Scotland, he gives a certificate to that effect, which is entered in the Votes and Proceedings. Part of the proceedings on the bill may then, unless a sufficient number of members object to this course, be transferred from the floor of the House to the Scottish Grand Committee. When the bill comes up for second reading, a motion may be made by a minister of the Crown to refer the bill to the Scottish Grand Committee. This motion may not be amended or debated, and it is not carried if as many as ten members rise in their places and object. If it is carried (as it almost invariably is), the committee must consider the bill " in relation to its principle ", and then report to the House that it has done so. It should be noted that the committee cannot reject the bill ; it can only debate it. The bill thus returned to the House has not yet been read a second time ; but when it comes up for second reading again (provided that notice of an amendment to the second reading has not been given by at least six members), a motion may be made by a minister to commit the bill to a Scottish Standing Committee. This motion may be neither amended nor debated. If it is carried, the bill is deemed to have been read a second time and proceeds in the normal way through committee.

A bill which has been considered by the Scottish Grand Committee at the second reading stage may, after it has been reported from committee, be referred again to the Scottish Grand Committee for " consideration on report " (*see* COMMITTEE TO CONSIDER BILL ON REPORT). A motion so to refer a bill must be made after notice by a minister of the crown at the commencement of public business, may not be amended or debated, and is not carried if as many as twenty members rise in their places and object.

SCOTTISH GRAND COMMITTEE

The name by which one of the Scottish Standing Committees is known. The function of this Committee is to consider (*a*) bills certified by the Speaker as relating exclusively to Scotland which have not been read a second time and have been referred to the Committee for consideration " in relation to their principle ", (*b*) bills which, having been so referrred to the Committee for consideration, are again referred to it for consideration on report, (*c*) Scottish estimates, and (*d*) specific matters relating exclusively to Scotland which have been referred to the Committee. The Committee consists of all the members for Scottish constituencies together with from ten to fifteen additional members drawn from the various parties in such proportions as will ensure that the parties are represented in the Committee in approximately the same proportions as in the House itself. This would not necessarily be the case if the Committee consisted solely of the members for Scottish constituencies.

For the reference to the Scottish Grand Committee of bills which have not been read a second time and estimates *see* SCOTTISH BILLS *and* ESTIMATES.

Matters relating exclusively to Scotland may be referred to the Committee only on the motion of a Minister of the Crown at the commencement of public business. Such a motion may not be amended or debated and is not carried if as many as ten members rise in their places and object.

When estimates are referred to the Committee, it cannot reject or reduce any grant ; it can only discuss them and report that it has considered them. Similarly, when a matter is referred to the Committee it cannot come to any resolution or vote upon it ; it can only discuss it and report that it has considered it.

The Scottish Grand Committee may not consider estimates on more than six days in the session, nor matters which have been referred to it on more than two.

SCOTTISH PRIVATE LEGISLATION

As far as Scotland is concerned procedure by provisional order has almost entirely replaced procedure by private bill. By the Private Legislation Procedure (Scotland) Act 1936 (which superseded an Act of 1899 with a similar title), local authorities, companies or persons who wish to obtain parliamentary powers in regard to any matter affecting public or private interests in Scotland, instead of petitioning the House of Commons for a private bill, must petition the Secretary of State for Scotland for a provisional order. Such petitions may be presented at two periods of the year, viz., November 24–27 or March 24–27. Copies of the draft order (which must accompany the petition) have to be deposited with the Clerk of the Parliaments, the Private Bill

SCOTTISH PRIVATE LEGISLATION—*continued*
Office of the House of Commons, the Treasury and certain other offices. Applicants for provisional orders have to publish and serve notices, to obtain consents and to deposit plans and other documents in various offices in much the same way as in the case of a private bill.

The draft orders, together with any dissents from or objections to any of their provisions which have been duly stated in the prescribed manner, are then considered by the Lord Chairman and the Chairman of Ways and Means. If these officers report that either of them considers that the powers sought by a particular application relate to matters outside Scotland to such an extent, or raise questions of public policy of such novelty and importance that the application ought to be dealt with by Parliament itself, the Secretary of State is bound to refuse to issue the order. It is, however, open to the applicants to proceed with their application by a private bill. It is not unusual for the chairmen to report that part of the proposed order should proceed as a private bill and the remainder as a provisional order. If the chairmen report that a particular application may proceed as a provisional order, the next step depends on whether or not it is opposed, *i.e.* whether a petition against it is deposited at the Scottish Office within the prescribed time.

If the order is opposed the Secretary of State must refer it to a commission for inquiry. He may also refer an order which is not opposed to a commission if he thinks it advisable. The commission of inquiry consists as a rule of two members of the House of Lords and two members of the House of Commons, selected by the Lord Chairman and the Chairman of Ways and Means respectively from panels chosen by the Committees of Selection of the respective Houses. If necessary, however, three or even all four commissioners may be taken from either panel. If sufficient commissioners cannot be drawn from the parliamentary panels, the number is made up by the Secretary of State from the "extra-parliamentary panel". This consists of twenty persons "qualified by experience of affairs to act as commissioners", nominated for a term of five years by the Chairmen acting jointly with the Secretary of State for Scotland. One of the commissioners is appointed as chairman. (The chairmen of commissions of inquiry are appointed alternately by the Lord Chairman and the Chairman of Ways and Means.) The chairman has a deliberative as well as a casting vote. Three commissioners form a quorum.

The inquiry is usually held at Edinburgh or Glasgow, but sometimes at Aberdeen. It is held in public and the proceedings are similar to the proceedings before a committee on an opposed private bill. Questions of *locus standi* are determined by the commissioners, who have power to award costs.

If the commissioners report against the order the Secretary of State is bound to refuse to issue it. But if they report in favour of it, the Secretary of State may issue the order either as prayed for or with modifications. In deciding whether to issue the order with or without modification he must have regard to any recommendations the commissioners, the Chairmen, the Treasury and other government departments may have made.

If the order is not opposed, or any petitions presented against it are withdrawn before an inquiry has been held by commissioners the preamble has to be proved before the Counsel to the Secretary of State. The order is then issued either as prayed for, or with such modifications as appear necessary in view of any recommendations the Chairmen, the Treasury and other government departments may have made.

The procedure on a bill to confirm a provisional order issued under the Private Legislation Procedure (Scotland) Act differs according as an inquiry has or has not been held by commissioners in Scotland. If no inquiry has been held, the bill is deemed to have passed through all the stages in each House up to and including the committee stage (s. 7.) If, however, an inquiry has been held the bill must be given a second reading and may, if a petition against the order is presented within seven days from the introduction of the bill, be referred, on motion, to a joint committee of both Houses (s. 9). Such a motion requires notice and must be made immediately after the bill has been given a second reading.

In order to give an opportunity for making such a motion at least seven days are allowed to elapse between the introduction of the bill and its second reading. If a motion to refer the bill to a joint committee is carried, the bill stands referred to a joint committee, the concurrence of the other House not being required. The joint committee consists of six members, three from each House, nominated by the Committees of Selection of the respective Houses. The applicants for the order and the petitioners are heard, in person or by counsel, in support of the order and against it. Any question of *locus standi* is determined by the committee which may, by a majority, award costs.

If no motion for referring the bill to a joint committee is carried, the bill is deemed to have passed the committee stage and is ordered to be considered as if reported from a committee. Whether or not the bill has been referred to a joint committee, it is deemed to have passed the committee stage in the second House, *i.e.* the bill goes straight from the second reading to the report stage.

There have been several attempts to refer bills for confirming provisional orders issued under the Private Legislation Procedure (Scotland) Act to joint committees, but up to the present time only one such motion has been carried. It is the House in which the

SCOTTISH PRIVATE LEGISLATION—*continued*

bill is introduced which decides whether there shall be a second inquiry. No motion to refer the bill to a joint committee may be made in the second House even though such a motion was not made in the first House.

If the Lord Chairman and the Chairman of Ways and Means decide that a provisional order or part thereof should not be allowed to proceed as a provisional order, the applicants may promote a private bill for the same objects. In this event they must give notice of their intention to all opponents, and must deposit copies of the substituted bill (as it is called) in every office in which copies of the draft provisional order were deposited. They are, however, not required to deposit a petition for the bill, the petition for the provisional order, when transmitted from the Scottish Office, being received as the petition for the bill. Nor are they required to give fresh notices or deposit fresh plans, etc. Opponents who have petitioned against the draft order do not have to petition against the bill, the petitions against the draft order, when transmitted from the Scottish Office to the Private Bill Office of the House of Commons or the corresponding office of the House of Lords, being received as petitions against the bill.

SCOTTISH STANDING COMMITTEE

The Standing Orders provide for the appointment of not more than two standing committees to consider public bills certified by the Speaker as relating exclusively to Scotland when they have been read a second time and committed to a standing committee, or have been deemed to be read a second time under the procedure applicable to Scottish Bills (*q.v.*) and committed to a standing committee. The term " Scottish Standing Committee " is generally used to mean either of these two committees, but in fact the Scottish Grand Committee (*q.v.*) is also a Scottish Standing Committee.

Bills which are considered by the two Scottish Standing Committees referred to above at their committee stage are subject to the same procedure as bills which are considered by any other standing committee at the committee stage.

The first of these two Scottish Standing Committees consists of thirty members representing Scottish constituencies, and not more than twenty other members; this Committee normally considers major government bills. The second Scottish Standing Committee consists of not less than sixteen members and not more than fifty, of whom not less than sixteen must represent Scottish constituencies; this Committee is mainly concerned with the consideration of private members' bills. The members of the committee are appointed from time to time for the period when a particular bill is under consideration. They are selected by the Committee of Selection which is directed, in choosing them " to have regard to their qualifications and to the composition of the House ", *i.e.* they are to be drawn from the various parties in such proportions as will ensure that the parties are represented on the committee as nearly as possible in proportion to their strength in the House, but that, subject to this, special knowledge of, or interest in, the subject with which the bill deals shall be the criterion in choosing the personnel of the committee.

SEATS OR PLACES

The present arrangement of seats in the debating chamber of the House of Commons is modelled on that of St. Stephen's Chapel, which the House occupied for some three hundred years before it was destroyed by fire in 1834. Consequently the members sit in long rows facing each other, on either side of the chamber, across a long narrow stretch of carpet which extends from the Table of the House to the bar and beyond that to the doors. By a long-established custom the Government and their supporters occupy one side of the House, on the right hand of the Speaker, and the opposition party or parties the other. This arrangement, whereby a member must by his position declare himself either in support of the Government or against it, is generally considered to have influenced the formation of the two-party system which has usually obtained in this country.

Generally speaking, no member is entitled, as of permanent right, to any particular seat in the chamber ; but there are certain qualifications to be made to this statement. The front bench on the government side, known as the Treasury Bench, is reserved for Her Majesty's ministers. The most important seat on it is that opposite the despatch box, at which ministers stand when speaking. The two members for the City of London, until the abolition in 1950 of the City's separate representation, had the right of sitting on the Treasury Bench on the first day of a new session. The bench immediately behind is occupied by the ministers' parliamentary private secretaries. Opposite the Treasury bench is the Opposition front bench, the most important seat in which is opposite the despatch box on that side of the Table. The right to occupy a seat on this bench belongs, again by custom, to ex-ministers, privy counsellors, and other prominent members in opposition to the Government.

Apart from the two front benches no particular significance attaches to any seat in the House ; though a member who wishes to indicate a measure of independence of, or disagreement with, a government or party that in general he supports, often chooses a seat " below the gangway ", that is, on the far side (from the Speaker's chair) of the gangway which runs across the benches on either side of the House. A place just below the gangway is a favourite position for an ex-minister to occupy when he makes a

SEATS OR PLACES—*continued*

statement explaining the reasons which have led him to resign office. Distinguished members of long standing are sometimes accorded a particular seat by courtesy of their fellow members.

Within these limits, and bearing in mind that the government majority may be so large that their supporters have to occupy some of the seats on the Opposition side of the House, members sit where they like, or where they can. Since the House only seats some four hundred out of more than six hundred members (including a hundred in the side galleries, from which, though technically within the House, members never speak), there is naturally great competition to secure a place on important occasions such as Budget Day. On these occasions all seats are filled, and members may be seen sitting on the steps leading to the Speaker's chair and standing crowded in the space behind the chair and between the bar and the doors. A member may, however, reserve for himself a particular seat for one day, by placing on it a white card (which he obtains from an attendant) before the beginning of the sitting, provided that he is then present at prayers. If he cannot attend prayers because he is in a select or standing committee, he may use a pink card, which will secure him the same privilege.

SECONDING OF MOTIONS

The expression by a member of his approval of a motion preliminary to its being considered by the House. In the House of Commons no motion now requires to be seconded ; it is, however, still the practice for two kinds of motion to be seconded, namely, the motion for an address in reply to the Queen's speech and that for the election of the Speaker.

In the House of Lords the only motion which requires to be seconded is the motion for the address in reply to the speech from the throne.

SECRET SESSION

A sitting of either House of Parliament which, or the remainder of which, that House has resolved shall be a secret session. Each House has also sometimes resolved that particular proceedings shall be held in secret session. Not only members of the public, but officers of the House who are not members (with the exception of the Clerks at the Table and, in the Commons, the Serjeant at Arms and the Deputy and Assistant Serjeant, and, in the Lords, the Gentleman Usher of the Black Rod and the Yeoman Usher and the Serjeant at Arms) are excluded. Members of the House of Lords are, however, allowed to be present at secret sessions of the House of Commons, and members of that House are allowed to be present at secret sessions of the House of Lords.

It is a contempt of the House for a member to disclose or purport to disclose anything said in the course of a secret session. It is also a contempt for any person to publish a report or what purports to be a report of the proceedings at a secret session. When it is desired to hold a secret session, the leader of the House or some other member of the Government "spies strangers", and when strangers have been ordered to withdraw, moves either that the remainder of the day's sitting be a secret session or that certain specified proceedings be held in secret session (*see* SPYING STRANGERS). Secret sessions have hitherto been held only in war-time.

During the late war a member was alleged to have disclosed the substance of part of a speech made by the Prime Minister in the course of proceedings which had been held in secret session. The matter was referred to the Committee of Privileges, which investigated the charge and reported that it had not been proved.

SELECTION, COMMITTEE OF

A committee appointed in each House by standing order. The Commons Committee of Selection consists of eleven members. The quorum is three. The functions of the Committee are to refer private bills and provisional order bills to committees and, in the case of opposed bills, to appoint the chairmen and members of the committees on such bills, to fix the date and the time of first meeting and to name the bill or bills to be considered thereat. The Committee also nominates the members of standing committees and the commons members of joint committees on petitions against special procedure orders, as well as certain other committees and panels of members.

The Lords Committee of Selection consists of the Lord Chairman and such other lords as are named by the House. Its functions are to select the members of committees on opposed private or provisional order bills, to appoint the chairmen and to name the bill or bills to be considered on the first or any later day of meeting, and to appoint the Lords members of joint committees on petitions against special procedure orders.

In each House the Committee of Selection is regularly entrusted with the selection of members to serve on select committees on hybrid bills and specially constituted committees on private and provisional order bills.

In the Lords all appointments made by the Committee of Selection have to be approved by the House; this, however, is merely a formal proceeding.

SELECTION OF AMENDMENTS

A method of avoiding unnecessary debates or the duplication of debates when an amendment or a series of amendments is proposed to a motion or a bill. In the House of Commons, the Speaker and, when the House is in committee, the Chairman and Deputy Chairman of Ways and Means have power to select which amendments, if any, shall be moved to the motion or bill under consideration and in the case of bills which, if any, new clauses and

SELECTION OF AMENDMENTS—*continued*

new schedules shall be proposed. When notice has been given of a series of amendments covering related matters, only one of them is normally selected to be moved on the understanding that in the debate on that amendment the subject matter of the related amendments may also be discussed. Where in the view of the Chair the subject matter of any of the related amendments so warrants, one or more of them may subsequently be moved on the express understanding that the question thereon is decided immediately without further debate.

The Chairman of Ways and Means, when acting as Deputy Speaker, cannot exercise the power of selecting amendments unless the unavoidable absence of the Speaker has been formally notified to the House; while the Deputy Chairman of Ways and Means, when acting as Deputy Speaker, cannot exercise the power unless the unavoidable absence both of the Speaker and of the Chairman of Ways and Means has been announced. Before deciding whether or not to allow a particular amendment to be moved the Speaker or the Chairman or Deputy Chairman of Ways and Means, as the case may be, may call on the member in whose name the amendment stands on the notice paper to explain its object. The Speaker or the Chairman of Ways and Means sometimes announces in advance what amendments he proposes to call or states why he is not calling a particular amendment. The chairman of a standing committee also has power to select amendments.

The power of the Chair to select amendments is given in a standing order first made in 1919 to combat the kind of obstruction which consisted of moving amendments to every line of a bill.

SERJEANT AT ARMS

Two of the Queen's Serjeants at Arms in Ordinary are appointed, one to attend upon the Speaker of the House of Commons, the other "to attend upon the Chancellor or Keeper or Commissioners for the custody of the Great Seal of the Realm for the time being".

When no Parliament is in existence, it is the duty of the Serjeant in the House of Commons (like the other Serjeants at Arms) to attend the Queen herself, but in practice this duty is not carried out. When the Speaker goes to and from the chamber before and after the sitting he is preceded by the Serjeant carrying the mace on his shoulder. The same ceremony is observed when the Speaker, with the House, leaves the chamber to proceed elsewhere; for example, to the House of Lords, to attend the Queen at the opening of Parliament or when the royal assent is to be given to bills, or to attend divine service in Saint Margaret's Church.

The Serjeant is generally responsible for keeping order in the lobbies and precincts of the House, and for controlling the admission of strangers to the galleries. He appoints and controls the doorkeepers and assistant doorkeepers of the House. He may be called upon to arrest a person guilty of an offence against the privileges of the House: orders for the attendance of persons required as witnesses by the House or any of its committees are served by doorkeepers acting under his instructions. The Serjeant acts, in fact, as the executive officer of the House, but, if force is needed outside the precincts, he relies on the assistance of the police. Within the precincts he is aided in maintaining order by the doorkeepers and by the policemen who are regularly employed there to carry out his instructions.

The Serjeant, as Housekeeper of the House of Commons (under the House of Commons Offices Act 1812), is generally responsible for the domestic arrangements in that part of the Palace of Westminster which is occupied by the House of Commons, and for the supervision of the employees of the Ministry of Works, cleaners, liftmen, attendants, etc., who work there; in carrying out his duties he acts on the directions of the Speaker, who himself acts on the advice of the Select Committee on House of Commons (Services).

The Serjeant at Arms is assisted by a Deputy and an Assistant and a Deputy Assistant Serjeant, who are appointed by him and share with him his duties both inside the chamber and elsewhere.

The Serjeant at Arms in the House of Lords is appointed by Her Majesty to attend the Lord Chancellor at all times, not only when he is acting as Speaker of the House of Lords, but also when he is carrying out his functions as head of the judiciary, *e.g.* at the opening of the Law Courts. The Serjeant carries the mace in front of the Lord Chancellor when the latter goes to or from the Parliament Chamber (the House of Lords); he similarly attends the Lord Chairman or other peer who takes the Woolsack as Lord Speaker in the Lord Chancellor's absence. He also, when necessary, arrests persons outside London on the order of the House. Other duties, comparable to those of the Serjeant at Arms in the House of Commons, are performed for the House of Lords by the Gentleman Usher of the Black Rod (*q.v.*). The Serjeant has a deputy who is appointed by the Lord Chancellor and acts as the latter's secretary.

The Serjeants at Arms in both Houses wear a court suit of black cloth with a sword.

SESSION

Each Parliament consists of one or more terms or periods known as sessions. The first of these begins on the day on which the new Parliament is directed by royal proclamation to meet, and continues until Parliament is prorogued by the Queen. The Lord Chancellor, in announcing the prorogation on behalf of the Queen,

SESSION—*continued*

names the day on which Parliament is to reassemble, when the new session begins. The length of each session is therefore determined by royal proclamation. The session usually lasts about a year, but may last for longer (like that of 1966–67, which lasted from April 21, 1966, to October 27, 1967); it may also be much shorter (like that of 1948, which lasted from September 14 to October 25). If a Parliament itself lasts for only one year, it may comprise only one session, as happened in 1924.

The business of a session is begun by the speech with which the Queen opens Parliament, and is closed by another speech, normally delivered by the Lord Chancellor on the Queen's behalf. Each speech is a statement by the Queen's ministers, through the Sovereign, on the work of the Government and Parliament during the session. All proceedings on public bills and other matters are brought to an end by the close of the session, unless the House in which they are in progress expressly makes provision for their continuance; a bill therefore, which has not received the royal assent before Parliament is prorogued must, if it is to become law, be begun afresh in the next session and pass through all its stages anew. Arrangements are, however, often made in the case of private bills, and sometimes in the case of hybrid bills, which have not been completed before the prorogation for carrying them over into the new session. A bill thus carried over is said to be "suspended" in the session in which it is introduced (*see* BILL, PRIVATE; PROROGATION).

SESSIONAL ORDERS AND RESOLUTIONS

A sessional order or resolution is one which is renewed each session. A number of such orders or resolutions are passed by the House of Commons at the beginning of each session. They relate to double elections, inability of peers to vote at elections, bribery and corruption at elections, tampering with witnesses, false evidence, clearing the approaches to the House, the printing of the Votes and Proceedings of the House, the appointment of a Committee of Privileges and the printing of the Journal of the House.

SHORT TITLE

The name by which a bill is described in the notice or order paper, the Votes and Proceedings, and the Journal of the House of Commons and the corresponding publications of the House of Lords. The short title must not be confused with the title proper (*q.v.*) (often called the long title) which is prefixed to the bill.

A clause, generally called the citation clause, appears in every bill, declaring that the intended act may be cited by its short title.

SITTINGS OF THE HOUSE OF COMMONS

The House meets on Mondays, Tuesdays, Wednesdays and Thursdays at 2.30 p.m., and on Fridays at 11 a.m. These are the normal days and hours of sitting prescribed by standing order. If the House wishes to vary them for a particular occasion, it does so by resolution. This occurs most commonly when the House is about to adjourn for a period longer than a week-end, on a day other than Friday. For example, the House usually adjourns for the Easter holiday on Maundy Thursday, and on that and similar occasions meets at 11 a.m., and rises not later than 5 p.m. Occasionally, and usually only in times of crisis, the House meets on Saturday or Sunday. This happened in 1939 on Saturday, September 2, and Sunday, September 3 (on which day war broke out), when the House met at 2.45 p.m. (then the usual hour of meeting) and at 12 noon respectively. On Saturday, July 30, 1949, the House sat (at 11 a.m.) in order to deal with unfinished business before adjourning for the summer recess, and on Saturday, November 3, 1956, the House met (at 12 noon) to debate the Suez operations.

The arrangements for terminating the sitting are complicated by the need to make provision for (1) the interruption and disposal of the business in progress, followed by a short interval during which only unopposed business may be taken, (2) the inclusion of a short debate on a motion for the adjournment of the House, and (3) the prolongation of the sitting in certain cases by the exemption of business from interruption.

The sitting may be brought to an end by a simple resolution "That this House do now adjourn". If, however, as usually happens, business is still proceeding at 10 p.m. (4 p.m. on Fridays), the Speaker must interrupt it; this he does by rising, saying "Order, order", and asking what day the business is to be resumed. If the House is in committee, the chairman interrupts the proceedings by saying "Order, order", and then leaves the chair of the committee, subsequently making a report when the chair of the House is resumed by the Speaker (*see* COMMITTEE OF THE WHOLE HOUSE). When the business in progress at the moment of interruption has thus been disposed of, only unopposed business may be dealt with. Either a motion for the adjournment of the House is moved forthwith (by a government whip), or the remaining orders of the day are read. An order of the day in these circumstances may only be proceeded with if no member opposes it or objects to its being taken. Many a bill has thus received a second or third reading "on the nod", without any debate taking place, during the time reserved for unopposed business. If, however, any objection be made (the single word "Object" is enough to stop any further proceeding), the order must be deferred to a future day. A motion for the adjournment may be interposed after some, but not all, the orders have been read or the government whip may allow them all to be taken before rising to move "That this House do now adjourn". This motion may be agreed to without a debate, on which the

SITTINGS OF THE HOUSE OF COMMONS—*continued*
House adjourns forthwith, or, as usually happens, a member (either having been successful in the ballot which is regularly held to allot this much-sought privilege or having been selected by the Speaker) may take the opportunity to raise some matter in which he is interested, and secure an answer or statement of policy from the responsible minister. If the debate is not over, and the adjournment agreed to, within half an hour after it has been moved, the Speaker must himself adjourn the House without putting any question. This he does by rising, saying " Order, order! The House now stands adjourned ", and leaving the chair (*see* ADJOURNMENT OF THE HOUSE).

If the House (or a committee of the whole House) is in process of taking a decision when the hour of interruption is reached, the business is not interrupted until that process is completed. This covers not merely the putting of a question, but includes any consequential questions, and divisions if necessary. Thus, for example, if a debate were in progress on a motion, an amendment to the motion having been moved, the closure might be moved as the clock struck ; the question could be put on that and decided in favour by a division, followed by the question on the amendment, and, after that, by the question on the motion itself, each accompanied by a division, making three divisions in all. The business would not be interrupted until the last division had been completed.

Certain kinds of business are exempt from interruption at 10 p.m. and may be either begun, or, if already begun, proceeded with after that hour, even though opposed ; this business, known to members as " exempted business ", includes bills brought in on resolutions (such as the Finance, Consolidated Fund and Appropriation Bills), proceedings in pursuance of certain standing orders, notably motions to approve mail or telegraphic contracts (this includes contracts with the British Broadcasting Corporation), proceedings on motions authorising expenditure in connection with bills (" money resolutions ") and proceedings in pursuance of any Act of Parliament. The time during which proceedings in the last two categories are exempted is limited. In the case of " money resolutions " the question must be put at 10.45 p.m. or three-quarters of an hour after the proceedings have been begun (whichever is the later). Proceedings in pursuance of an Act of Parliament comprise chiefly motions for the approval and for the annulment of statutory instruments. Proceedings on motions for approval may continue until 11.30 p.m. or for one and a half hours (whichever is the longer period) ; the Speaker then either puts the question, or, if he thinks the importance of the subject matter warrants further discussion, adjourns the debate till the next sitting (other than a Friday). Proceedings on motions for annulment may not be entered upon at or after 11.30 p.m.; if such a motion is under consideration at that hour, the Speaker must put the question necessary for its decision but here, too, he may, if he thinks fit, adjourn the debate as explained above (*see also* EXEMPTED BUSINESS).

Other business may be given the status of "exempted business" at any particular sitting by order of the House. For this purpose a motion "That the proceedings on (some specified business) may be entered upon and proceeded with at this day's sitting at any hour, though opposed", must appear on the order paper in the name of a minister at the commencement of public business; it is not however taken at that point but stands over until the interruption of business at 10 p.m. and may then be moved when such business has been disposed of, no amendment or debate being allowed. If the business in progress is itself exempted business it must be interrupted and may be resumed after the motion has been decided. The motion must specify the business to be exempted, a requirement which is satisfied by the use of the term "Government business", and the exemption may be for an indefinite period or it may be limited, for example, to one hour, or it may be indefinite for some items of business and limited for others. Any business which has been postponed in order to make way for a motion for the adjournment "on a specific and important matter that should have urgent consideration" (when the Speaker has directed that the urgency of the matter requires it to be discussed on the day on which it is raised) becomes exempted business for a period of time equal to the duration of the proceedings in favour of which it was postponed. At the conclusion of the exempted business unopposed business may be taken in the same way as after 10 p.m. Usually, however, the adjournment is moved at once, and, if the debate thereon is not finished and the motion agreed to within half an hour, the Speaker adjourns the House without putting any question, as after an ordinary sitting. The rules given above for bringing the sitting to an end apply to Fridays, with the substitution of 4 p.m. for 10 p.m.

The importance of the procedure for exempting business lies in the fact that by enabling the sitting to be extended indefinitely it ensures that the House shall not fail to come to a decision for want of time. This, like the closure and the guillotine, is one of the devices at the Government's disposal for countering the minority's weapon of obstruction. It is, however, most often used to make time for business which it would otherwise be difficult or impossible to fit into the time-table of the House. Few weeks pass without an extra hour or two thus being added to the hours of sitting, and as the session proceeds and the time-table becomes more congested, late sittings till twelve or one o'clock become more frequent.

SITTINGS OF THE HOUSE OF COMMONS—*continued*

"All-night sittings", till 5 or 6 a.m. or later, are rare, but a year seldom passes without two or three. The record length was reached on January 31, 1881, when the House sat for $41\frac{1}{2}$ hours, most of which was spent in discussing the Protection of Person and Property (Ireland) Bill (commonly called the "Coercion Bill"). This, however, was before the standing order for bringing the sitting to an end had been passed. The longest sitting of recent years was that of July 23, 1935, which lasted for $34\frac{1}{2}$ hours; certain Unemployment Assistance Regulations (relating to the "Means Test") were the main item of business on this occasion. In theory a sitting may last indefinitely for the consideration of exempted business, but some limit is imposed by the rule that if it extends beyond the hour of meeting of the following day (11 a.m. on Fridays, 2.30 p.m. on other days), the latter sitting is cancelled and its business deferred till another day. Such a result is inconvenient for the Government, if they lose a day for business which has to be accommodated later on in a crowded session. The sitting may be suspended in certain circumstances (*see* SUSPENSION OF SITTING), notably under the Standing Order which provides for the possibility of suspension at any time after 10 p.m. and for the resumption of proceedings on the following morning.

SPEAKER

The title of the presiding officers in the two Houses of Parliament. The Speaker of the House of Commons was originally so called because his function was to speak for the Commons in all the proceedings of the Parliament in which they were allowed or required to take part. The title was borrowed from the Commons by the Lords, who did not become a "House" until a considerable time after the House of Commons.

The Speaker of the House of Commons is elected at the beginning of each new Parliament by the members from among themselves, not on their own initiative, but in obedience to the Queen's command.*

On the day appointed for the meeting of Parliament the members of the House of Commons, who have assembled in their House, are summoned to the House of Lords, where the Lord Chancellor, as mouthpiece of the commissioners for opening the Parliament, informs the members of both Houses that as soon as they have taken the oath of allegiance the Queen will declare the causes of her calling the Parliament. He then directs the members of the House of Commons, in the Queen's name, to repair to the place where they are to sit and there proceed to the choice of some proper person to be their Speaker and present the person

* The first recorded instance of the Commons being directed to choose a Speaker occurred in 1384.

whom they so choose in the House of Lords on the morrow at an hour named for the royal approbation.

The members of the House of Commons then return to their House and elect their Speaker. The election is usually little more than a formality, the member who was Speaker in the preceding Parliament, if he is a member of the new one, being re-elected unanimously. (There has been no instance to the contrary since 1835, when the Whig majority refused to re-elect Sir Charles Manners Sutton, who had been Speaker since 1817, on the ground that he had assisted with others in the formation of the Tory administration on Lord Melbourne's dismissal by the King.)

Arrangements are if possible made beforehand by the Government for the re-election of the Speaker to be proposed by one of their leading supporters and seconded by a member from the other side of the House. The proposal for the Speaker's re-election takes the form of a motion "That Mr. So-and-so do take the Chair of this House as Speaker". The proposer and seconder address their speeches to the Clerk of the House, who acts as chairman during the election. He does not, however, call on members who rise to speak by name; he stands up and points with his finger at them, and then sits down.

If no other candidate is nominated and no member rises to oppose the motion,* the member whose re-election as Speaker is proposed, after expressing his sense of the honour proposed to be conferred on him, "submits himself to the will of the House". His proposer and seconder then lead him to the chair. Before taking his seat, the Speaker elect (as he is called until approved by the Queen) thanks the House for the honour they have conferred on him. The mace, which up to this point has been under the Table of the House, is now placed on it, and after the leader of the House, the leader of the Oppposition and the leaders of the other parties have congratulated the Speaker elect, the House, on the motion of the leader of the House, adjourns to the following day.

Should two candidates be nominated as Speaker, both candidates address the House, and, after their comparative merits have been debated, the Clerk puts the question that the member who was first proposed "do take the chair of the House as Speaker".† If this question is decided in the affirmative, the member is led to the chair in the manner already described. If, however, it is decided in the negative, the Clerk puts a similar question in respect of the other member who has been proposed as Speaker.

* In 1911, although no other candidate was nominated, a member spoke in opposition to the motion for re-electing Mr. Lowther Speaker. In 1698 and again in 1700, although only one candidate was nominated, the Tories on the first occasion and the Whigs on the second divided the House on the question that he "do take the chair as Speaker".

† This last happened in 1951 on the first election of Mr. Speaker Morrison.

SPEAKER—*continued*

If this question is agreed to, the member is led to the chair by his proposers and seconder.

On the following day the Speaker elect takes the chair shortly before the time at which the Commons have been directed to present him for the royal approbation and awaits the summons to the House of Lords. When this is received he proceeds to the House of Lords, accompanied by a number of members. There he informs the Lords Commissioners that the choice of the Commons has fallen on him, and "submits himself with all humility to Her Majesty's gracious approbation", which is signified by the Lord Chancellor. (The only instance of the royal approbation being refused occurred in 1678, when Charles II refused to approve Sir Edward Seymour's election.) The Speaker then "lays claim, by humble petition", to the Commons' ancient and undoubted rights and privileges, and when these have been confirmed returns to the House of Commons, and reports what has taken place.

Duties of the Speaker. The duties of the Speaker may be divided into those which are performed by him in virtue of the authority derived from the House itself, and those which he is either required or authorised by statute to perform. Some of these duties are necessarily performed in the chair of the House, while others are performed out of the House, at the foot of the throne, at the bar of the House of Lords, in his own room at the House, at his own residence or elsewhere.

Those duties which are performed in the chair, by authority of the House, are as follows: he presides at all sittings of the House except when the House is in committee. He calls upon members to speak, to ask questions and move motions of which they have given notice, and to present bills. (If two or more members rise at the same time, he decides which shall speak.) He *proposes* questions for the consideration of the House, and *puts* them for its decision. He maintains order in the House and enforces the observance of the rules and orders by which the proceedings of the House are regulated. (In the discharge of this duty he declines to submit to the House motions and amendments which infringe its rules.) The Speaker has power to direct a member who disregards the authority of the chair or conducts himself in a grossly disorderly manner to withdraw from the House, or, if he thinks the offence calls for punishment, to "name" the offender. (A member named by the Speaker is invariably suspended from the service of the House on a motion made by the leader of the House and agreed to without discussion.) In the event of grave disorder the Speaker has power either to adjourn the House or to suspend the sitting for a definite period. In the case of persistent irrelevance or tedious repetition of arguments the Speaker may direct the member to discontinue speaking. If he thinks a motion for the adjournment either of the House or of the debate is " an abuse of the rules of the House " (*q.v.*), he may either refuse to accept it, or put the question on it at once without allowing the motion to be discussed. He has power to accept a motion for the closure or to refuse to accept it. He has also power to select which amendments to a bill or motion shall be discussed. He may, if he thinks a division is unnecessarily claimed, take the vote of the House by calling in turn on the members who support and who challenge his decision to stand up, and then either declare the determination of the House or name tellers for a division. He decides doubtful points of order.

When any member calls his attention to the fact that forty members are not present, the Speaker counts the House and, if less than forty members are present, adjourns the House. On returning from attending the Queen or the Lords Commissioners in the House of Lords the Speaker reports what has passed there. When a written message from the Queen is brought by a member the Speaker reads it to the House. At his discretion he communicates to the House letters and documents addressed to him as representing the House. It is also occasionally his duty to examine witnesses at the bar, and, by order of the House, to thank persons or to reprimand or admonish them. By order of the House also he issues warrants for writs to fill vacancies among its members, for the arrest and imprisonment of offenders and for their discharge from custody, for bringing prisoners whose evidence is required before committees, and, in short, for giving effect to all orders of the House which require the sanction of a legal form.

On other occasions the Speaker, still acting by authority of the House, appears as its spokesman and representative beyond the precincts of its own chamber. When an address from the Commons is presented by the whole House, the Speaker reads it to Her Majesty. The Speaker has frequently to represent the Commons at the bar of the House of Lords. His first duty, on being approved by the Crown, is there to lay claim to their ancient and undoubted rights and privileges. When the Queen delivers her speech from the throne at the opening of a session, and when the Queen's speech is read to both Houses of Parliament at the conclusion of a session and whenever the royal assent is given to bills by royal commission, the Speaker attends at the bar of the House of Lords. When any bills of aids and supplies are to receive the royal assent, he presents them for such assent.

By order of the House he appoints the printer of the Journal of the House. He has charge of the arrangements for the official report of the debates (Hansard), and, control of that part of the Palace of Westminster which is occupied by the House of Commons having been transferred at the Queen's direction to the Speaker from the Lord Great Chamberlain, the Speaker now makes the necessary arrangements on the advice of the

SPEAKER—*continued*
Select Committee on House of Commons (Services). By standing order he is required, at the beginning of each session, to nominate a panel of not less than ten members to act as temporary chairmen of committees of the whole House when requested by the Chairman of Ways and Means. He names the five members who, with the members of the Chairmen's Panel, constitute the Business Committee (*q.v.*). He distributes bills which stand committed to a standing committee among the several standing committees, appoints the chairmen of these committees and performs other functions in reference thereto. By standing order he is empowered to call the House together during an adjournment if, on representations from the Government, such a course seems desirable.

During a recess by prorogation or adjournment the Speaker, under certain conditions, in pursuance of certain Acts of Parliament, issues warrants to the Clerk of the Crown to make out new writs to fill up vacancies among members caused by death, acceptance of office (other than the stewardship of either the Chiltern Hundreds or the Manor of Northstead), summons to the House of Lords, or bankruptcy. By statute he is also required, at the beginning of each Parliament, to appoint not more than seven, nor less than three members to execute these duties in case of his own death, the vacation of his seat, or his absence from the realm. The duty of issuing a warrant to the Clerk of the Crown to make out a new writ for electing another member in the room of a member of unsound mind is also imposed on the Speaker by the Mental Health Act 1961. He is one of the commissioners for regulating the Offices of the House of Commons and by usage acts as their chairman (*see* House of Commons Offices Commission). By the House of Commons Costs Taxation Act 1847 and the House of Lords Taxation Act 1849 the Speaker signs certificates of the costs allowed in promoting and opposing private bills. He decides whether a bill is or is not a money bill within the meaning of the Parliament Act, 1911 (*q.v.*). He nominates the Commons members of the Ecclesiastical Committee (*q.v.*) constituted under the Church of England Assembly (Powers) Act 1919. He determines who, as the leader of the party in opposition to the Government having the greatest numerical strength in the House of Commons, is entitled, under the Ministers of the Crown Act 1937, to be paid a salary as leader of the Opposition. By virtue of other Acts of Parliament the Speaker is entrusted with duties which have no reference to the House of Commons and his functions as Speaker and therefore do not fall within the purview of this work.

The Speaker must always be treated with the greatest respect and attention by the individual members of the House. Whenever he rises during a debate any member who is speaking or standing must sit down, and the whole House must be silent. The conduct of the Speaker cannot be criticised or discussed except on a substantive motion. It cannot be brought under the consideration of the House by an amendment or a motion for the adjournment of the House under Standing Order No. 9. A member may give the Speaker notice privately that he intends to submit a question of order for his decision, but he may not table a question to the Speaker.

Term of Office. The Speaker holds office during the whole term of the Parliament in which he is elected. When it is dissolved his office comes to an end ; but for certain purposes he is, by statute, even after the dissolution, deemed to be the Speaker until a Speaker is chosen in the new Parliament.

The Speaker takes no part in the debates in the House or, since 1870, in committee. He never votes except in the case of a tie, and then votes, if possible, in such a way as to give the House another chance to decide the question.

When he enters or leaves the House at the end of a sitting or to attend the Queen or the Lords Commissioners in the House of Lords, the Serjeant at Arms precedes him carrying his mace. When he is in the chair the mace is placed on the table.

He takes precedence immediately after the Lord President of the Council, *i.e.* he ranks sixth after the members of the royal family.

His salary of £8,500 a year is charged on the Consolidated Fund (*q.v.*), like the judges' salaries, and has not to be voted annually. When he retires he gives up his membership of the House, is given a pension and is usually made a peer (a viscount). But even if, like Mr. Whitley in 1928, he refuses the offer of a peerage, he gives up his membership of the House of Commons.

Death or Resignation of Speaker. If the Speaker dies or resigns, a new Speaker is elected in the manner already described. But the House does not proceed to choose a new Speaker until it has received the royal permission to do so. The Queen's permission to proceed to the choice of a new Speaker is usually communicated to the House by the Leader of the House. When the new Speaker has been elected, the Leader of the House or some other member of the Government announces the time at which the Speaker elect is to be presented at the bar of the House of Lords for the royal approbation. When the new Speaker has been approved by the Queen he does not lay claim to the Commons' privileges.

Absence of Speaker. The House of Commons, unlike the House of Lords, has no Deputy Speaker. If the Speaker is unavoidably absent, the Clerk of the House informs the House of the fact and the Chairman of Ways and Means, or, in his absence, the Deputy Chairman of Ways and Means, takes the chair and is invested with all the Speaker's powers until the next meeting of

SPEAKER—*continued*

the House. If, however, the House adjourns for more than twenty-four hours, the powers of the Speaker continue vested in his deputy for twenty-four hours only after the rising of the House. The Speaker can also ask the Chairman or the Deputy Chairman of Ways and Means to take the chair temporarily or until the rising of the House without announcing the substitution to the House. When either the Chairman or the Deputy Chairman of Ways and Means thus takes the chair temporarily at the Speaker's request he has no power to accept a motion for the closure or to select amendments for discussion, except during proceedings on or in relation to the business of Supply or during consideration of a bill on report.

SPEAKER OF THE HOUSE OF LORDS

The Lord Chancellor is Speaker of the House of Lords *ex officio*.

The Queen appoints a number of peers to act as Speaker in the absence of the Lord Chancellor. If neither the Lord Chancellor nor any of the lords named in the commission of appointment is present, the House elects a Speaker *pro tempore*.

If, while any of the royal appointees or a Speaker elected *pro tempore* occupies the woolsack, the Lord Chancellor enters the House, the lord who is acting as Speaker must at once surrender the woolsack to him. Similarly, a Speaker elected *pro tempore* must immediately give up the woolsack to any of the royal appointees who enters the House.

The Speaker of the House of Lords has no authority beyond that of any other peer to determine questions of order. Such questions can be settled only by the House itself. He has no power to enforce the rules of the House or to maintain order in debate. He cannot adjourn the House or do anything else without the consent of the House, except put the question, collect the voices, and announce the decision.

If the Lord Chancellor is a peer, he can and usually does take part in debates, and can vote in divisions, but he has no casting vote. When he takes part in a debate, he stands a few feet to the left of the woolsack. When he votes he gives his vote first and gives it to the tellers without leaving the woolsack.

If the Lord Chancellor or the Speaker is not a peer he cannot take part in debate, but he can put the questions and perform various other acts.

SPEAKER OUT OF THE CHAIR, MOVING THE

This somewhat curious expression is explained by the fact that the Speaker used formerly to put the question, " That I do now leave the Chair ", whenever an order of the day for committee was reached ; he is now, however, directed by a standing order to leave the chair without putting the question, on an order of the day for committee being read. This change in procedure, like many other changes which dispensed with the putting of questions, and therefore opportunities for debate, was made in order to lessen delay. The practice survived, until recently, on one occasion in each year, on going into the Committee of Supply. With the abolition of that Committee in 1967 the practice became obsolete.

SPEAKER'S COUNSEL

The title borne by an officer of the House who assists the Chairman of Ways and Means in his examination of private bills. He also assists committees on unopposed bills, the Standing Orders Committee and the Select Committee on Statutory Instruments. He is a member of the Court of Referees. The title of Speaker's Counsel is somewhat misleading because in fact he is rarely called upon to advise the Speaker. He owes his title to the fact that he was originally appointed by the Speaker to prepare breviates of private bills containing a statement of the object of the bill and a summary of its provisions for the information of members.

SPEAKER'S SECRETARY

This officer is responsible for arranging the Speaker's official dinners, levees and receptions. He issues tickets for the Distinguished Strangers' Gallery and deals with applications for tickets for the gallery allotted to the Speaker's wife. He is secretary to the Commissioners for Regulating the Offices of the House of Commons (*see* HOUSE OF COMMONS OFFICES COMMISSION). He deals with the Speaker's correspondence. He prepares the Speaker's warrants authorising the Clerk of the Crown to make out writs for the election of members in the room of deceased members or members whose seats have become vacant, as well as any other warrants which the Speaker may be directed by the House to issue, *e.g.* warrants authorising the Serjeant at Arms to arrest offenders.

SPECIAL ORDER

A term applied by standing order in the House of Lords to any order or regulations (with certain exceptions) or draft order or regulations which do not acquire the force of law until they have been approved by resolutions passed by both Houses of Parliament (known as " affirmative resolutions ") or do not continue to have the force of law unless affirmative resolutions are passed by both Houses within a certain time. The chief exceptions are measures passed by the General Synod of the Church of England and orders made under the Sunday Entertainments Act 1932 permitting the opening of cinemas on Sundays.

Every special order laid before the House stands referred to the Special Orders Committee (*q.v.*). A motion approving a

SPECIAL ORDER—*continued*

special order may not be moved until the Special Orders Committee has reported thereon.

SPECIAL ORDERS COMMITTEE

A select committee appointed by the House of Lords at the beginning of each session to which every special order (*q.v.*) laid before that House stands referred. It is the function of the Committee in each case to consider and report—

(*a*) whether the order raises important questions of policy or principle,

(*b*) how far it is founded on precedent, and

(*c*) whether, having regard to the answers to (*a*) and (*b*) and any other relevant circumstances, the order can be approved by the House without further inquiry, and, if not, what form the inquiry should take.

The Committee is not empowered to inquire into or express any opinion as to the merits of the order, but only to report where there is a *prima facie* case for further inquiry. (If the Committee has any doubt whether the order is *intra vires*, it must make a report to that effect.) The Committee consists of the Lord Chairman and a number of other lords. The lord in charge of a special order is a member of the Committee while that order is under consideration. An officer of the department by which the order was made attends the Committee to explain the order and answer any questions which members of the Committee may put to him.

SPECIAL PROCEDURE ORDER

A term applied by the standing orders of both Houses to an order, made or confirmed by a minister, in relation to which the Statutory Orders (Special Procedure) Act 1945, as amended by the Statutory Orders (Special Procedure) Act 1965, applies. These Acts provide a quicker procedure for conferring powers on local authorities, etc., than the former procedure of special Acts of Parliament. The procedure applies to orders made under four Acts which were already on the statute book in 1945 and to orders made under any subsequent Act which provides that such orders shall be "subject to special parliamentary procedure". The procedure may be applied to orders made under other Acts passed before 1945 if addresses are presented to the Queen by both Houses asking for the application of the procedure to be so extended.

Special procedure orders do not require confirmation by Parliament except in the circumstances described below; but they can be annulled by resolution of either House. Parties whose private interests are affected by an order may petition against it.

As in the case of a provisional order, before a special procedure order is made or confirmed notice of the proposed order must be published in the "London Gazette" and in a local newspaper, copies of the proposed order must be made available for inspection by parties interested, an opportunity of lodging objections must be given, any objections lodged must receive due consideration and, as a rule, a local inquiry must be held.

Copies of all special procedure orders must be presented to both Houses. Petitions against the order as a whole or asking for amendments (which must be specified) may be presented to either House of Parliament within the following twenty days. A petition of the former kind is known as a " petition of general objection " ; a petition of the latter kind as a " petition for amendment ".

When the time allowed for presenting petitions has elapsed, the Chairman of Committees in the House of Lords (*q.v.*) and the Chairman of Ways and Means (*q.v.*) examine any petitions that have been presented. If they are satisfied that a petition is in order, they certify it as " proper to be received " as a petition of general objection or a petition for amendment, as the case may be. When the two chairmen have completed their examination of the petitions they make a report to both Houses stating what petitions have been certified as proper to be received and into which category they fall. If no petition has been presented, the chairmen make a report to that effect.

During the twenty days after the chairmen have made their report any member of either House may move that the order be annulled. If such a motion is carried, the order drops, though a fresh one can subsequently be made. A motion for the annulment of an order may be moved whether or not any petitions have been presented against it. In the Commons such a motion is exempted business (*q.v.*). If a petition of general objection has been certified as " proper to be received ", it stands referrred to a joint committee of both Houses unless a motion is carried in one House or the other that it be not so referred. The effect of carrying such a motion is that the order comes into force in the form in which it was laid before the House. A petition for amendment, if certified as proper to be received, automatically stands referred to a joint committee. Thus if no motion for the annulment of the order is carried within the time allowed, the order will become law unless a petition stands referred to a joint committee and no motion that it be not so referred is carried.

The joint committee consists of six members, three from each House. The order stands referred to it " for the consideration of the petition (or petitions) ". The committee is a committee on the petitions, not on the order. The issues to be decided by the committee are those raised by the petitioners, *e.g.* the committee cannot entertain the question of the expediency of the order unless a petition of general objection is before it. The onus of

SPECIAL PROCEDURE ORDER—*continued*
showing that the order requires amendment or, when a petition of general objection is before the committee, of proving that the order ought not to be approved, is on the opponents. The minister or, if he delegates his right of being heard to the applicant for the order, the applicant, has not to " prove the preamble ". The proceedings in committee open with a short explanatory statement by counsel for the minister. The petitioners or their advocates are then heard and call witnesses if they wish. Counsel for the minister is then heard against the petitions. If he calls witnesses the petitioners have a right of reply. In other respects the proceedings are similar to the proceedings before a committee on an opposed private bill. The committee can amend the order, but only so as to give effect wholly or partly to the prayer of a petition. If a petition of general objection is before the committee, it may, if satisfied that the order ought not to become law, report that it " be not approved ". If, however, the committee thinks that the objections raised by the petitioner can be met by amendments, it may amend the order. The committee can award costs.

If the committee thinks that the prayer of none of the petitions, whether for amendment or of general objection, ought to be complied with, it reports the order without amendment, and the order becomes law. If the order is reported with amendments, it becomes law in its amended form unless the minister either withdraws it or appeals to Parliament from the committee's decision. If the committee reports that the order be not approved, there is an end of it unless the minister appeals successfully against the decision. The minister appeals from the decision of the joint committee by introducing a bill to confirm the order. If the order has been reported with amendments, the order is scheduled to the bill in its amended, not its original form. On the report stage the minister endeavours to persuade the House to strike out those amendments which he is unwilling to accept. (In the case of the Mid-Northamptonshire Water Board Order 1948 the Minister of Health appealed successfully to Parliament against some of the amendments which the joint committee had made.)

Bills to confirm special procedure orders are treated for all purposes as public bills, but (except in cases where a petition for amendment, as well as a petition of general objection, stood referred to the joint committee) do not have to pass the second reading or committee stage in either House. On being introduced, and on reaching the second House, they go straight to the report stage. Where a petition for amendment, as well as a petition of general objection, stood referred to, but was not dealt with by, the joint committee (as will usually be the case) the bill has to pass through all stages in the House in which it is introduced. After second reading it is referred to the joint committee for the purpose of considering the petition for amendment. When the bill reaches the second House, however, it goes straight to the report stage.

In the case of special procedure orders which relate exclusively to Scotland the procedure is somewhat different. When a proposed order is objected to an inquiry is held in Scotland by commissioners who are usually drawn from the panels of members of the two Houses of Parliament from whom commissioners in inquiries under the Private Legislative Procedure (Scotland) Act 1936 (*see* SCOTTISH PRIVATE LEGISLATION) are drawn. If the minister concerned accepts the commissioners' recommendations, he makes an order giving effect to them. A copy of this order is presented to both Houses of Parliament and the subsequent procedure is with one exception the same as that described above. The exception is that a petition does not go to a joint committee automatically; a motion to refer it must be moved and carried. If the Minister is not prepared to accept the commissioners' recommendations, he can introduce a bill to confirm the order. Such a bill goes straight to the report stage.

SPYING STRANGERS

Drawing attention to the presence of strangers with a view to having them excluded. A member who wishes to have the galleries cleared may at any time rise and "take notice that strangers are present". The formula usually employed is: "Mr. Speaker, I spy strangers". (This formula is a relic of the time when the proceedings of the House of Commons were theoretically conducted with closed doors, and, though strangers were often allowed to be present by the connivance of the officers or members, a single member could at any time secure their exclusion by drawing attention to their presence, whereupon the Speaker was obliged to order them to withdraw.) When notice is thus taken of the presence of strangers the Speaker or, if the House is in committee, the chairman at once puts the question "that strangers do withdraw" without allowing any member to speak. If the question is agreed to, all members of the public who have been admitted to the galleries, as well as the reporters and journalists in the press gallery, must withdraw at once. The official reporters also withdraw. The last occasion on which strangers were ordered to withdraw was on November 18, 1958. Questions for the withdrawal of strangers were negatived on April 6, 1965, June 28, 1966, and July 12, 1967.

STANDING ORDER

An order made by either House of Parliament for the government and regulation of its proceedings and declared by that House to be a standing order. Orders of this description do not expire with the session in which they are made, but remain in

STANDING ORDER—*continued*

force until they are vacated or repealed by the House by which they are made. If it is intended that an order shall be a standing order, it is at once declared to be such, but an order or a resolution of a previous session or Parliament is sometimes revived and declared to be a standing order.

Standing orders are sometimes suspended by order of the House either temporarily or for a particular purpose. Notice is usually required of a motion to suspend a standing order.

Some orders and resolutions are in practice observed and held good in succeeding sessions and by different Parliaments without having been turned into standing orders, *e.g.* the rule against smoking in the House.

In neither House do the standing orders provide a complete code of procedure. Much of the procedure of both Houses is governed by custom and precedent, supplemented in the case of the House of Commons by rulings from the chair. In the House of Commons the standing orders are largely restrictive of rights which members enjoyed under its older practice.

STANDING ORDERS COMMITTEE

A committee appointed by standing order in each House. The principal function of these committees is, upon the report of the Examiners of Petitions for Private Bills that the standing orders have not been complied with in the case of a particular petition or bill, to determine and report whether they ought or ought not to be dispensed with ; whether the parties should be permitted to proceed with their bill or any part of it, and, if so, under what conditions, if any, as to giving notices, publishing advertisements, depositing plans and procuring consents, when such conditions seem proper.

In the House of Commons the Standing Orders Committee consists of the Chairman and the Deputy Chairman of Ways and Means, and eight members named by the Committee of Selection. The Chairman of Ways and Means is *ex officio* chairman of the committee, the quorum of which is three. The Committee is assisted by the Speaker's Counsel.

In the House of Lords the Standing Orders Committee consists of the Lord Chairman and such other lords as are named by the House.

STATUTORY INSTRUMENT

A statutory instrument may be defined, broadly speaking, as an order or regulation made by the Queen in Council or one of her ministers, as the case may be, under an Act of Parliament and either having the force of law or acquiring such force on being approved by either or both Houses of Parliament. The Statutory Instruments Act 1946 laid down a uniform procedure for the parliamentary control of such "delegated legislation" in place of the diverse requirements of the many Acts passed previously, and applies to all except an insignificant minority of such orders, etc. In those cases where an Act confers the power to make instruments on the Queen in Council, the instrument is designated an Order in Council; instruments made by ministers generally take the form of rules, orders, regulations, schemes, licences or directions, according as the enabling Act in each case provides. The Statutory Instruments Act provides that the procedure which it lays down shall apply to all subsequent Acts conferring the power to make statutory instruments and may be applied by Order in Council to other Acts; it applies also in the case of previous Acts which conferred similar powers on a "rule-making authority" as defined in the Rules Publication Act 1893.

A statutory instrument which is required, by the Act under which it is made, to be laid before Parliament, must be so laid before it comes into operation; if the requisite copies cannot be delivered to the Houses in time, the Lord Chancellor and the Speaker must be informed of the fact and the reasons therefor.

The instrument must be printed and published by the Stationery Office.

The Statutory Instruments Act 1946 prescribes a uniform period for all cases where action may be taken for the annulment of an instrument. This period is forty days, beginning with the day on which the instrument is laid before each House. In reckoning the duration of this period, no account is taken of any time during which Parliament is dissolved or prorogued, or either House is adjourned for more than four days. This means, in effect, that the period during which action may be taken to annul an instrument is only interrupted, not brought to an end, by a dissolution or prorogation, and continues to run in the new Parliament or session; and that, while the normal adjournment over the week-end (which usually lasts longer in the case of the Lords than of the Commons) does not affect the counting of the forty days, the period is interrupted by a longer adjournment (such as for Easter or the summer holiday) in exactly the same way as by a prorogation.

If a statutory instrument is subject to annulment, an address may be moved, praying that Her Majesty will be graciously pleased to annul it; if the address is agreed to, the Queen revokes the instrument; in the case of instruments made under acts passed before the coming into force of the Statutory Instruments Act, the motion takes the form "that such-and-such an order (or as the case may be) be annulled". In either case the effect, if the motion is agreed to, is the same; the instrument ceases to have effect. But this is without prejudice to the validity of anything done under the instrument or to the making of a new instrument.

STATUTORY INSTRUMENT—*continued*

In cases where the relevant Act provides for the laying of a draft of an instrument but does not forbid the making of the instrument itself without the approval of Parliament, a period of forty days (beginning with the day of laying) must elapse before the draft is submitted to the Queen (if an Order in Council is concerned) or, in other cases, before the instrument is made. If during this time either House resolves that the draft be not submitted, or that the instrument be not made, no further action may be taken thereon; but this does not prevent a new instrument being laid before Parliament.

Some statutory instruments—those dealing with financial matters—are laid before the House of Commons only, in accordance with the Act under which each is made.

In either House, if (as is most unusual) a statutory instrument is laid before the House in the form of a "dummy", the time during which a resolution for the annulment of the instrument may be moved does not begin to run until a full copy of the instrument is available to members. Both Houses publish lists of instruments subject to such resolutions; in the House of Commons the list appears every Saturday, in the House of Lords every other Tuesday.

STATUTORY INSTRUMENTS, SELECT COMMITTEE ON

A select committee appointed by the House of Commons at the beginning of each session. Its function is to consider all statutory instruments (*q.v.*) and analogous delegated legislation including special procedure orders (*q.v.*) laid or laid in draft before the House which either must be approved by resolution of the House or of both Houses before they acquire the force of law or are annulled if either House passes a resolution or votes an address to that effect, and every other general statutory instrument (but not local statutory instruments), and to draw the special attention of the House to any instrument or draft—

(1) which involves the expenditure of public moneys or imposes or fixes fees for licences or for services;
(2) which cannot be challenged in the courts on the ground that it is *ultra vires* or is only temporarily so challengeable;
(3) the making of which appears to constitute an unusual or unexpected use of the powers conferred by the Act under which it was made;
(4) which purports to have retrospective effect although the Act under which it was made does not in terms give the minister power to make such orders;
(5) the publication or the laying before Parliament of which appears to have been unduly delayed;

(6) in the case of which there has been unjustifiable delay in notifying the Speaker that the instrument had come into operation before it was laid before Parliament ;
(7) the purport or form of which appears to require elucidation ; or
(8) the drafting of which appears to be defective.

The Committee cannot consider or report on the merits or policy of any instrument.

The Committee consists of eleven members. The quorum is three. The Committee is assisted by the Speaker's Counsel (*q.v.*). It is given power to require any government department concerned to submit a memorandum explaining any instrument or draft which the Committee is considering or to depute a representative to attend the Committee and explain the instrument or draft. Before the Committee reports that an instrument or draft requires the attention of the House, the Committee must give any government department concerned an opportunity of furnishing orally or in writing such explanation as the department thinks fit. It is also given power to take evidence from the Stationery Office with regard to the printing or publication of any instrument, but has otherwise no power to take evidence. The Committee usually meets once a fortnight, or more often if necessary. It is given power to meet during an adjournment of the House but has never exercised it.

STRANGERS, ADMISSION OF

In the parliamentary vocabulary all persons who are not either members or officers of the House of Lords or the House of Commons, as the case may be, are termed strangers. In the House of Commons accommodation for strangers is provided in the South Gallery and in parts of the side galleries. There is also room for a few strangers under the South Gallery on the Opposition side of the House. The first two rows in the South Gallery are reserved for peers, ambassadors and other heads of foreign missions, High Commissioners of Commonwealth countries and other distinguished strangers. The third row of the South Gallery and certain seats in the side galleries are known as the Special Gallery. The remaining rows in the South Gallery form the Strangers' Gallery.

A limited number of orders admitting strangers when the House meets to the galleries and seats appropriated to them can be obtained in advance through members.

Holders of orders of admission to the Strangers' Gallery are admitted immediately after prayers have been read. In order to make sure of being admitted without delay holders of these orders of admission must present themselves at the entrance to

STRANGERS, ADMISSION OF—*continued*
the Strangers' Gallery not later than 3 p.m. (11.30 a.m. on Fridays). After 3 p.m. holders of these orders of admission are admitted only as and when seats become vacant. The holder of an original order for the Strangers' Gallery is given precedence over the holder of an order issued from the Admission Order Office after 2.30 p.m.

Each member receives two orders of admission to the Strangers' Gallery every nine sitting days (Fridays excepted). Orders of admission to the Strangers' Gallery on Friday can be obtained by members from the Admission Order Office off the Central Lobby. Such orders for Friday are allotted to members in order of application, not more than two orders being issued to a member.

Orders of admission to the Special Gallery and to the seats under the South Gallery are intended primarily for those with a direct interest in the debate and may be obtained by members from the Admission Order Office. A member may not apply for more than two orders for any one day and must state the names of the visitors for whom the orders are sought and give some indication of the interest which they have in the subject which is to be debated. The Serjeant at Arms decides to whom the seats are to be allocated. No allocation is made until the business of the House for the following week has been announced. When there is a large demand for seats the final allocation has sometimes to be delayed until shortly before the House meets. Members are informed by the Admission Order Office if their applications have been successful or not. Orders for the Special Gallery are issued to members as soon as the allocation is made.

Orders admitting visitors to the Special Gallery and to the seats under the South Gallery at specified times during the sitting may be obtained by members from the Serjeant at Arms in his chair at the Bar of the House provided (*a*) that before the House meets they have entered the name or names of the persons for whom the orders are required and the time for which they are required in a book which is kept for the purpose in the Admission Order Office, and (*b*) that there are vacant seats. On the arrival of the hour for which the orders of admission have been bespoken the member goes to the Serjeant at Arms in the House, who, if seats are vacant, hands him the orders.

After 4.15 p.m. (11.30 a.m. on Fridays) members of the public may without applying to a member obtain from the Admission Order Office off the Central Lobby orders admitting them to seats in the Strangers' Gallery as and when these become vacant. When matters of special interest are being debated, it may, however, be a long time before any seats become available.

If any member draws attention to the fact that strangers are present, the Speaker, or if the House is in committee, the chairman, must at once put a question "that strangers do withdraw". If the question is resolved in the affirmative, members of the House of Lords are not required to withdraw, though reporters, including the official reporters, must do so. The Speaker, and, when the House is in committee, the chairman, may, at their discretion, order strangers to withdraw from the House.

By standing order members are forbidden to bring strangers into any part of the House or gallery appropriated to the members while the House or a committee of the whole House is sitting.

Any strangers who enter any part of the House or gallery which is appropriated to the members are taken into custody and detained until the rising of the House, as are strangers who misconduct themselves in any other part of the House while the House or a committee of the whole House is sitting or do not withdraw when strangers are directed to withdraw.

Members of the public are allowed to be present at sittings of standing committees, but may be excluded if the committee thinks fit. They are also allowed to be present at sittings of select committees on private bills or hybrid bills except while the committee is deliberating. In other select committees strangers must withdraw if any member of the committee takes notice that they are present, unless the House has provided otherwise when appointing the committee. In recent years a number of committees have in fact been given the power to admit strangers during the examination of witnesses unless the Committee otherwise order. This power is interpreted to mean that strangers can be excluded during the examination of witnesses only at the wish of a majority of the committee.

In the House of Lords accommodation for distinguished strangers is provided below the bar and in the West Gallery. Members of the Diplomatic Corps are admitted to seats near the north end of the East Gallery. A number of seats near the north end of the West Gallery are reserved for High Commissioners and other distinguished visitors from the Commonwealth.

Accommodation for other strangers is provided in the Strangers' Gallery at the north end of the House, *i.e.* the end furthest from the throne. Peers and officers of the House of Lords are allowed to issue two orders admitting visitors to the Strangers' Gallery. Members and officers of the House of Commons may obtain orders in advance issued by the Lord Great Chamberlain or Black Rod or during the sitting by Black Rod.

After 2.40 p.m. on Tuesdays and Wednesdays (4.10 p.m. on Thursdays) members of the general public may, without applying to a member or officer of either House, secure admission to the Strangers' Gallery by queueing up outside St. Stephen's Entrance.

SUPERSEDED QUESTIONS

A question which has been proposed to the House, whether or not a debate has arisen thereupon, must be disposed of before the House can proceed to other business. The question may be put and decided; or debate may be adjourned to another day; or the motion may be withdrawn (*see* MOTION; QUESTION, PUTTING THE). It may, however, in certain circumstances, be *superseded*, in which case the business is dropped from the order paper and can only be reinstated either at the request of the member in charge or by order of the House (*see* DROPPED ORDER). This can happen if a motion for the adjournment of the House is moved and carried during a debate, or the House is counted out, or if the previous question (*q.v.*) is moved and agreed to.* In any of these cases the question before the House at the time is superseded. If, on the other hand, a motion for the adjournment of the *debate* is agreed to in the same circumstances, the debate is ordered to be resumed on a specified day unless the member in charge of the business refrains from naming a day for its resumption.

SUPPLY

The provision of money to the Crown for the public services. Until 1966 the Committee of Supply was set up at the beginning of every session " to consider of the supply to be granted to Her Majesty ", but in that year the Committee was abolished, and all resolutions authorising the expenditure set forth in the estimates are now approved by resolutions of the House, known as " supply resolutions ".

The business of supply must, under standing order, be appointed as an order of the day as soon as the address in answer to the Queen's speech has been agreed to, at the beginning of the session, and must be set down every day thereafter; but such business is, as a rule, only considered on the twenty-nine days allotted to it (although it may be considered on other days in case of need). Even on the " allotted days " the application of the term " business of supply " is somewhat misleading, as such business now includes, by definition, proceedings on substantive motions and on motions for the adjournment of the House, as well as proceedings on the estimates, and on consideration of reports of the Committee of Public Accounts and of the Estimates Committee. The choice of the business to be considered on an " allotted day " rests, by long-established custom, with the Opposition and, more often than not, such days are now devoted to matters which are not directly connected with the authorisation of public expenditure. It is also open to a minister to move that business other than the business of supply may be taken before 10 p.m. on an allotted day, thus enabling business not comprised within the

* Or negatived in the House of Lords.

categories named above to be taken on an allotted day, though this is only done with the agreement of the Opposition.

The system under which a fixed number of days is allotted each session to the business of supply has thus become a convenient method of ensuring that the Opposition can count on a minimum number of sittings in which the House must consider business of the Opposition's choice (other than legislation) ; but the standing order also provides that on three days in the year the estimates must be submitted for the approval of the House and voted on, even if they are not actually debated. On these three days the Speaker must, at 10 p.m., put the question on certain votes which are set down for consideration by the House. On the first of these days (which must not be later than the 6th February) the Speaker is directed to put the question, in respect of all outstanding supplementary estimates for the current year, that the total amount of those estimates be approved, and also on a vote on account to provide enough money to carry the civil departments through the first few months of the coming financial year. On the second occasion (which must be before the 25th March) the Speaker must put similar questions on any vote on account for the defence services for the coming year, on any supplementary estimate which is still outstanding in respect of the current year and also on any excess vote which may be necessary in respect of the last completed year (*e.g.* in March 1969 for the financial year 1967–68). On the third occasion, which is on the last of the allotted days, the Speaker must put the question on all outstanding votes for the current year, whether on main or supplementary estimates.

The standing order now includes a provision which requires the questions put from the chair on each of these occasions to be reduced, in the absence of opposition, to the smallest possible number. The Speaker is directed in the first place to put the question in respect of the " total amount " of any of the votes, referred to above, only if any member has given notice of objection to such amount ; and when such votes have been disposed of, or if no notice of objection has been given, he puts one question only in respect of all the votes for each financial year in respect of which money is to be voted (*see* ALLOTTED DAY).

SUSPENSION FROM THE SERVICE OF THE HOUSE

The punishment inflicted by the House of Commons upon a member who has been " named " by the Speaker or by the chairman of a committee of the whole House for grossly disorderly conduct, disregard of the authority of the chair, or persistent and wilful obstruction of the business of the House by abusing the rules of the House or otherwise. Under Standing Order No. 24 the question on a motion for the suspension from the service of

SUSPENSION FROM THE SERVICE OF THE HOUSE —*continued*

the House of a member who has been "named" for committing any of these offences must be put at once, no debate being allowed. The motion cannot be amended nor can its consideration be adjourned. A member so suspended from the service of the House is excluded from the precincts of the House until the fifth day on which the House sits after the day on which he was suspended on the first occasion, on the second occasion until the twentieth day on which the House sits after the day on which he was suspended, and on any subsequent occasion until either the House terminates his suspension or the session comes to an end. The first or second occasion means the first (or second) occasion that session. Suspension from the service of the House does not exempt a member from serving on a private bill committee of which he has been appointed a member.

The punishment of suspension from the service of the House may also be inflicted on members for breach of privilege, contempt or other offences, without their being named. Thus, in 1911, Mr. Ginnell was suspended from the service of the House for publishing, in a newspaper of which he was editor, a letter from another member, reflecting on the Speaker's conduct. A motion for the suspension from the service of the House of a member who has not been named is debatable and can be amended and the debate thereon may be adjourned. A member who is suspended from the service of the House in these circumstances is debarred from the exercise of his functions as a member, but is not excluded from the precincts of the House unless the order suspending him expressly so provides.

SUSPENSION OF SITTING

A temporary suspension of the sitting of the House of Commons always takes place on the first day of the session after the House returns from attending the Queen or the Lords Commissioners in the House of Lords. The sitting is also suspended—

(1) if there is no business to be transacted, pending the return of a bill from the Lords, with amendments, or the arrival of a message from the Lords Commissioners desiring the attendance of the House in the House of Lords;

(2) if the business of the day is finished before 7 p.m. on a day on which a member has obtained leave to move the adjournment for the purpose of discussing a specific and important matter which should have urgent consideration and the Speaker has directed that the urgency of the matter requires it to be moved at that hour or on which opposed private business is set down for consideration at 7 p.m. by direction of the Chairman of Ways and Means;

(3) if the House is counted before 4 p.m. (or before 1 p.m. on a Friday) and less than forty members are found to be present (in which event the Speaker suspends the sitting till 4 p.m. or till 1 p.m. on a Friday, or until sufficient members arrive);

(4) in the event of grave disorder arising in the House,

(5) to afford a minister who is making an unusually long speech a breathing space,

(6) if a member is suddenly taken ill in the House, or

(7) on days when private members' motions have precedence till 7 p.m., if the proceedings on such motions should end before that hour.

The sitting may also be suspended under a Standing Order made in 1968, which enables the House to avoid the inconvenience of an unduly long sitting by breaking off its work at a reasonable hour and continuing it instead on the following morning. For this purpose a minister of the Crown must first move "that the proceedings of this day's sitting be suspended"; this motion (which may not be made before 10 p.m.) must be decided immediately without amendment or debate. If it is agreed to, it is immediately followed by a motion for the adjournment of the House; at the conclusion of the debate on this motion, which may not last for more than half an hour, the Speaker must suspend the sitting till 10 a.m. on the following day. At that hour the interrupted sitting continues; it is brought to an end:—

(1) on a motion for the adjournment of the House, moved by a minister, being agreed to (no debate being allowed), or

(2) by the Speaker adjourning the House, after the business has been concluded, or

(3) if the House has not adjourned before 2 p.m. by the Speaker interrupting the business and adjourning the House forthwith.

If it is desired to suspend the proceedings when the House is in committee, the motion must take the form "that the proceedings of the committee be suspended". If this is agreed to, the chairman leaves the chair and the Speaker must then put the question, "That the proceedings of this day's sitting be suspended"; if this is agreed to the subsequent proceedings are as described above, except that if the resumed sitting continues in committee till 2 p.m., the chairman must then leave the chair and report progress before the Speaker adjourns the House. If the question, put by the Speaker, for the suspension of the sitting (after the committee's proceedings have been suspended) should be negatived, the House must immediately resolve itself into the committee again.

TABLE OF THE HOUSE

The Table of the House (strictly speaking the Clerk's table), a piece of furniture measuring some fifteen feet in length by six feet in breadth, occupies the space in front of the dais on which the Speaker's chair rests and between the two front benches. At the end nearest the Speaker's chair, with their backs to the Speaker, sit the Clerk of the House and any clerks assisting him there. At the opposite end are the resting places of the mace (*q.v.*) and, on either side, the two despatch boxes before which the ministers and the principal members of the Opposition stand, when they make their speeches. Newly elected members come to the Table to take the oath (which is administered by the Clerk of the House) or make affirmation, and sign the test roll, standing between the Table and the Government front bench. All documents which are presented to the House for the information of members were formerly, as they are still in theory, laid upon the Table ; in fact they have, for the last hundred years, been delivered to the Votes and Proceedings Office and sent thence to the Library (*see* PAPERS). Notices of motions and questions to ministers must be handed in at the Table (or to the Table Office), and are there scrutinised by the Clerks Assistant (or the clerks in the Table Office) to ensure that they are in order. In carrying out this function, which they exercise (under the Speaker's authority) on behalf of the House, the clerks are commonly referred to by members as " the Table " (*see also* TABLE OFFICE).

TABLE OFFICE

The duty of the Clerks in the Table Office (which is situated close to the Commons debating chamber at the end nearest to the Speaker's chair) is to assist the Clerks at the Table, principally by scrutinising the notices of questions handed in by members to determine whether or not they comply with the rules of the House. Notices of questions, amendments and motions may be handed to the Clerks in the Table Office as well as to the Clerks at the Table. Notice of the intention to present a public petition is also given in the Table Office.

TAXES, PROVISIONAL COLLECTION OF

Where it is necessary that a tax, or an altered rate of tax, should come into force immediately, a declaration to that effect may be included in a Ways and Means resolution agreed to by the House and the tax thereupon becomes effective. This is done by virtue of the Provisional Collection of Taxes Act, 1968, which was passed in its original form in 1913 in consequence of a successful challenge by Mr. Gibson Bowles, a former member of the House, to the Treasury practice at that time of collecting taxes in advance of the passing of the Finance Act. The declaration, which is made in the words " It is hereby declared that it is expedient in the public interest that this Resolution should have statutory effect under the provisions of the Provisional Collection of Taxes Act 1968 ", is effective in the case of a resolution passed in March or April, till the 5th August and in the case of any other resolution for four months from the date on which it takes effect, provided that a bill to give effect to the resolution is read a second time within twenty-five sitting days after the date of the resolution, or a bill already before the House is amended by the House to the same effect.

Where, as regularly happens in the case of the annual budget, a number of motions requiring provisional statutory effect are to be moved by a minister, that minister (who is normally the Chancellor of the Exchequer) may move a preliminary motion, without notice, to give such immediate effect to all the motions, and the question on this motion is put forthwith, the other motions being moved at the end of the budget debate. If this preliminary motion is agreed to, the other motions (although not yet moved) have immediate effect, provided that they are agreed to by the House within a period of ten sitting days (*see* FINANCE ; BUDGET).

TAXING OFFICER

An officer of each House of Parliament whose duty it is, on application, to tax, *i.e.* to go through and if necessary reduce, a parliamentary agent's or solicitor's bill of costs incurred in promoting or opposing a private bill, provisional order or special procedure order. Applications for the taxation of a bill of costs must be made either by the party for whom the work has been done, or by the agent or solicitor or by the party to whom or against whom costs have been awarded by a committee. Section 256 of the Local Government Act 1933 provides that no expenses incurred in the promotion of, or opposition to, a bill under Part XIII of that Act, being expenses which are liable to be taxed under the Parliamentary Costs Acts 1847 to 1879, may be charged to the funds of a local authority, unless they have been taxed and allowed.

Maximum charges which parliamentary agents and solicitors may make for the various services usually rendered by them are fixed in lists of charges prepared in the House of Commons by the Speaker and in the House of Lords by the Clerk of the Parliaments.

TELLERS

Members appointed by the Speaker (or, in a committee of the whole House, by the chairman) to tell, or count, the members as they emerge from the lobbies in a division. Two tellers are appointed for the Ayes, and two for the Noes, their names being supplied to the Speaker by the whips on each side, or, if the

TELLERS—*continued*

matter has been left to a free vote of the House, by the members interested on both sides in pressing the matter to a division. If no member or only one member can be found willing to act as teller for either side, the Speaker declares that the Ayes, or the Noes, have it (that is, that the question is decided in favour of the other side). When the tellers have been appointed, they take up their positions at the doors leading out of the division lobbies; one teller from each side goes to each lobby, where the two stand facing each other, the members voting passing between them. As each member passes the doors he bows, and the teller representing the Government pronounces the number loud enough for all to hear.

When the lobbies are empty, the tellers return to the House; one teller from each lobby gives the number from that lobby to one of the Clerks at the Table, who writes the figures on a slip of paper, which he hands to the teller for the majority. The tellers then take up their position near the foot of the Table, facing the Speaker, those for the majority being on his left. On his command "Order, order", they advance, bow, and the senior teller for the majority announces the numbers. The Speaker then states the numbers to the House, and says "so the Ayes (or Noes) have it", whereupon the tellers bow again and return to their seats.

TEN-MINUTE RULE

The colloquial name for a standing order of the House of Commons which allows a brief discussion to take place on a motion for leave to introduce a bill. Notice must be given of the motion, which may be set down for a Tuesday or Wednesday (and, if in a minister's name, for a Monday or Thursday as well). Except in the case of notices of motions given by ministers at least a week's notice must be given of a motion under the ten-minute rule and no such notice may be given for a day on which notice of a motion under the rule already stands on the order paper; nor may such notice be given until after the private members' bills which have won precedence in the annual ballot (*see* BALLOT) have been presented to the House on the fifth Wednesday on which the House sits in every session. It is taken "at the commencement of public business"; that is, just before the main business of the day. The Speaker may allow a brief statement from the members respectively moving and opposing. The expression "ten-minute rule" is derived from the conventional limit allowed to each speech.

The chief value of this procedure is in giving an opportunity for a brief statement of the arguments for and against a private member's bill which has not succeeded in gaining a place in the ballot. If such a motion is successful, further progress is unlikely unless the bill is unopposed or the Government can be induced to provide time for its consideration.

The standing order allows motions similarly to be made for the nomination (not the appointment) of select committees; a purpose for which, however, it is rarely used.

TEN O'CLOCK RULE

At 10 p.m. on Mondays, Tuesdays, Wednesdays and Thursdays the Speaker interrupts the business under discussion, unless it falls within the category of "exempted business" (but such "exempted business" is itself liable to interruption to allow a motion to be moved to bring some other business within the same category for that day's sitting, in which case it may be resumed after the motion has been disposed of) (*see* EXEMPTED BUSINESS). If the House is in committee on the arrival of that hour the chairman leaves the chair and reports progress. If, however, a division is in progress at 10 p.m. the Speaker does not interrupt the business, and, if the House is in committee, the chairman does not leave the chair, until the division is over and, unless a member rises to speak or objects to further proceeding, the main, the original, or any further questions consequent upon the question on which the House or committee was dividing at 10 p.m. have been put. If, however, a member objects to further proceeding or merely rises to speak, the Speaker or the chairman, as the case may be, interrupts the business. Business interrupted under the ten o'clock rule stands adjourned till whatever day the member in charge of it names.

When the Speaker or the chairman interrupts the business the closure may be moved (*see* CLOSURE).

After the business under consideration at 10 p.m. has been disposed of, no opposed business can be taken unless it falls within the category of exempted business.

TEST ROLL

When a newly elected member takes his seat, he goes to the Table and either takes the oath of allegiance or makes affirmation. Immediately afterwards he signs his name below the printed oath in a book, made of parchment bound in black leather and known as the Test Roll.

TITLE

A short statement prefixed to a bill, setting out its purpose or object, *e.g.* "A Bill to grant certain duties, to alter other duties, and to amend the law relating to the National Debt and the Public Revenue, and to make further provision in connection with Finance".*

* The title quoted is that of the Finance Bill of 1969.

TITLE—*continued*

It must not be confused with the short title (*q.v.*) by which the bill is described in the notice or order paper, the Votes and Proceedings of the House of Commons or the Minutes of Proceedings of the House of Lords, and the Journal of the House of Commons or the House of Lords, as the case may be, or with the short title given to the proposed Act by the citation clause (*q.v.*). The title of a bill may be amended at any stage in the progress of the bill at which amendments may be made to the bill, *e.g.* in the House of Commons the title may be amended in committee or on the report stage; in the House of Lords it may be amended in committee or on third reading. In the House of Commons, if a committee makes amendments to a bill which are not within the title of the bill, it must amend the title. Strictly speaking, it is only in these circumstances that the title of a bill may be amended in committee, but it has also been amended in cases where the bill as introduced was narrower than the title of the bill as set out in the notice of presentation. Amendments to the title of a bill are moved after the committee has gone through all the clauses and schedules and any new clauses or schedules have been disposed of. The procedure on an amendment to the title of a bill is similar to the procedure on an amendment to a clause. Apart from this, no question is put on the title or the title as amended. In the House of Lords, the first proceeding in committee on a bill is to postpone the title, and when the committee has gone through the bill, the chairman puts the question " That this be the title of the bill ".

TREASURY BENCH

The name given to the bench occupied by the ministers; that is, the front bench, as far as the gangway, on the right of the Speaker. It is also called the Government front bench.

UNOPPOSED BUSINESS

Business to the transaction of which no member objects. Only unopposed business may be taken at the time of private business (*q.v.*), or, unless it falls within the category of exempted business (*q.v.*), after the business under consideration at 10 p.m. on Monday, Tuesday, Wednesday or Thursday or at 4 p.m. on Friday has been disposed of. Business becomes opposed if a member (*a*) rises in his place and says " I object " or (*b*) challenges the Speaker's declaration, made after he has put a question and collected the voices, that he thinks that the Ayes or the Noes " have it " (*see* DIVISION; QUESTION, PUTTING THE).

UNPARLIAMENTARY LANGUAGE

Words or expressions which, because they make improper accusations or imputations against a member of either House or by reason of their abusive nature, ought not to be used in debate. The use of such language is a breach of order and, if the member using it does not immediately withdraw the offensive words at the request of the Speaker or chairman, he may be called upon to withdraw from the House or "named" (*see* ORDER IN THE HOUSE).

USUAL CHANNELS

An arrangement made between the parties in the House of Commons is said to be made "through the usual channels", *i.e.* the whips of the respective parties. The use of this expression dates, no doubt, from the days when the existence of these officers was not admitted in the more formal public statements. Much of the business and other arrangements of the House are thus discussed informally between the whips, and agreement between the parties secured thereby.

VOTE

This word is used in three different senses in parliamentary language. (1) In the first place, a vote means a formal expression by an individual of his will or opinion in regard to some question put from the chair. From this is derived its colloquial use to indicate the process of voting in either House or in a committee, which is technically called a division. (2) Secondly, decisions of the House were formerly often referred to as votes, whence the title of the Votes and Proceedings, the daily record or minutes of the House of Commons. (3) Thirdly, each class of the Estimates is divided into a number of headings known as votes; thus, the salaries and expenses of each of the government departments are contained in a single vote. In theory, each vote should be approved separately by a Supply resolution, though in practice, under the guillotine, the Civil Estimates as a whole are usually voted.

VOTE OF CENSURE

A motion, usually moved by the leader of the Opposition, expressing lack of confidence in the Government. If the leader of the Opposition asks the Government to give time for the discussion of such a motion, the Government invariably allots a reasonably early day for the purpose. If the motion is carried, the Government either resigns or asks the Queen to dissolve Parliament.

VOTE OFFICE

An office in the House of Commons from which members may obtain copies of all parliamentary papers, including the Votes and Proceedings, Hansard, order papers, bills, etc., as well as papers laid upon the Table. Messengers from this office deliver papers to members' addresses in London; to those in the country papers are sent by post.

VOTE ON ACCOUNT (*see also* ESTIMATES; FINANCE; SUPPLY).

Just before the close of the financial year the House of Commons must provide the necessary money to enable government departments to carry on their work from the beginning of the new financial year (April 1) until the Appropriation Act, which provides in detail for their full annual expenditure, becomes law. In the case of the Civil Departments a "vote on account" is agreed to in the form of a single supply resolution. For the Service Departments, since they had the power, sanctioned by "Monk" Resolutions, to apply a surplus realised on one vote to meet a deficiency on another, it was formerly customary merely to authorise some of the votes, into which each estimate was divided, in full. The use of the vote on account has now replaced this process of "virement" in the case of the Service Departments; one vote on account is now required for the three defence services, and two such votes therefore provide all the money which can be foreseen to be required at the end of the financial year to meet the needs of government until the first week in August.

Each vote on account is divided into a number of items, each of which corresponds to one of the votes under which money is allotted in the estimates. The sum provided under each item is about five-twelfths of the total amount provided in the estimates, being an amount which is calculated to be enough to cover the departmental needs under that heading until the passing of the Appropriation Act. Thus the vote on account may be regarded as an estimate of an advance payment which is required on the full estimates.

Each of these votes on account is covered by the provision in the Standing Orders applying a "guillotine" procedure to certain Supply business. Thus, provided that the vote on account has been put down for consideration at least once on a previous day, the Speaker is required to put the question at 10 p.m. on the appointed day, which must be not earlier than the sixth allotted day and not later than February 6 in the case of the vote on account for Civil Departments and not earlier than the tenth allotted day (and before March 25) in the case of the Defence vote on account. The resulting expenditure must be finally authorised by the passing into law of a Consolidated Fund Bill.

A Member may oppose a vote on account by moving that the whole vote be reduced by a token amount, such as £1,000 or £100, or by moving that one of the items in the vote be similarly reduced. The latter course narrows the scope of the debate to the subject of the expenditure included in the item. As on all allotted days, the Opposition have the right to choose the subject for debate on those days when the votes on account are put down for consideration, and it may happen that, although both votes must be submitted for consideration and approval by the House, each one is agreed to without being discussed at all.

VOTES AND PROCEEDINGS

The title of the daily record or minutes of the House of Commons. The Votes and Proceedings are a provisional record of the House's proceedings, of which the Journal provides a more formal and permanent record. Whereas the Journal is not published till some time after the end of the session to which it relates, the Votes are issued regularly in the morning of the day following every sitting. The authority for their publication is provided by an order made at the beginning of every session " That the Votes and Proceedings of this House be printed, being first perused by Mr. Speaker ; and that he do appoint the printing thereof, and that no person but such as he shall appoint do presume to print the same ". The original order was made on October 30, 1680 ; it was repeated in 1681, after which there was a gap till 1690, since when the Votes, as they are colloquially called, have been printed daily under a sessional order.

The form of the Votes was originally similar to that of the Journals ; that is, each issue was a continuous narrative of the day's proceedings. But in 1817, when their volume had grown to such an extent that a year's issues sometimes amounted to more than two thousand sheets and at least four days were needed for the preparation of each issue, a select committee was appointed " to consider a more convenient and expeditious method of preparing and distributing the printed Votes ". As a result of this committee's inquiries and recommendations the daily Vote was cut down to a series of minutes, based on the former marginal notes or headings, and giving the required information in the fewest possible words. The Votes continued in this form with little change up till the end of session 1968–69. In the following session another change was made ; the Votes now appear in almost exactly the same form and language as the Journal, which has itself been made shorter, though still narrative in form. Some of the information has been relegated to appendices. The resulting document is little longer than its precedessor.

VOTES AND PROCEEDINGS OFFICE

The clerks in this office are responsible for compiling the Votes and Proceedings (*q.v.*) and for receiving copies of statutory instruments and other documents presented to the House of Commons (*see* PAPERS, PARLIAMENTARY). The office is only notionally distinct from the Journal Office. It is staffed by clerks from the latter office and occupies the same set of rooms.

WAYS AND MEANS

The Committee of Ways and Means having been abolished in 1967, proposals for authorising (*a*) taxation and (*b*) the payment

WAYS AND MEANS—*continued*

of money into the Consolidated Fund, which were formally required to originate as resolutions of the Committee of Ways and Means, now take the form of simple resolutions of the House, known as Ways and Means resolutions. The authority for payment of money *out* of the Consolidated Fund, formerly also given by resolution of the Committee of Ways and Means, is now given by the Supply resolutions which authorise the expenditure for which that money is required. A motion for a Ways and Means resolution may be made any day, with or without notice, once the address in reply to the Queen's speech which opens the Session has been agreed to.

The annual budget, in which the Chancellor of the Exchequer lays before the House his proposals for changes in taxation (usually in April), is embodied in the Ways and Means (or budget) resolutions. These are preceded by a resolution which gives provisional statutory effect (in accordance with the Provisional Collection of Taxes Act 1968) to the motions to which the House is to be asked to give its approval. The main budget debate then takes place on the motion to authorise changes in the taxation law and the questions on the subsequent motions dealing with new taxes and changes in rates of tax must be put without amendment or debate. The Finance Bill, which is then introduced, is said to be "founded" on these resolutions and gives legislative authority to them; the contents of the resolutions define and limit the scope of the bill.

In addition to the budget resolutions, Ways and Means resolutions may be needed at other times during the year to approve proposals dealing with matters of taxation, such as customs, excise, import duties and the like, if public policy requires legislation thereon. If a bill is to be brought in on more than one such resolution, the question on each motion after the first must be decided without amendment or debate. Resolutions may also be required to sanction the payment *into* the Exchequer of moneys accruing to the Crown under the provisions of bills before the House.

WELSH GRAND COMMITTEE

A standing committee appointed by standing order for the consideration of specific matters relating exclusively to Wales and Monmouthshire referred to it by the House. It consists of all the members for constituencies in those areas together with not more than five other members chosen by the Committee of Selection. These additional members are drawn from the various parties in such proportions as will ensure that the proportions of party representation in the Committee thus enlarged shall reflect as nearly as possible those in the House. The Committee of Selection may discharge these additional members or some of them from time to time and appoint others in their stead.

Motions to refer matters to the Welsh Grand Committee may be made only by ministers of the Crown at the commencement of public business. They may not be amended or debated. It cannot come to any resolutions on the matters which have been referred to it; it can only discuss them and report that it has considered them.

WHARNCLIFFE ORDERS

The name commonly applied to certain standing orders of both Houses of Parliament which require (1) that private bills promoted by companies, societies, associations or partnerships shall be submitted to, and approved by, the proprietors or members of the companies, etc., at meetings specially held for the purpose; (2) that a similar course shall be followed in the event of certain provisions being inserted in the bill, or of any such provisions originally contained in the bill being materially altered, during its progress through the House in which it is first considered; and (3) that provisions in private bills conferring powers on, or altering the constitution of, companies, etc., other than the promoters (whether contained in the bill as deposited or inserted in the bill during its progress through the House in which it is first considered) shall be submitted to, and approved by, the proprietors or members of the companies, etc., affected, and that a similar course shall be followed in the event of any such provision originally contained in the bill being materially altered during its progress through the House in which the bill is first considered. In the House in which a bill promoted by a company, etc., or which confers powers on, or alters the constitution of, a company, etc., originates proof of compliance with these standing orders is not given until after the bill has received a second reading.

WHIPS

In both Houses the peers and members whose duty it is to manage the affairs of the parties and to organise their forces in divisions and debates are known as "whips". This expression is derived from the whippers-in or whips employed by a hunt to look after the hounds and keep them together in the field. The whips are not officially recognised in the written rules of either House, but long tradition has given them a secure place in the parliamentary machine, and their status and function are now well recognised and similar in all parties.

Their chief duty is to arrange the business of their party in the House and inform their members of all forthcoming business; they provide a vital link between the leaders and the rank and

WHIPS—*continued*

file of the parliamentary armies. The government chief whip in the House of Commons is a most important person, since he is responsible, with the Leader of the House, for arranging the timetable of the Government's business in the House; which means the main framework and many of the details of the work of the House. He must ensure that the time at the Government's disposal—which is seldom or never enough for the work to be done—is properly distributed, and that the House never has too much or too little to do. The opposition chief whip is similarly responsible to his party for ensuring that the considerable opportunities available to the Opposition are properly used. Other duties of the whips are to marshal their party's forces for divisions, and to maintain some degree of order and discipline among its members.

The government chief whip always holds the office of Parliamentary Secretary to the Treasury and is therefore a minister, though not in the Cabinet. Other government whips hold minor salaried office as Lords Commissioners of the Treasury or as officers of the royal household, and others yet are unpaid, as are those of opposition parties.* In addition the whips employ a number of clerks and "runners" or messengers, in the two Houses, and occupy offices which are placed for the sake of convenience as near as possible to the debating chamber. The duties of a government chief whip in the Commons are arduous as well as important; he must attend at all hours, and know how to combine tact and patience with firmness in the maintenance of his authority. A good chief whip contributes much to the ease and efficiency with which the House gets through its work.

The word "whip" is used to describe also the circular announcement of forthcoming business which is sent out from time to time by the whips of each party to its members. In this, attention is drawn to the more important business by the appended words "Your attendance is particularly requested". This sentence is underlined once, twice or thrice according to the importance of the business, a "three-line whip" being the most urgent communication of all.

WHITE PAPER

Government publications of all kinds, presented to Parliament, are known as white papers. The distinction between white and blue papers is related to the length of the document, since a stiff blue paper cover is used for the bulkier sort. The term is associated chiefly with such command papers (*i.e.* papers presented by the Queen's command to Parliament) as are not of sufficient size to need a blue cover.

* The opposition chief whip now receives an official salary.

WITHDRAWAL OF MOTIONS, AMENDMENTS AND BILLS

With the leave of the House or the committee a motion or an amendment may be withdrawn by the mover at any time before the question is fully put upon it even if the debate has been adjourned. If the mover asks leave to withdraw a motion or an amendment, the Speaker (or the chairman) asks: " Is it your pleasure that the motion (or amendment) be withdrawn ? " If no-one dissents, he declares that the motion (or amendment) is, by leave, withdrawn. If, however, even one member objects, the Speaker (or the chairman) proceeds to put the question, unless, of course, a member rises to continue the debate. If further debate takes place after a request has been made to withdraw an amendment, the request to withdraw may not be made again.

If an amendment has been moved to a motion, the motion cannot be withdrawn until the amendment has been withdrawn.

A private member's bill may be withdrawn by the member in charge of it on any day on which the House is sitting, unless a proceeding on the bill appears on the order paper (*q.v.*) as an effective proceeding for that day, *i.e.* among the orders which are intended to be proceeded with on that day, and not among the list of " remaining orders of the day ". He does not move any motion, but simply informs the Clerks at the Table during a sitting of the House that he wishes to withdraw the bill. If he wishes to withdraw the bill on a day on which a proceeding on the bill appears on the order paper as an effective proceeding, he must wait until the order for the proceeding is read, and then move that the order be discharged.

If the government wish to withdraw one of their bills, they will arrange for the next stage of the bill to appear on the order paper as an effective proceeding, and when the order for the proceeding is read, move that it be discharged.

Bills can also be withdrawn at the end of debate at any stage. In that case, at the end of the debate the motion (*e.g.*, that the bill be read a second time) is, with the leave of the House, withdrawn, and immediately afterwards the member in charge of the bill asks leave to withdraw the bill.

In practice a motion to withdraw a bill is never opposed. If it was, the Speaker would probably overrule the objection. A Lords bill cannot be withdrawn in the House of Commons, or *vice versa*.

WITNESS

Attendance of Witnesses. Select committees appointed by the House of Commons (those on hybrid bills excepted) are usually given power " to send for persons, papers, and records ". A committee so empowered may require any person (other than a member of either House or an officer of the House of Lords) to attend

WITNESS—*continued*

for the purpose either of being examined or of producing a document. The power is not often exercised. Persons from whom committees wish to take evidence will usually attend at the request of the chairman. If, however, a person who has been requested to attend refuses to do so, or if (as in the case of a person charged with breach of privilege) it would be inconsistent with the dignity of the committee to request him to attend, an order signed by the chairman is either served on him personally or sent to him by registered post. If he fails to attend or to produce a document which he has been directed to produce, the fact is reported to the House, which will enforce obedience to the summons, if necessary, by imprisoning the recalcitrant witness.

The House of Lords does not give its select committees authority to require the attendance of witnesses or the production of documents. If a person from whom a committee wishes to take evidence will not attend at its request, the committee must apply (through its chairman) to the House for an order for his attendance or for the production of the document.

If a select committee of the House of Commons wishes to take evidence from a person who is in prison, the House, on the motion of the chairman, will direct the Speaker to issue a warrant to the governor of the prison requiring him to bring the witness in safe custody to the committee. The attendance before a Lords committee of a witness who is in prison is obtained by an order of the House of Lords, signed by the Clerk of the Parliaments.

A select committee may not require (though it may request) a member of the House to attend as a witness. If he refuses, the committee can only report the fact to the House, which may order him to attend.

If a select committee of either House wishes to call a member or an officer of the other House as a witness, a message is sent by the House to which the committee belongs to the other House asking it to give him leave to attend. This is given as a matter of course, unless the member is unwilling to give evidence. Neither House, however, will *compel* one of its members to give evidence before a committee of the other House. A committee may take evidence from one of its own members.

Expenses of Witnesses. Witnesses summoned to attend select committees on public bills or other matters are entitled to be paid their reasonable expenses.

Examination of Witnesses. By statute committees of either House have power to administer an oath to witnesses examined before them. The oath or affirmation is usually administered by the committee clerk. In both Houses witnesses before committees on opposed private bills are sworn, but in the House of Lords witnesses before other committees are sworn only when the House so orders, and in the House of Commons they are sworn only in inquiries of a quasi-judicial character.

In committees of the House of Lords it is customary for the chairman to take the lead in the examination of the witnesses and put such introductory questions to each witness as are necessary to bring out the facts relating to the subject of the inquiry which are within his knowledge. In Commons committees, however, the chairman sometimes invites the other members in turn to put any questions they wish to the witness before himself examining him.

Committees on private bills cannot, without express authority from the House, take evidence from any witness who is not called by the parties. Other committees appointed by the House of Commons cannot take evidence unless they have been invested with the power of sending for persons.

In committees on private bills the examination of witnesses is conducted by the parties or their counsel though members may take part in it. In other committees, when a party is given a *right* to be heard, he (or, if he is legally represented, his counsel) may call and examine witnesses, but if the hearing of parties is at the discretion of the committee (as is usually the case), the witnesses are called by the committee and can be cross-examined by parties or their counsel only with the leave of the committee.

The evidence is taken down in shorthand and is printed for the use of the committee. A copy of the evidence given at his own examination is sent to each witness for his revision. A witness to whom copies are sent for revision is not at liberty to publish any portion of the evidence until it has been reported to the House.

Witnesses who refuse to be sworn or to answer questions or produce papers which they have been directed to produce, or who give false evidence or prevaricate in their evidence or suppress the truth, or otherwise misbehave themselves, are reported to the House, which will, if it think fit, punish them for their contempt. A witness is not entitled to refuse to answer a question on the ground that, if he does so, he may incriminate himself.

Protection and Privileges of Witnesses. Witnesses before committees of either House and persons summoned as witnesses are privileged from arrest except on a criminal charge while they are in attendance on the committee or on their way to give evidence or returning after giving it. No action for defamation will lie for statements made in evidence before a committee of either House. Answers to questions given before such a committee are probably not admissible against the witness on a subsequent criminal charge.

For anyone to insult, abuse, threaten or commence legal proceedings, or take any other action against any person on account of evidence given by him before a committee of either House, is a breach of privilege. Anyone who threatens or in any way

WITNESS—*continued*

punishes, damnifies, or injures a witness before a committee of either House of Parliament on account of his evidence commits a criminal offence for which he may be fined and imprisoned unless such evidence was given in bad faith. He may also be ordered to pay the costs of the prosecution as well as a sum by way of compensation to the injured person.

To tamper with a witness in respect of his evidence, *i.e.* to endeavour to induce him to give false evidence or to suppress the truth, or to endeavour, directly or indirectly, to deter or hinder any person from appearing or giving evidence, is declared, by a resolution passed at the beginning of each session, to be a high crime and misdemeanour.

In 1892 a select committee which had been appointed to " inquire whether and, if so, in what way the hours worked by railway servants should be restricted by legislation " reported that John Hood, an employee of the Cambrian Railway Company, had been dismissed by the directors of the company mainly in consequence of charges arising out of the evidence he had given before a committee on the same subject in the preceding session. The committee further reported that the manager of the company had laid Hood's evidence before the directors and that at a directors' meeting held in consequence of an application by Hood for a re-hearing of his case (at which Hood was present), three of the directors (one of whom was a member of the House) and the manager had called Hood to account and censured him for the evidence he had given in a manner calculated to deter other railway servants from giving evidence before the committee. After hearing the three directors and the manager in their defence, the House resolved that they had been guilty of a breach of privilege and ordered the Speaker to admonish them.

WOOLSACK

The seat of the Speaker of the House of Lords (usually the Lord Chancellor). A large square cushion of wool, without back or arms, and covered with red cloth, the woolsack is the sole survivor of the four woolsacks on which in the middle ages the King's counsellors sat in the midst of the Parliament. The woolsack is said to be technically not in the House of Lords, but this has been questioned on the ground that the Act for the placing of the Lords (31 Hen. 8 c. 10) describes it as being " in the midst of the Parliament Chamber ". However this may be, when the Lord Chancellor wishes to take part in a debate, he must stand aside from the woolsack. When the House of Lords is in committee, the Chairman replaces the Lord Chancellor on the woolsack

WRIT

Writs are, for parliamentary purposes, of three kinds. First they are issued, in accordance with a royal proclamation, at the

Lord Chancellor's direction from the Crown Office by the Clerk of the Crown to peers individually to summon them to a new Parliament, and also to new peers on creation and to all peers who on succession have established their claim to be issued with a writ (*see* PEER) and to all bishops on their becoming entitled to a seat in the House of Lords (*see* WRIT OF SUMMONS). Secondly, a general writ is similarly issued from the same source to returning officers for the election of members to serve in a new Parliament. To returning officers in Northern Ireland this is issued by the Clerk of the Crown in Northern Ireland. Thirdly, on a seat becoming vacant during the existence of a Parliament, a writ for the holding of a by-election is issued, on receipt of a warrant from the Speaker, by the Clerk of the Crown to the returning officer concerned.

WRIT OF SUMMONS

A document issued out of Chancery to a peer commanding him to be on a certain day personally present at Westminster with the Queen and the "Prelates, Great Men and Peers" of the Realm to treat and give his counsel upon "certain arduous and urgent affairs" concerning the Queen, the State and defence of the United Kingdom and the Church. When a new Parliament is called writs of summons are issued by direction of the Lord Chancellor in pursuance of an order in council directing him to cause writs of summons to be issued by the Clerk of the Crown in Chancery to every member of the House of Lords. Writs of summons are also issued during the lifetime of Parliament to new peers on creation and (on application) to all peers who on succeeding to a peerage establish their claim to be issued with a writ to the satisfaction of the Lord Chancellor (*see* PEER), and to all Bishops on their becoming entitled to a seat in the House (*see* LORDS, HOUSE OF).

INDEX

The figures in bold type show the pages on which the subject is principally treated